Pengui

AIR G

Anthony Griffis was born in 1969 in Taree, New South Wales. When his career as a rock star failed dismally, he took a job as a writer/presenter on the television program *Beyond 2000*, and later on the series *Sex Life*. Since leaving television, he has worked as an artist and freelance writer. He lives on Queensland's Sunshine Coast with his wife Paula and son Sam.

Also by Anthony Griffis

Above and Beyond:
On the Road with Beyond 2000
(with Paula Bycroft)

AIR GUITAR

THE TRUE LIFE AND DAGGY TIMES OF A LOUNGE-ROOM ROCK STAR

ANTHONY GRIFFIS

Penguin Books

Penguin Books

Published by the Penguin Group
Penguin Books Australia Ltd
250 Camberwell Road, Camberwell, Victoria 3124, Australia
Penguin Books Ltd
80 Strand, London WC2R 0RL, England
Penguin Putnam Inc.
375 Hudson Street, New York, New York 10014, USA
Penguin Books, a division of Pearson Canada
10 Alcorn Avenue, Toronto, Ontario, Canada M4V 3B2
Penguin Books (NZ) Ltd
Cnr Rosedale and Airborne Roads, Albany, Auckland, New Zealand
Penguin Books (South Africa) (Pty) Ltd
24 Sturdee Avenue, Rosebank, Johannesburg 2196, South Africa
Penguin Books India (P) Ltd
11, Community Centre, Panchsheel Park, New Delhi 110 017, India

First published by Penguin Books Australia Ltd 2003

1 3 5 7 9 10 8 6 4 2

Cover design by Tony Palmer, Penguin Design Studio
Text design by Brad Maxwell, Penguin Design Studio
Cover and text illustrations by Julie Knoblock
Cover photographs courtesy of EMI Music Australia
Typeset in 10.5/15 pt Sabon by Post Pre-press Group, Brisbane, Queensland
Printed and bound in Australia by McPherson's Printing Group,
Maryborough, Victoria

National Library of Australia
Cataloguing-in-Publication data:

Griffis, Anthony.
Air guitar: the true life and daggy times of a
lounge-room rock star.

ISBN 0 14 300035 7.

1. Griffis, Anthony. 2. Rock musicians –
Australia – Biography. I. Title.

782.42166092

www.penguin.com.au

For Gordon, Leila and Darren, with love

ACKNOWLEDGEMENTS

Heartfelt thanks and love to my groupies
Paula and Sammy; everyone at Penguin,
especially Clare Forster and Meredith Rose,
whose sharp editor's eye and advice proved
invaluable. Also the gang at Curtis Brown,
in particular Fiona Inglis for her unbridled
enthusiasm; Alison Pressley, who got the
ball rolling; and everyone who's had the
misfortune to share a stage with me.

My family aside, some names of people and
bands in this book have been changed.

I sang backing vocals on Oasis' debut CD, *Definitely Maybe*. It's right there in the liner notes. It says, and I quote, 'Backing vocals on "Supersonic" by Anthony Griffiths.' Okay, so it wasn't really me, but it was *almost* me. It was me but for a stray 'th'. And besides, I've had my surname misspelled so many times that I feel justified in holding my hand up for this one.

I love the fact that I – sort of – made an appearance on what many music critics regard as one of the most important rock CDs of the 1990s. It tickles me that some geezer with the same name got to sing on a breakthrough album recorded by a group of then unknown, belligerent lads from Manchester who spearheaded the resurgence of Britpop and became, for a time, the most famous – and infamous – rock'n'roll outfit on the planet.

I wonder what my namesake is like. I wonder is he actually a singer, does he have his own music career? Or is he just a friend of the Gallagher brothers, another shaggy-haired Mancunian in an oversized tracksuit top who fronted up to the recording session with a six-pack of lager and was roped into having a squawk? Did Noel Gallagher say, 'Ay, Griffo mate (for surely he too is called Griffo), ta fa the lager, son. 'Ow'd ya lark ta sing backup wi' our Liam on this nex' wun, then?'

The mere fact that I would sit around ruminating on such unimportant drivel nicely sets the tone for much of what follows. *Air Guitar* is simply about loving pop music – although there's precious little that's simple about that. (By the way, when I say pop music, I mean popular music in the wider sense, not the narrow strand of bubblegum bollocks that judders across TV screens on Saturday mornings.) For something which is, on the face of it, so shallow, so completely and utterly lacking in substance, so breathtakingly stupid for the most part, pop music sure is a tricky bugger. It gets under your skin, like tattooist's ink, and it's just as indelible. Pop has been, to borrow from the poet Kenneth Slessor, my 'witless lover enemy'. It has provided me with some of my most memorable moments – moments of sheer, unadulterated, ecstatic, orgasmic bliss. Then, when I've least expected it, pop music has turned round and delivered a stinging blow to the solar plexus of my ego, a quick forearm to the chin of my self-confidence, a well-aimed knee to the crotch of my dignity. Gasping, I make excuses for it, rationalise that somehow it was my fault, convince myself that I had it coming, and stumble on in its wake like a faithful puppy.

This is a book about that hopelessly misguided teenage longing for fame and rock'n'roll riches. You'll read strange and improbable stories about playing in bands, all of which are true, honest. Along the way, you'll be privy to various pearls of wisdom and observations regarding music. It's basically a big, three-day rock festival of a book. Which you may or may not find enticing, depending on whether you've ever tramped through a muddy field to see some second-rate band and arrived just in time to have a soft-drink bottle full of urine tipped over you.

Sometimes I put on *Definitely Maybe*, skip to 'Supersonic', and study those liner notes with far more intensity than is strictly called for, trying to distinguish my namesake's voice amid the metal din. I gaze at my name, printed in bold sanserif type –

just centimetres separating me and Liam Gallagher. Sad, sad, sad. I can only wonder what my life would be like if my name happened to be Bono, or P. McCartney, or V. Morrison. I'd be paralysed into inaction, staring endlessly at liner notes like Narcissus gazing at his own reflection.

Anyway, I'd better be off. One of the Young brothers from AC/DC owns a sandstone mansion not far from where I live, and I'm going to go stand outside the high fence and look at it for a while.

Pity me, for I am a poor addled creature. A besotted pop music fan. And this is my story.

Sydney, Parramatta Road
4:30pm, 15 May 2000
The band Bait in transit

'Where are we playing?'
    'East Glen Touch Football Club.'
    'Where the hell's that?'
    'Dunno.'
    'What d'you mean, you don't know?'
    'I mean, I don't know. They didn't give me directions.'
Incredulous pause.
    'You didn't ask?'
    'Nup.'
Another pause, even more incredulous than the first.
    'For Christ's sake, why not?'
    'Thought we'd just turn up and suss it out. It's only Goulburn.
Can't be too hard to find, can it?'

Goulburn's outskirts
A bit later

The service-station attendant scratches his head. 'Fark. East

Glen? Never heard of it, mate.'

'You've never heard of East Glen?' I ask.

'Nup.'

'It's not a suburb or something? A new estate?'

'If it is, I haven't heard of it.'

'Touch football clubs? Any at all?'

'Touch footy? Nah, wouldn't have a clue, mate. Only got four clubs 'ere as far as I know.' He counts them off on his fingers. 'We got the RSL club, the workers' club, the bowling club, and the gentlemen's club.' (The *gentlemen's* club? Bloody hell, not only have we travelled a couple of hundred kilometres, we've gone back in time as well.)

'So no touch footy clubs?'

'Nah, mate. Never heard of any. Sure you're not mixin' us up with Canberra?'

'Don't think so.'

'Whya lookin' forrit anyway? Ya not gonna play touch footy *now*, are ya? It's almost dark and farkin' freezin'.'

'No, there's a surprise fortieth birthday party on. We're the band. From Sydney.' I don't know why I mention the Sydney bit. As if it should impress him or something.

'Sydney, eh?' Eyebrows raise. 'Well, sorry, mate.' Shrugs. 'Can't help ya.'

I get back in the warm car. Darren is wearing a familiar expression. A suppressed smirk. I know that look. He can't fool me, we've been brothers for the best part of thirty years. And for some of the worst parts too, come to think of it. He knows what I'm going to say.

'East Glen doesn't exist, does it? You just made it up. You can't fucking well remember where it is we have to go, can you?'

'Not exactly,' he owns up. 'I do know it's a touch footy club. And I'm pretty sure it's East-something. Yeah, East definitely rings a bell.'

Why am I doing this again? I wonder as Goulburn's frosty streetlights flash by. How is it that I find myself once more cramped in a clapped-out hatchback, hemmed in on all sides by the flotsam of an all-but-forgotten time – microphone stands and coiled leads and plectrums and old fast-food wrappers and empty guitar-string packets? It's been eight years since I was in a band. I was twenty-three when the Ripchords played their farewell gig at the Snake Gully Hotel in Newcastle. The papers weren't falling over themselves to cover it. I don't recall a lot of wailing and gnashing of teeth, unless you count Darren jamming his finger in the car door as he tried to wrestle his bass drum from the back seat. As a send-off, the Ripchords' last hurrah does not compare favourably with, say, Crowded House's farewell concert on the Opera House steps. Certainly not in terms of – well, any terms you'd care to mention, actually. But it meant something to us.

It wasn't an acrimonious split. There was no infighting, no bickering, none of that self-important, pretentious carry-on you normally associate with band breakups. No-one was displeased with the musical direction the band was taking. No-one was hankering after a solo career. None of us had been poached to join a rival band. I don't recall any clashes of ego. No-one was sleeping with anyone else's girlfriend – at least, not as far as I was aware. The songwriting team wasn't taking the lion's share of the money, thus relegating the rest of the band to session muso status. All in all, it wasn't terribly dramatic. It was just life, folks. Reality beckoned, and we were savvy enough to understand that we probably, all things considered, were never going to play Wembley. Leighton Buzzard or Sputum darts club, maybe. But not Wembley. So we packed away our toys, divvied up the cash, gave each other a hug and went our separate ways. (In what was I think a subconscious stroke of genius, we eased the pain of splitting up by making our last show the worst of our lives. Of anybody's life, in fact. We were spectacularly bad. Complete and utter, unadulterated, high-grade, class-A crap. By the time we'd ground our way to the end, amid much torturous squealing of feedback and rending of bum notes, we were so relieved we couldn't get out of there fast enough.)

The bass player – a boilermaker by trade – headed to South Africa to work in a mine. The lead/rhythm guitarist made tracks for Queensland to work on the roads, twirling a Stop/Go lollipop sign. Darren moved to Adelaide to take up a position in a bank. And I, who spent my daylight hours gainfully employed as a journalist, legged it to Sydney to start an exciting career in the heady world of infotainment TV.

That was the very early '90s. I'm now thirty-three. I am married. I consider myself to be a normal, functioning member of society. I have owned real estate and tended my own little slice of suburbia. I have gardened. I have paved. I have retiled a bathroom. (That is to say, I have employed a tiler to retile a bathroom – I merely selected the tiles.) I enjoy football and happily bay for blood at the big game. I enjoy the odd drink, though I'm not in Ronnie Wood's league (meaning I don't need several drinks in one room, stationed at regular intervals, so that alcohol and I need never be more than a metre apart). The sort of things, I guess, which just happen without you noticing as you mature. One minute, there you are air-guitaring to Angus Young, throttling a TV remote as you struggle to reach the twiddly-widdly bits at the start of 'Thunderstruck', the next you're using the same remote to switch on home make-over shows.

Don't get me wrong. Music still plays a starring role in my life. It's just that these days I'm happy to be a bit more passive. You know, buy the odd CD, see a band, watch video clips, that sort of thing. I don't care so much any more about actually *producing* music. Frankly, I don't miss being in smoke-choked dives at three in the morning, staring out at the human debris. I don't pine for the days when being the support band meant having the dubious honour of lugging around Midnight Oil's front-of-house speakers while Midnight Oil kicked back in their motel. Nor do I miss whiling away the wee hours in a grotty, smelly rehearsal room with slabs of noxious foam soundproofing peeling off the walls and fag ends all over the floor.

So why then, when Darren phoned and said, 'Let's do the band thing again. Just you and me, a duo,' didn't I reply, 'Thank you for the kind offer, dear brother, but I would rather gnaw off my own scrotum and mash the contents with a fork,' and hang up? As hoary as it sounds, I guess it was simply because 'the band thing' gets in your blood, gets under your skin, erupts from time to time like some dermatological disorder. You itch, you scratch, but relief never lasts long. One phone call and it flares up again. You break out all over. And that voice starts whispering to you. *Psst . . . Hey, maybe it'll be different this time. Maybe you'll make money. You might even be discovered. It's not too late, you're only thirty-one. Plenty of time yet . . .*

Trust me, it's not just my diseased logic. The second-rate muso's capacity for self-delusion is as close to infinite as doesn't matter. One bloody phone call is all it takes, and you're fourteen again, bracing yourself for an all-out assault on the charts. It *is* in the blood, no question. Pathetic, really. And the way I'm feeling right now, as we meander bemusedly along Goulburn's wide, country-town streets towards our first gig, I'm going to book into that Swiss clinic Keith Richards visited in the early '70s, and get myself a full fucking body transfusion.

The doorman at the Goulburn RSL is impassive.

'East Glen Touch Football Club? Never heard of it.'

'Any name like it?'

'Sorry, mate.'

'Any place with East in the name?'

'Not that I can think of.'

Darren, I'm considerably cheered to note, is starting to show signs of desperation. Time is getting on, and so far we've wasted huge chunks of it asking people for directions to a non-existent club in an apparently fictitious suburb. We're about to walk out when he has a flash of inspiration and changes tack.

'Well, where do they play touch footy round here?'

Without missing a beat, the doorman replies, 'Eastgrove. Just out along the highway. Past the Big Merino, first on your left.'

Stunned silence.

'Eastgrove,' Darren says slowly.

'That's right.'

'*East*grove.'

The doorman nods. Darren's voice rises in pitch, becoming a little strangled. 'Well, that's got bloody East in the name, hasn't it? You've got to admit, East*grove* is not a million bloody miles from East *Glen*, is it?'

The doorman doesn't reply. He just looks at Darren as if to say, What's your point?

Just as the doorman promised, we spy the Eastgrove Touch

Football Club on the edge of town. Then again, with a three-storey concrete sheep as your reference point it's hard to go wrong. My wife Paula, who has sat quietly throughout most of this, leans forward from the back seat and observes dryly, 'You're playing in a tuckshop.'

It's hard to argue. The clubhouse does indeed resemble a school lunch facility. It is a tiny, red-brick shed with metal shutters on its windows, a solitary building surrounded by an expanse of flat green sporting fields, interrupted only by the white H of goalposts. Inside, gaily coloured balloons cluster on the ceiling, and paper plates brim with little hillocks of potato chips and nuts and other assorted salt-choked nibblies. Three walls are dotted with photographs of various Eastgrove touch football teams from years gone by, and on the fourth there is a whiteboard with 'HAPPY 40TH BIRTDAY PAT' scrawled in huge happy red letters.

'Oh shit, will you look at that,' says Debbie, Pat's wife. 'Left the bloody "h" outta birthday. Christ fellas, I've had a day.'

At Pat's party there's no warm-up period, no easing into it. There's no sitting on a drink, no pacing yourself. The creed seems to be, Why have just one drink when you've got two hands? One minute people are arriving, kissing, shaking hands, hugging, and the next there're fifty or so extraordinarily pissed people staggering about. With no middle bit.

We lug in the gear. We set up. Darren plugs in the PA and all the lights go out. There's general mayhem. A man-mountain called Len grabs a torch, locates the fusebox and trips the safety switch. The lights come back on. Take two. Darren plugs in the PA. The lights stay on. We breathe a huge sigh of relief.

Without asking, a drunken reveller grabs Darren's thankfully unamplified acoustic guitar and strums a jumble of chords which don't seem to bear any relation to each other. TWANG, STROMMM, FNANGH. He pores over the instrument like a flamenco virtuoso, eyes closed, *feeling* the music. After a minute or two, he looks up.

''Owassat? Made that up meself, ay. Useta have me own guitar, did'n'I, a real beauty, but it's in the hock shop now. I'll get it out soon but, ay. Next cuppla weeks I reckon I'll be able to get 'er back.' Just for a moment he looks as if he might burst into tears. 'Anyway, thanks fer the play, fellas.'

The part I dread is the level check. 'Check . . . check one . . . check one tsyoo . . . tsyoo . . . one . . . tsyoo,' I say into the microphone, while Darren twiddles knobs and sets the levels. You might have noticed, if you're a regular gig-goer, that the person performing the mic check never just says 'two'. It's always 'tsyoo'. That is ssseriouss sssibilance for a word that doesn't even have an 's' in it. I'm sure there's probably a reason, but I've never found out. I just follow suit in the time-honoured tradition. It's also time-honoured tradition for a drunken plonker to yell out, 'Three, four, five, mate. That's what comes after two!' I'm not to be disappointed on this occasion, either, and everyone duly falls about in fits of mirth.

Not long after we start playing, I reach the conclusion that Debbie should have shelled out a little more and hired the Wiggles instead. There are no men in the shed. Not one. The men, all coalminers and shearers, are outside in the bitter night, laying waste to two kegs of beer. They stand around a bonfire, a ring of jeans and cracked leather, slapping Pat on the back and laughing at his jokes. The duo Bait, meanwhile, is playing to a shed full of mothers and small children. The children sit on their mothers' denim-clad laps, eyeing us warily as we yomp through a blues number. The women hold their offsprings' little arms and clap their pudgy little hands together in time with the music. But this enforced musical participation can't hide the truth. Darren's delicately fingered minor chords and my mournful harmonica are no match for 'Wake Up Jeff!' To be honest, there's nothing like playing Muddy Waters and Buddy Guy to a roomful of three-year-olds to make you feel a bit of a prat. They don't understand. The longing of the blues is lost on them. The sexual euphemisms – 'someone's diggin' my potatoes', or 'there's another mule kickin' in your stall', or 'while I was slippin' out, someone else was slippin' in' – are not so much saucy as vaguely embarrassing. Preschoolers don't know what a mojo is. Hell, I'm not too sure myself.

(On this point, someone once told me I had no right singing the blues because I owned a laptop computer. That I had a credibility problem. They said it didn't matter even if my big old mean woman done sit down on it, I was going nowhere with blues like that. I laughed at the time, but I can see their point. I do love the blues but they bear no relation to my life. I ain't fixin' to die. I ain't goin' to the chair or the chamber for shooting a backdoor man in St Louis. I once had a guy throw half a kebab at me in Balmain, but that ain't really the blues, that's just unfortunate. I wasn't brung up in a shotgun shack. I've never driven a Chevy or a pick-up. I did own a Datsun 200B once, but that doesn't have quite the same ring. Likewise, I've never jumped a Greyhound bus or a southbound train full of hoboes. And while you can get the blues someplace like Chicago or Louisiana, getting the blues in Coffs Harbour or Singleton just doesn't have the same ring to it.)

Anyway, we're playing the blues in Goulburn. One little girl overcomes her initial fear. She toddles over and stands right next to me, gripping my mic stand for support. The tiny chanteuse stares dolefully out at the adoring audience, who bill and coo and go, 'Ooohhh, isn't she cute,' and there's a barrage of flash photography.

For our part, we are tentative. My vocals are a little dusty. As I say, it's been a while since anyone paid me to sing in public. It feels, I don't know, *different* somehow. I feel different. Like an imposter. I remember the words all right, it's just that I'm not sure I believe them any more. After about eight songs, Debbie wisely decides that we better have the speeches while her beloved is still conscious. We hear from Debbie herself, a perfunctory speech thanking people for coming from so far away. (Why is it *de rigueur* during thankyou speeches for some local wag to pipe up at this point, demanding a special mention for coming from down the road?)

Her husband's speech is a little more, well, free-form, shall we say. Bald head shining under the fluorescent glare, Pat rambles about his intense, all-pervading love for everyone in the room, even the band, but especially his kids, his two little boys, who are the most special things that have ever happened to him, and who, just this minute, are causing a sensation by locking themselves in the women's toilet. As Pat slurs on, a team of female negotiators armed with coloured gelatine snakes and a battery of 'C'mon now, darlings' and 'There's good boys' and even 'Open this door or you'll get bloody good hidings' eventually coaxes the recalcitrants from the cubicle. Even then, they crawl out *under* the locked door, and so the women's toilet is rendered inaccessible for the rest of the evening.

The men duly come to the rescue, offering the women exclusive use of their amenity. As they reasonably point out, they don't need it. 'Christ,' says one chivalrous gent, 'we're surrounded by two square kilometres of farkin' footy field. And then there's the shower cubicles. A bloke's fairly spoilt for choice when it comes to places to piss. You go forrit.'

Pat, meanwhile, has had the mic prised from him and now his father is delivering the most entertaining and enlightening speech of the evening. The crusty old shearer grips the microphone as if it might suddenly come alive and attack him.

'I useta haveta be away from 'ome a lot,' he drawls at one point. 'Always thought me boys wer behavin' 'emselves while I was gone. Maybe I was wrong. Useta wonder why we kept losing chooks all the time. Find out just the other day that bloody Pat, the li'l bastard, was getten 'em an' buryin' 'em up to their necks, then runnin' over their 'eads with the bloody mower.'

The room erupts. I've got to give it to Pat, that does have a touch of cruel Caligulan ingenuity about it.

One of Pat's mates is called, for reasons not explained, Looby. Looby's long hair has been fashioned into a mullet – short on the top and sides, long at the back – and he has a straggly beard which begins life full of vim on his chin but gradually loses interest as it climbs his thin cheeks. Looby loves us. He loves the band. We know because he keeps telling us.

'Youse guys are the farkin' best,' he says over and over again. 'Youse guys are the farkin' *best*!' Looby is the drunkest person I have ever met. I don't mean to imply that the two facts are related. It doesn't automatically follow that to appreciate our musical talents, one must be utterly stonkered. Looby might well have liked us if he had been sober, but I fear that being totally inebriated did have some bearing on his level of appreciation. Which, as I say, was fulsome.

'Larv that shit youse are playin', ay,' he says. Then, quite touchingly, 'It's great that youse blokes come down here to play for us blokes in the bush.' He throws an arm around my shoulders. 'We really farkin' appreciate it. Nah, mate, really. I know the guys aren't dancin' or nothin', an' that they just stand out 'ere ignorin' ya an' stuff, but mate, they love ya. Believe me. You'd know it if they didn't. Youse are playin' some great shit.'

Looby, as far as I can make out, works in the roofing business.

'Best farkin' job inna world, ay,' he says as Darren, Paula and I huddle around the fire during one of Bait's short breaks. Looby uses only one side of his mouth for speaking. The other side is clamped on a cigarette. ''S the best life, ay. Spend me days up on roofs in the outdoors, ripped off me farkin' tits with me mates. What could be betta en 'at, ay?'

We concur.

'Just as long as you don't fall off,' Darren offers chummily.

Looby looks at him hard through bleary eyes and a haze of blue smoke. 'Never farkin' fall off, mate. No way. I know me roofs, right enough.'

A little while later, talk turns to our compact PA, which, when packed up, is the size of a large suitcase. Two speakers and a basic control panel. Or as Looby would have it, 'Ya little knob box.' Switch on, plug in, let her rip. Ideal for your smaller venue. Looby expresses his approval and is suddenly struck by a thought.

'Had a mate, ay, an' he had this little box with little, like, ear-phones comin' out of it. Said you could play music on it. I said, Bullshit, but he said, Yeah, ya can, here havva listen. So I puts these little farkin' things in me ears and –' he mimes shock – 'BOOM, BOOM, BOOM, the sound was clear as a farkin' bell. Couldn' farkin' believe me ears! An' all outta this li'l box. Y'seen those?'

Darren and I are not game to speak. Paula answers. 'Yeah, they're called Walkmans.'

'Wassat?'

'Walkmans. You can get them for cassettes or CDs.'

'CDs too? Fark me.' Looby shakes his head in wonderment and stubs out his cigarette. 'Whatlay think up next?'

Later, I introduce a song thusly: 'This is a song all about having to get married and not being terribly pleased about it,' and a woman goes completely berserk. Until now she has sat quietly drinking alone in a corner. She has long, lank black hair and a couple of teeth missing. Her jeans are so tight you can read the dates on the coins in her pocket. Now she is jumping around and waving her arms, yelling in a cackly voice, 'Yes! Me! Me! This song is all about me!' Heads turn. Darren and I exchange glances. Still screaming, she runs from the room and disappears into the night.

Paula later solves the mystery. 'She's married to Looby. She's Mrs Looby.'

Oh. Right.

It's getting messy. It's only 10:30 and both beer kegs are empty. Debbie's in a flap. She's already been reduced to tears once tonight, after some mysterious incident. Now she and a girlfriend jump into a ute and roar off to see if they can find more alcohol, before there's a riot. With there being no drink outside, the men are all *inside*, juiced up and sloppy and taking an unsettling amount of interest in us. It's brewing. Onstage, Darren and I can both feel it coming, and we're dreading it. On any night, playing almost any venue in Australia, you reach a certain moment. If you play in covers bands long enough, you can *smell* it. You can see it in the punters' eyes. That moment is now. The crowd surges forward as one, a brawny, slobbery, slurring tide of flannelette.

'Play "Khe-farkin'-Sanh"!'

'CHISEL! CHISEL!'

'Farkin' Barnesy!'

'"Workin' Class Man!"'

'ACCADACCA!'

Oh dear. See, it's like this. When I agreed to come back to do 'the band thing', I made a proviso. I said, 'No more playing those songs we were playing ten years ago, okay? No more Cold Chisel, no more Angels. No Radiators. I'm not singing "Gimme Head" again. No way. If we do it, we play obscure songs. Songs that people don't hear every day in every corner pub in every bloody town in the country.' What I secretly meant by obscure songs was songs people might mistake as having been penned by us. Not that I'd admit that, even to myself.

Darren was in agreement. 'Sure thing,' he said. 'Besides,' he pointed out, 'we are a duo. We have one guitar and vocals and harmonica. We *can't* play pure rock. I mean, we can hardly play "High Voltage" with one acoustic guitar now, can we? We'll have to have a different repertoire. Anyone can see that.'

How's that for ridiculous? Bait, the covers band with principles. Too lazy to write our own material, we also refuse to play the songs most people want to hear when they go to see a covers band.

If teen pop and boy bands are the fast food of music – synthetic, interchangeable and formulaic – then the blues are akin to your average RSL smorgasbord – undoubtedly healthier and heartier, yet still samey and doled out from a large bain-marie. Now, I don't want to offend. I'm not looking to attract sackloads of abusive correspondence from irate blues devotees. I am one of you. I love the blues. You know where you stand with the blues. You think you know the songs even if you've never heard them before. Their structure is familiar, the chords progress in a reassuringly predictable way. That is, I think, the blues' great strength. If you're in a blues band and running short of material, you need only call out, 'Blues in G, lads!' and make up the lyrics as you go. If it's a slow blues, you've got heaps of time to think of the next line. Something along the lines of your baby done left you, or you worked hard to keep a woman happy and now she's kicked you out, or you came home in the wee small hours and found your woman in bed with a backdoor man usually does the trick.

Unfortunately, unless you happen to be playing somewhere in Chicago or the Mississippi Delta, or at some outdoor event with the words 'Blues Festival' in the title, people tire of the blues. They get bored. On this occasion Darren and I had made a grave error of judgement. We had entered the Church of the Covers Band Staple Song List and urinated copiously on its holy of holies. It was time to atone for our sins. We would immediately observe this church's number one commandment – He Who Pays the Piper Calls the Tune.

'High Voltage' goes over quite well, actually. I'm surprised, given that it suddenly sounds as if John Denver wrote it, and not Bon Scott. From that precarious point, Darren launches straight into 'TNT', followed by 'Jailbreak', which he blends with the old Van Morrison classic 'Gloria' (they are strikingly similar). It's like pulling on an old and comfortable slipper. Back and forth we travel between the two songs, effortlessly mixing up verses and choruses. The crowd love it. They're jumping around, screaming the words, red in the face, spittle flying, cannoning into each other, falling down, tripping over children, unknowingly stomping on little feet. And the men are quite unruly as well.

Off to one side Looby sits alone, a joint dangling from his bottom lip. He surveys the manic scene and a dreamy smile spreads over his face. You were right, Looby. We *are* playing some great shit. We've clicked and the cobwebs have been swept away. We are cooking, my friend. In the groove. Darren is sweating and grinning, his arm cranking across the face of his poor old guitar. The speakers tremble with the effort of unloading the volume. I'm in grave danger of bursting a blood vessel. I pose, I strain, I sneer, I leer; my neck muscles are taut and quivering. Ladies and gentlemen, I am a complete tosser, the quintessential frontman – Jagger/Plant/Scott/Mercury all rolled into one, carrying on like a load of old bollocks and loving it. The only things missing are my long, permed hair and my skin-tight grey jeans with the tear right beneath the left buttock.

Just when I think it can't get any better, two young women grab Darren's mic and start doing backup vocals. Just like that. Unbidden. And they can sing, *really* sing. Not only that, they harmonise. Furthermore, they know when *not* to sing. And when they're not singing, they pout and thrust and generally act all pneumatic in the background. They unabashedly *sell*, as if they're being filmed. It's like one of those movies when people break into song and everybody mysteriously knows all the words and actions. Unbelievable. These women add a whole new dimension. Who the hell are they? Where did they come from? Darren is gazing at them in real admiration. Well, I think it's admiration.

After several encores – you find remarkable energy reserves when a crowd loves you – and after someone's five-year-old son has grabbed the microphone between songs and suggested that everyone go and get fucked, we wind things up with a stupendous, fifteen-minute version of the Troggs' party anthem 'Wild Thing', which sends the place into meltdown. Then, in a voice that sounds as if I've been gargling loose gravel, I bring the curtain down on Bait's first outing with those immortal words: 'You've been a great audience. Thank you . . . and GOODNIGHT!'

Whoops, whistles, applause, cries of 'More!'

Yesss!

2

It's a good crowd. The *best* crowd. A sea of upturned faces –
forty, maybe fifty thousand people – receding into the distance.
All cheering and chanting, going completely in*sane*. I glance over
to my left. Keith's there, swaggering about on vermilion boot
heels, cigarette welded to his bloodless lips. Don't know where
Ronnie's got to. Probably strutting around on one of the cat-
walks jutting out over the crowd. Behind me, Charlie's perched
on his drum stool, pounding away like a blacksmith over a forge.
As usual, he looks utterly bored. Great bloke, Charlie.

'Awriight, Chicago! Rock and *rollll*!' I yell into the microphone. Chicago responds, the noise is deafening. I'm touched,
and not a little relieved. I was worried they might miss Mick.
I remember saying to Keith when he initially approached
me about taking over as frontman in the World's Greatest
Rock'n'Roll Band, 'Keith,' I said, 'won't they miss Mick? I mean,
I'm flattered to be asked and everything, but how on earth can
you have the Rolling Stones without Mick Jagger?'

'Listen, man,' Keith had replied in that boozy rasp of his.
'If ol' bum's-rush Jagger wants to concentrate on his "acting"
career, then let the cat go. This thing that is the Stones has a
life of its own, man, its own momentum. The road goes on forever. You'll be *fine*.'

And it is fine. 'Let's spend the night together!' I yell to the
crowd, by way of clever introduction to the next song, and

we're away, with me playing additional guitar, freeing up Ronnie and Keith so that they can swap solos. I turn to look at Bill Wyman, who gives me a slight smile and a nod, and when I turn back my father is standing at the bedroom door, mouthing words I can't hear because the volume in my headphones is turned right up. He's wearing the sort of expression that might be expected from any parent who's just caught their pyjama-clad progeny miming song lyrics to an empty room while strumming a wooden tennis racquet – an expression somewhere between amusement and disgust. Embarrassed, I throw the racquet onto my bed and snatch the cans off my head. The Stones' live album *Still Life* blares out tinnily.

'Come out here. Your mother wants you,' my father says. And as he turns to leave, he adds quietly, 'Son, you are a complete dickhead.'

This, sad to say, was a regular occurrence in our house. I lost count of the number of times a fantasy gig or imaginary studio session was rudely curtailed by a family member bursting into my bedroom. (That previous sentence gives you some clue as to the extent of my rock music affliction. Not only did I imagine myself playing to packed stadiums worldwide, I also entertained recording-studio fantasies. There I was, alone in my room wearing headphones, pretending I was alone in some *other* room wearing headphones.)

I was never sure who was more embarrassed, my parents or me. At first I assumed it was me. After all, I was the one jumping around pretending to play a tennis racquet, pulling faces and striking poses I'd lifted directly from the latest video clips. Then, after a while, I noticed that whenever my father felt compelled to disrupt yet another of my sell-out concerts, he would avoid looking at me. He'd fling open the bedroom door, turn his head away, and deliver whatever message he had while look-ing intently at the linen cupboard. He'd then retreat down the hallway without checking whether I'd actually heard him. And it dawned on me that he was more uncomfortable glimpsing me in the act than I was being glimpsed. This is the thing, see. I *was* embarrassed, sure, but I had to learn to accept the fact that I would, on occasion, be caught acting like a pubescent sex god because I knew there was *no way I was going to stop*. Giving it up wasn't an option. I was addicted. That is the weird influence pop music exerts on you. Your dignity is the first casualty. My father's 'dickhead' remark, the numerous entreaties to 'grow up', 'stop all that nonsense' and 'wake up to yourself' made not one iota of difference.

$$\bigcap$$

So where did all this start? Well, if I'm to be totally honest, it can probably all be traced back to the Sherbet poster. Much as it disappoints me, this is my earliest memory of pop music fan-dom – a poster of five long-haired men clad in choice, mid-'70s pop livery, crammed into the basket of a hot-air balloon, all waving and smiling cheery, mid-'70s smiles. The poster was given to me in exchange for two chocolate biscuits, and I can tell you who got the better of that deal. They were very nice chocolate biscuits.

The poster went up not on my bedroom wall, but on the side of my wardrobe. This sort of defeated the purpose of having a poster, because you could only see it as you entered or left the room, or if you happened to be passing in the hall. In many ways it was a fitting beginning, for so much of being a pop music fan makes absolutely no rational sense whatsoever. Not only did I put up the poster in a spot where I had only the slimmest chance of viewing it, but it was a poster of a band I didn't like. Sherbet were big at the time – huge, in fact – but I don't recall taking an active interest in them, beyond singing the odd chorus of 'Howzat' during schoolyard cricket matches. Which we all found terribly amusing at the time.

No, the whole poster thing is a mystery to me. But, interestingly, it does mark the earliest glimmerings of recognition, the dawn of a new awareness. Something was stirring inside me. The moment the crinkled Sherbet poster touched my choc-soiled fingers, musical cogs creaked into action, synapses fired, ganglions tingled, and a whole other part of my young brain wheezed into life like a puffing steam train pulling out from a station. So in that regard, I guess I owe Sherbet – later renamed Highway, later still the Sherbs, each name change marking a new low-point in their slide into obscurity – a debt of gratitude. Two partially melted Tim Tams were a small price to pay for a life-time on board the rock'n'roll express.

The fire was lit. All it needed now was an injection of oxygen to fan the flames. Which brings us nicely back to the subject of air-guitaring. Over the next few years, my furiously whirling arms created such strong air currents, I could have run a generator and powered a small island from my bedroom.

Now, I know I'm not the only person to have wielded the imaginary axe, but I made a fully-fledged hobby out of it. Air-guitaring was my recreation of choice. Other kids loved getting out in the local park and enacting their footy fantasies. Equally, I looked forward to taking my grass stains and itchy legs home again so I could transfix the adoring crowd that awaited in my bedroom.

What is the origin of the air guitar? I wonder. I don't remember what put the idea into my head, apart from the obvious fact that we didn't have a real guitar. It just seemed a natural thing to do. Later, of course, I discovered that others did it too. Millions of people, in fact, the world over. Even people who play real guitar sometimes play air guitar. I've seen them do it. Something else to ponder: is the guitar the only instrument to be faked in this way? Anyone ever heard of air-tromboning? I know for sure that there's another generation of air-guitarists out there right now miming licks, but is there a kid somewhere playing air glockenspiel? Air cello? Air French horn? I doubt it, though I'm happy to be proven wrong. (Given the shift in modern musical tastes, are there people now air-DJ-ing? Swaying in their bedrooms, manipulating pretend decks? Making fingery gestures to heaving, imaginary nightclubs?)

While we're on board this train of thought, I've just discovered that my father, in his salad days, did quite a nice line in air-conducting. He is a huge classical music buff and once or twice was caught out using a ruler as a baton, waving it around energetically as the violins swelled, thinking no-one was watching. He was immensely embarrassed when this little tidbit was divulged; I was hugely indignant. After all the grief he'd given me!

Maybe it's a genetic thing, this propensity to musical delusion. Not just musical, either. My brother used to drive an imaginary car around the house. A battered orange saucepan lid was his steering wheel and he growled like an engine as he went, his little legs carrying him at speed. He was always careful to slow and stop at doorways, so as not to have a head-on collision with any of us, and he always indicated, making *dit-daw, dit-daw* noises. Recently I was laughing with my mother Leila about all this. 'Aren't you lucky,' I said, 'that your kids were blessed with such vivid and active imaginations?'

'Are you joking?' my mother replied. 'You were completely

bloody bonkers, the pair of you. I seriously thought you'd both have to be put away.'

But back to the guitar. It lends itself to emulation, I think, because it's sexy. I'm well aware that at this point we're entering a world of Freudian subtext. I've heard the talk about the guitar being an extension of the penis, about the masturbatory connotations of rock-guitaring, about the even stronger masturbatory overtones associated with air-guitaring, and I'm here to quash all that right now. Masturbation and air-guitaring are two entirely unrelated activities. One gives you an enormous thrill of doing something you know is illicit and frowned upon, leaving you panting and sweaty. The other is playing with yourself.

Air-guitaring has taken a nosedive recently in terms of social acceptance. I've been to parties where I think people would quite frankly prefer you flopped out your tadger and started feeding the chooks, as it were. During some drunken revelry a little while back, I made the mistake of running off a couple of mid-air licks while a group of us were dancing. I mean, the *looks* they gave me. It was as if I'd just vomited on their feet. That was someone else, a bit later. Air-guitaring is considered such an utterly juvenile thing to do in mixed company. It says you still harbour adolescent rock'n'roll fantasies. Or maybe it's just that I looked a little too authentic, my proficiency betraying the fact that I did have, after all, some twenty-odd years of experience to draw on. (Twenty years? My God, it's just dawned on me. Had I persevered with learning the real instrument, I could have been a bloody axe god by now. A veritable Yo-Yo Ma of the guitar. Another Jimi Hendrix. Eric Clapton. Heaven knows, I'd have settled for *Richard* Clapton.)

When I started air-guitaring, at the age of about seven or eight, I did it without props. One hand I held out in mid-air, ranging up and down an imaginary fretboard; with the other I clutched a make-believe plectrum and tapped out a sort of morse code on my right thigh. So positioned, I 'cut my chops', as they say. Every Sunday night found me standing in front of *Countdown*, twitching away to Mother Goose's one and only hit, 'Baked Beans', or Jon English. (Needless to say, the part of my brain housing music appreciation was still very much under-developed.) I soon had that technique conquered and craved more. I needed to expand.

That's when the old wooden tennis racquet with Ken Rosewall's face on the handle became the object of my desire. I slowly drew it from the back of my father's wardrobe, as if I were drawing Excalibur from the stone. I examined it in excitement. As a tennis racquet, it was completely useless. We were in the age of aluminium, my friends. Carbon fibre was just around the corner. Wooden racquets were already finding their way into second-hand shops, curios from the past. But as a surrogate guitar, it was the business – sturdy yet lightweight. Its catgut strings proved to be perfect for plucking, particularly ballads. As time passed, the sweat from my furiously hammering fingers ate away at Ken's smiling visage. He gradually disappeared, along with bits of the logo. The black rubber grip perished and uncoiled like an apple peel.

Sometimes my fantasies blossomed even before the music started. I would bound into my room like a rock star coming onstage, in my mind gearing up for another breathtaking, panty-dampening performance. I'd set my face in what I imagined to be a mask of cool detachment. I could hear the vast, seething crowd and the piercing whistles. I could see hundreds of tiny guttering flames – cigarette lighters held aloft in the ultimate rock'n'roll salute.

The whole facade crumbled one day when I found the tennis racquet gone. Indignant, I burst into Darren's room to find him bouncing on his chenille-covered bed, headphones clamped to his ears, racquet slung around his midriff with a length of nylon rope. Bastard! Not only had my brother discovered my faux Fender, he'd gone one up on me and made a bloody *strap* for it. The 'guitar' dangled around his groin as he clapped his hands above his head, urging his imaginary crowd to join in. I felt anger, admiration and envy all at once. I also felt a fleeting flush of embarrassment, as I now had a pretty good idea of how ridiculous *I* looked alone in my bedroom.

This situation presented us both with a problem and introduced us to the eggshell-fragile world of sibling diplomacy. Normally we'd simply run to our parents, one of us whining, the other protesting his innocence, and let them sort it out. But although neither of us said as much, we both knew Gordon and Leila couldn't solve this impasse. It was far too humiliating. Neither of us was going to run to Mum and say, 'He stole the tennis racquet I was using as a guitar and I've got thirty thousand people waiting in my bedroom. Tell him to give it back.' We had to work it out sensibly and maturely. And so, once we'd finished wrestling, we lit upon the idea of a racquet roster. We took turns a day about, which sounds like an amicable arrangement, except that you could lay odds that, come your day, you wouldn't have time for a concert, or you wouldn't feel like performing for some reason.

However, the nylon strap, it has to be said, was a brilliant innovation. With my hands free, a whole new range of air-guitar shenanigans presented themselves. My favourite was the wedging of an imaginary ciggie behind the pretend strings at the pretend head of the pretend guitar. I'd seen Keith Richards do this in the video clip for 'Angie' and thought it the coolest thing I'd ever witnessed. The anti-smoking lobby will undoubtedly be relieved to know that it didn't encourage me to actually take up the old cancer sticks (apart from a single surreptitious suck on one of Mum's which was followed by some not so surreptitious spluttering), but gee whillikers, it looked the epitome of rock chic, that smouldering fag and its wisping blue smoke. And so I went through several pretend packs a day, lighting up behind cupped hands and shaking the match dead, while the tennis racquet dangled at my groin. I snatched puffs between songs. I exhaled nonchalantly, never once coughing, and carefully lodged my smoke back in place before launching into the next intro. On good days, when my imagination was firing on all cylinders, the real world simply melted away. The pine bookcase, my bed with it's jungle-motif Woolworths spread, the wardrobe all disappeared, replaced by a vivid mirage in which I was adored by millions. In which I never struck a dodgy chord or sang off-key. Back in those golden days, reality was an optional extra.

My parents went to great lengths to purge me of my rock'n'roll fantasies. Initially they thought my school friends could succeed where they themselves had failed, and enlisted my chums' unwitting aid in their quest to Stop Anthony Behaving Like a Complete Tosser. Anyone who popped around to check on my availability for, say, backyard cricket, was sent straight to my room unannounced. 'Oh sure, Darcy,' my mother would say, 'Anthony's in his room. Go on in.' And she would chuckle evilly as poor unsuspecting Darcy walked in on me, right in the middle of a blistering solo, eyes squeezed shut and face contorted with the effort of reaching those top notes.

It didn't work. Yes, I was red-faced. Yes, I could feel my ears burning with embarrassment. Yes, Darcy played right into my parents' hands and taunted me exhaustively for days afterwards. In the end, though, it didn't matter. Rock'n'roll's gravitational pull was too strong. I was one-third of an unusual love triangle – my cassette player, the tennis racquet and I could never be parted for long. Until, that is, my mother brought her formidable domestic pride to bear against me in this ongoing battle, with rather more effect. One day she called me into my room.

'Look what you've done to the carpet,' she said.

'What *I've* done?' I looked. The patch of off-white Berber to which she was pointing ran between my bed and the window. It was worn, scuffed and discoloured, the pile wilted like the tendrils of an unwatered pot plant.

'How do you suppose that happened?' she asked, her voice steel dusted with icing-sugar.

'Don't know, Mum. Maybe it's the afternoon sun coming in the wind –'

'It is not the bloody sun at all.' My mother had no time for bullshit, even creative bullshit. 'It's you, dancing around all the time like a bloody idiot!' To illustrate her point, in the most horrifying manner, my mother started imitating me imitating a rock star. She jumped up and down, pulling faces that made her look like a fish stranded on the shoreline. Her arms waved around in what I assumed to be a stab at playing air guitar. My instincts told me this wasn't the time to correct her technique. I could only watch appalled as Mum jerked and twisted and grimaced all over my centre stage, making a show of grinding her slippers into the carpet. It's an image I will take with me to my grave. At the time I thought I mightn't have long to wait.

'You've ruined it!'

'But –'

'But nothing. I'm telling you, stay off this bit of carpet, right? Jesus Christ, what do you think this is, a bloody disco? I'm serious. Enough's enough. If you stop Mick-bloody-Jaggering all over it, it might just spring back.'

This was a disastrous turn of events. You see, my cassette player sat on a chest of drawers under the window. Were I to reposition my imaginary stage to the other side of the bed, for instance, the lead from my headphones wouldn't reach me. Besides, I didn't want to change the setup – the illusion I had created was etched in my brain. Changing the configuration now would ruin everything.

My mother was still talking. '. . . everyone else in the world is happy just to listen to music,' she was saying. 'They don't have to pretend they're playing it. It's time you acted your age.'

'Yes, Mum.'

'And another thing. This room is starting to smell like a zoo, what with all your sweating. From now on you're going to keep your door open so the air can circulate. Right?'

'Yes, Mum.'

'And if you don't stop, I'll confiscate that bloody cassette player and you'll have no music at all. That'll fix you.'

My mother stormed out, still muttering about demented kids ruining her house. I slumped on my bed, the very picture of surly adolescence. Everywhere I looked, the Stones stared balefully down at me from my bedroom walls. Their expressions seemed to challenge me. *Is that it then?* they mocked. *Man, we've been through drug busts, done porridge in the Scrubs, withstood the weight of the Establishment, even had people murdered at our gigs. Your mam tells you not to dance in your room and you give up? Just like that? Nice one. Tremendous spirit of rebellion. Don't know why we bothered. Might as well 'ave stayed at 'ome.*

It's all right for you, I thought back fiercely. Your mums probably didn't rope off parts of the house with red velvet and erect little Do Not Touch plaques everywhere. My mother didn't actually do that either, of course, but she did tend to view her role in our home as that of museum curator.

I knew, though, that it wasn't over. Far from it. I didn't care if Mum thought I was as 'nutty as a fruitcake', or as 'mad as a cut snake', phrases I seemed to hear on a daily basis. I would play again. I would take up the tennis racquet once more and give a seminal performance in front of a packed stadium in my mind. Soon after, my father, exhibiting his natty gift for retribution, also took up the tennis racquet and wielded it masterfully around my thighs and backside. His backhand was still good, I noticed. Quite soon after that, both the racquet and my cassette player disappeared into a cupboard for an extended period of confiscation.

I vowed then and there that one day my parents would watch me perform in front of a real live audience, for money. And at some point my father would take out his earplugs, turn to my mother and proudly say, 'Well, bugger me, Leila, would you look at that. Our boy's made a career out of being a complete dickhead.'

One or two things need some clearing up, I think, before we move on. Anyone possessing even a rudimentary grasp of mathematics might well be wondering why someone whose early teens coincided with the dawn of the 1980s was fantasising about being in the Rolling Stones. Or indeed listening to the Rolling Stones. Let alone having imaginary conversations with posters of the Rolling Stones, who, even back then, were thought to have done their best work and were generally considered to be bloated, irrelevant caricatures of their former hell-raising selves.

It's a question I've been asked many times over the years, one usually put to me in the following fashion after several beverages: 'You're a smart bloke, so how come you've got this thing about a bunch of crappy old has-beens who haven't made a good record since the early '70s?' Or words to that effect. Sometimes the bit about being a smart bloke is overlooked.

For twenty years I've been forced to defend my love for the Stones. Considering how big and influential a band they are, you'd be amazed at the amount of scorn I've had heaped upon me. I mean, it's not as if I'm admitting to liking some obscure Norwegian flugelhorn quartet or anything like that. In fact, now I think about it, liking an obscure Norwegian flugelhorn quartet would probably earn me a whole swag of credibility points. To many, the Rolling Stones are a byword for corpulent excess. They are seen as money-obsessed, stadium-rock behemoths who haven't had the good decency to either die or retire and run pubs in Kent. Back in the mid-'70s, so the story goes, the Stones sold out, betrayed the disenfranchised youth of the world by transforming the rock'n'roll concert into something that looked as if it had been dreamt up by Andrew Lloyd Webber – a naff, expensive, all-singing, all-dancing spectacular complete with whizzy lighting effects, fireworks and giant inflatable figures. They went from being symbols of revolution and anarchy to wealthy lotharios courted by the Establishment. And sometime amid all that, they left their relevance in a trashed hotel room somewhere.

I love this word 'relevance' when it's used to describe a band. In music, to say someone is irrelevant is just about the greatest put-down you can dish out. When you see a band dismissed as such in the music press, you can almost hear the sobs and the tantrum of feet and fists. People who like talking about music toss this term around with gay abandon. 'But they're just not *rel*evant,' people say to me, apropos the Stones. Others nod sagely, as if that's pretty much wrapped up the argument.

'Relevant to what?' I'll ask, if I'm feeling a little feisty. World oil prices? The situation in Gaza? 'Today's music-buying youth,' they sometimes reply. Yes, but it's not just today's youth who buy music, is it? We know now that rock music isn't just a stage we pass through before we take our well-rounded tastes and go swanning off to the opera or ballet. We're all in our thirties and we still buy pop music, don't we?

If I'm in a more expansive mode, I might offer a defence that goes something like this: The Stones were principally responsible for the blues' crossover into mainstream white music. There were others who caught on and followed suit, and some, like John Mayall, have taken it further, but Jagger and Richards led the way. In the course of doing that, they helped make household names of the classic bluesmen – people like Robert Johnson, Howlin' Wolf, Muddy Waters, Willie Dixon, John Lee Hooker and Buddy Guy. The Stones took their songs and catapulted them into the pop music stratosphere. Remember, while the Stones were sexing up a storm with Dixon's 'Little Red Rooster', the chart around them was filled with tiddly-pop like 'Mrs Brown You've Got A Lovely Daughter'. The Stones gave popular music some balls, and the essence of the Rolling Stones is the blues. Keith Richards often says that you only see the real Mick Jagger when he's blowing blues harp. Whatever else they might have done over the years – questionable forays into disco, country and rap spring to mind – they are still basically a band rooted in the blues. And the blues is a form of music which has nothing to do with youth. John Lee Hooker died at the age of eighty-three. Until the very end he was playing and recording, and I never heard anyone describe John Lee as being a crusty old fart, or attack him on ageist grounds. No-one ever suggests that B.B. King should put a rug over his knees, or that Bo Diddley should pack himself off to a retirement village. On the contrary, these artists are viewed like fine wines. As with a robust shiraz, age is a plus. So why, then, would one expect the Rolling Stones, a band still soaked in the blues and whose tours still break all records, to slip quietly off to a nursing home? 'I'm a bit old for job training,' Keith Richards once famously said when asked whether the Stones were starting to look a tad ridiculous. 'Whaddya want me to do, go off and be a fucking welder?'

Furthermore, the Rolling Stones laid down the template for what a rock'n'roll band should ideally be. They might or might not be the World's Greatest Rock'n'Roll Band, but they are most definitely the World's Most Rock'n'Roll Rock'n'Roll Band. Their *attitude* is arguably their greatest legacy. Countless bands, consciously or otherwise, have tried to be the Rolling Stones. I'm not even talking musically, I mean *behaviourally*. Led Zeppelin, the Black Crowes, Guns N' Roses and Aerosmith are the most obvious examples. In each case you've got the posturing front-man, the dark and dangerous guitarist. Crippling drug habits and wrecked hotel rooms (and lives) litter the path. In the case of the Black Crowes the music press simply can't see past the similarities. They are Stone clones, pure and simple, and, as such, worthy of no further critical consideration.

But, more tellingly, there's a band like Oasis. The Gallagher brothers hate the Stones and profess undying love and respect for the Beatles, John Lennon in particular. But who does Liam Gallagher remind you of? Is he like Lennon or McCartney? Or does he behave more like Keef? Oasis grab headlines around the world for assaulting photographers and doing drugs and getting themselves banned from airlines. Is any of this new? I think not. They adopt the behaviour that is more or less expected of any rock band worth its salt. And which band set the trend for rock band behaviour and tardiness on a monstrous scale? It's true that there were plenty of bad-boy rockers before the Stones came along, Chuck Berry and Jerry Lee Lewis most notably, but it was the Stones who made it an institution.

Of course, in the end, all this is a pointless, circular argument. It's like arguing about religion. I can come up with any number of theories on why someone like Michael Jackson shouldn't exist, not in any rational universe, but there are millions who still worship. Anyway, in matters of music, as in art, you don't have to justify liking something. It's subjective. But I've been subjected to some fairly vituperative opinions over the years, so I suppose it's got me thinking.

Having said all that, I'm not totally blind to the Stones'

shortcomings. When a band's output spans several decades, there are always going to be some lean spots, and the Stones have definitely had their troughs. I can't, for instance, with the best will in the world, defend 1967's *Their Satanic Majesties Request* album. A paltry, gormless attempt to match *Sgt. Pepper's Lonely Hearts Club Band*, *Satanic Majesties* is so bad that it stands as the only Stones album not in my collection. To tell the truth, I've never even listened to it all the way through. It really is that bad. Toe-crinkling, cringe-worthy metaphysical mush; drug-sodden hippie piffle wrapped in an admittedly groundbreaking 3-D cover with Jagger and his cronies looking like characters from a Tolkien novel, dressed in wizard robes and other medieval attire. Even taking into account the hooch-hazy era in which it was made, *Satanic Majesties* is a travesty.

Nor can I put my hand on my heart and say that the Stones' latter offerings have all the vigorous cut and thrust of, say, *Some Girls*, or even *Undercover*, let alone *Exile on Main Street*. And as for Jagger's solo work, both musical and theatrical, the less said, the better. Recently I watched a trailer for the abominable *Ned Kelly*, which was filmed in 1969 with Jagger in the lead role. I know there's nothing I can say about this film that hasn't been said before, but when the promo line is 'If he were alive today, they would have to kill him all over again' – well.

But the pros far outweigh the cons. For a start, there's Charlie Watts. Any band with Watts in it is already streets ahead. He is, without doubt, the coolest guy in the business. Suave, eccentric, funny, Charlie's a man who doesn't like rock music, yet somehow wound up in one of the biggest outfits of all time. 'You don't think I take this seriously, do you?' he once snapped at a journalist. 'It's just a fucking rock'n'roll band.' He always looks as if he'd much rather be off playing Charlie

Parker material in a jazz combo. Like a jazz drummer, he only ever plays a basic kit – one snare, one tom, one floor-tom, bass drum, high-hat, ride and crash cymbals; no wall of percussion, no huge gong behind him – and he grips his left drumstick underhand, with the stick nestled in his palm. No other rock drummer I've ever seen holds his sticks this way. I'm sure no other rock drummer gives a toss, but hey, I notice these things.

While the other Stones were notching sexual conquests on their bedheads, Charlie married a fan named Shirley, and thirty-odd years later they're still together. They live on their sprawling country estate, with their horse stud and Charlie's collection of antique artillery. He wears suits that are sharper than Freddy Krueger's fingernails. In the '80s, when the Stones reached their quarter-century milestone, an interviewer asked Charlie, who was waiting impatiently to go onstage, whether there'd been a lot of hanging around over the last twenty-five years (which is a bizarre question, really). 'Yep,' replied Charlie in his tired East London accent. 'Five years work 'n twenty years 'angin' rahnd.'

Then there's *Beggars Banquet*. Anyone doubting the Stones' credentials will have those doubts quashed by this single album. This is the CD I press into the hands of dubious friends when I embark on my occasional evangelical rampages. Recorded in 1968, this is out-and-out brilliance. Over the course of just ten tracks, Mick and the boys traverse several musical styles, kicking off with 'Sympathy For The Devil', a shuffling, insidious samba beat. From there we plunge into ballad ('No Expectations'); country-tinged folk ('Dear Doctor', 'Factory Girl', 'Jigsaw Puzzle'); blues ('Parachute Woman'); anthemic protest song ('Street Fighting Man'); gospel ('Prodigal Son'); and 'Stray Cat Blues', one of the dirtiest, lowdown, snarling, cranking, straight-ahead rock songs of all time. On this track Jagger is lechery personified, a predatory lowlife enticing an underage runaway to join his party, promising that she can bring her wild friend and that it's 'no hanging matter'. Anything the Stones recorded between '68 and '72 should have dissenters holding up their palms in surrender. *Let it Bleed*, *Sticky Fingers*, *Exile on Main Street*. Peerless rock'n'roll.

What's more, the Stones, even in their dotage, still look like rock stars. Crinkly ones, perhaps, but rock stars nonetheless. While most of their contemporaries have grown fat and grey and bald as they slide into obscurity and old age, the Stones still look like the Stones. Gerry and the Pacemakers might resemble paunchy accountants, they might actually *have* pacemakers, but the Stones are still thin. They still dress like cowboys and outlaws. Keith must have been chemically preserved, because he actually looks fit – healthy even. Within his own horrifying parameters, at any rate. Their cheeks might be hollower, their knuckles bonier, the famous lips thinner, the faces more scari-fied, but they still look the part. Jagger is still the consummate pants man, bedding supermodels a third his age. Even the most churlish would have to admit that that's not bad going for a bloke on the wrong side of fifty-five. Money is part of the attrac-tion, no question. Still, can you really imagine Luciana Morad agreeing to a little rumpy-pumpy with Eric Burdon from the Animals? Or Justin Hayward from the Moody Blues? I think not.

Looking back, I have to concede it *is* a touch bizarre that a twelve-year-old could possibly be interested in a band which, even then, was being derided as the Strolling Bones. To put it all in context, we have to rewind.

It's December 1980. I am eleven, teetering on the cusp

between primary school and the big, scary world of high school. The summer holidays stretch out before me, seemingly endless days of sun, surf, cricket, and dackings at the local pool. Ah, how we laugh as yet another set of young genitals is suddenly and unexpectedly exposed to all and sundry, pubic hair sprouting like new grass. Oh, how strange and wondrous it is, the sight of Narelle Worboys in a bikini already having a distinctly peculiar effect beneath the waistbands of our boardshorts.

I'll tell you which songs were around that year and you can perhaps hum them quietly to yourself, the better to help you get the feel for it all. My number one: 'Turning Japanese' by the Vapors. Also popular were Martha and the Muffins with 'Echo Beach'. The Korgis were singing the breathtakingly insipid 'Everybody's Got To Learn Sometime', while James Freud was in love with a 'Modern Girl', and Australian Crawl were feeling a little 'Downhearted'. (Loved how Gavin Wood on *Countdown* used to work the song titles into a sentence. Clever stuff, that.)

Anyway, it's an overcast afternoon and I'm lounging in the aptly named lounge room, reading. The Hardy Boys are foiling some dastardly plot, and the villains are bemoaning the fact that they'd have gotten away with it too, if it wasn't for those pesky kids. The TV is on, but I'm not paying any attention. Until, that is, the regular program is interrupted to make way for a news flash. John Lennon is dead. Shot. Outside an apartment block. New York. Pictures of a thin man with a long nose and little round glasses. World in shock. Tributes flooding in. All the usual stuff they say when someone famous dies. More details as they come to hand and a full report in tonight's news at six. Lassie's adventures resume.

'Dad?'

From the next room. 'Yeah?'

'John Lennon's been shot.'

'What?'

'John Lennon. He's been shot.'

My father enters the room. 'What, you mean dead?'

'Yeah, think so. That's what they just said.'

Pause. My father says, 'Oh,' and turns to walk out. (As I mentioned earlier, my father was only interested in classical music. Elvis, the Beatles, the Stones, the sexual revolution, the swinging '60s, give peace a chance – all so much water off a duck's back to my dad.)

'Dad, who's John Lennon?'

'One of the Beatles.'

'Who are they?'

'A famous pop band.'

Famous? Since when? I haven't seen hide nor hair of them on *Countdown*. Never been mentioned, far as I can recall. How famous can they be? But there's a splinter of doubt. After all, if my *father*'s heard of them . . .

'Oh yeah? What songs do they sing?'

'Hundreds.'

'Like what?'

'Oh, I dunno. "Love Me Do", "Yellow Submarine", "Let It Be", "Hey Jude".'

'Never 'eard of 'em.'

'Well, they split up before you were born, didn't they? Besides, they're my bloody age. I'm not surprised you haven't heard of them.'

A band my father's age? It was incredible. It hardly bore thinking about. Almost as difficult to contemplate now is the fact that I spent my first eleven years on the planet without knowing who the Beatles were. My hometown was a small place, but even so.

We watched the news that night, saw the candlelit vigils, the tears, the grief, the wreaths, the placards. Mark Chapman became the most loathed man on the face of the planet. A couple of days later, Ian 'Molly' Meldrum cried on *Countdown*. He walked onto a darkened set, perched on a stool and sobbed. It stunned me to see someone cry on national telly. Over the next few days, I took a crash course in the Beatles. The local radio station played nothing else for what seemed like a month. You couldn't turn on the TV without seeing Lennon seated at that white piano in that white room singing 'Imagine'. And who was that strange woman with the long black hair who just wandered in and plonked herself down beside him? She didn't do anything, just sat there. Didn't she know they were filming? And there were the old black and white clips of the Beatles playing, wearing their matching suits and shaking their shaggy heads and going 'Woooooo!' and taking a synchronised bow at the end of the show.

And you know what? It had absolutely no effect on me whatsoever. There was no epiphany. I still preferred 'Turning Japanese'.

While we're on the subject of great rock'n'roll deaths, the one before John Lennon's actually had a far greater impact on me. Well, the last but one for those of you who include Johnny O'Keefe's demise in 1978, I'm talking in global terms here. I was only eight, but I can remember the man on the morning radio news telling me Elvis was dead. You know something big has happened when they don't begin the bulletin with the usual, 'Good morning, So-and-so with the news at 7:30,' but with an interview grab or some other soundbite. In this case, the ponderous news theme died away and there was silence. Then there was Elvis singing the last strains of 'Bridge Over Troubled

Water' live. Then, over the tumultuous applause, the newsreader cut in and said, with all the studied gravity of someone who has terrible news and can hardly wait to tell you, 'Elvis Presley, the king of rock'n'roll . . . is dead.'

I rushed straight to the bathroom, where my mother was seated on the toilet smoking a cigarette, as she was wont to do in those days. I burst through the door. 'Mum, Elvis is dead!'

I can only imagine how we must have looked. My mother, still on the lavatory with her pants around her ankles, sobbing inconsolably, and me hugging her, also crying, not because Elvis was dead, but because my mother was crying and she rarely did.

So anyway, as I was saying, I'd never heard of the Beatles until the day John Lennon was murdered. I relate that story simply to put you in the picture, to give you an idea of my innocence, and ignorance. Mine had always been the *Countdown* world of Marcia ('You') Hines; Rupert ('Escape [The Pina Colada Song]') Holmes; Christie ('He's My Number One') Allen; The Little River Band ('The Long Jumping Jeweller'); The Ted Mulry Gang ('Jump In My Car'); John Paul ('Love Is In The Air') Young; Hush ('Boney Moroney'); Stars ('Mighty Rock'); Joe ('Shaddap You Face') Dolce; Judie ('Stay With Me Till Dawn') Tzuke; The Ferrets ('Don't Fall In Love') and Smokie ('Living Next Door To Alice'). Depressing, really, when you list them like that. But everything changed just twelve short months later.

Countdown is on and Molly has just thrown to the chartbusters of the week. Punk has packed its bags and made off with the lucre, leaving the way open for New Wave and the New

Romantics. Soft Cell are leading the charge with 'Tainted Love'. Tonight Molly's telling us to watch out for an English band called Duran Duran, they're going to be huge as well. The song's called 'Planet Earth'. The five members of Duran Duran are cavorting on a computer-generated plinth. They're all blousy white shirts, fru-fru hair and eyeshadow, *de rigueur* clobber for the time. 'Do yourself a favour,' Molly urges, his signature utterance. 'Do yourself a favour, get out to the shops, buy that, they're going to be huge.'

Abruptly Duran Duran vanish mid-chorus and we're confronted with the sight of Mick Jagger, alone against black drapes, wearing a very tight T-shirt and what look to be white tracky dacks. (All prick and ribs, as someone later said.) He has his hands on his hips and he pulls a variety of peacock poses, even before anything has really happened songwise. Molly, meanwhile, is telling us he can't believe it, but look who's just entered the Top Ten with a bullet, it's the Rolling Stones with 'Start Me Up'. The camera tracks back and two terrifying profiles swim into view – Ronnie Wood and Keith Richards. Grotesque, spiky marionettes orbiting each other unsteadily, wielding guitars like drunken duellists. You can almost smell cigarettes and booze. Off in the background, clad in a powder-blue suit, Bill Wyman stands motionless next to the drumkit, almost as if he's embarrassed and doesn't want to be associated with the antics of the other three. Nestled behind the high-hat and snare, Charlie Watts looks resigned, a wan smile plastered on his hangdog face. On the face of it, you'd have to say they are the sorriest-looking bunch of derelicts in all Christendom.

Bear in mind that at this stage I didn't know their names. It was John Lennon and the Beatles all over again. Except this time I was transfixed. Mesmerised. Maybe it's my memory cheating after all this time, maybe it was just that I'd seen Duran Duran only moments before, but even on our little black and white TV in the spare room the Stones seemed to be cast in sharp relief. They were a breath of refreshingly fetid air amid an unrelenting cloud of pancake, hairspray and ruffles. It was rock music pared back to almost nothing. No costumes, no makeup, no set, no effects, special or otherwise – nothing. There was a noticeable whiff of indolence. Jagger forgot to mime half the lyrics; at times they were laughing and pulling faces at each other when they should have been singing. They just didn't seem to care. Only later did I learn that they were so big, and had been around so long and had had so much success, that they *didn't* care. They had nothing to prove.

Ah, and the song itself. Keith's opening riff trips over almost straight away as Charlie hits the high-hat and immediately turns the beat around. The growling, guttural guitars. The sparseness of it. The empty spaces where there's nothing, save for the echo of the snare drum. The way it tumbles into that gloriously ragged chorus. Writing back in the mid-'80s in his definitive book on the Stones, cryptically titled *The Stones*, British rock journalist Philip Norman says that the effect of 'Start Me Up' was that of 'a Neanderthal painting, lit by primitive fire'. That's as may be. From where I stood, it was certainly a large, unsqueezed pimple on the cherubic, hairless, lightly rouged buttocks of the 1981 hit parade. Of course, it's heinous in its political incorrectness, comparing as it does a woman to a nice set of wheels, but all that went way over the head of the twelve-year-old me. (Believe it or not, the song actually started out as a *reggae* track. I can't imagine it.)

Some weeks later, my parents asked me what I'd like for Christmas and I told them I wanted a cassette called *Tattoo*

You by a band called the Rolling Stones. 'Start Me Up' was track one. They both stared at me dumbfounded.

'They're as old as us. Older even,' my mother said, as if that were some kind of warning I would be well advised to heed. My father just shook his head. Barely a year ago, I'd been wondering who on earth the Beatles were and sneering at their *alleged* popularity. Now here I was asking for a Rolling Stones record. Bloody kids. Who could fathom them?

Christmas 1981 is significant, then, for a couple of reasons. First, it marks the point of my departure. Many others my age continued down the eight-lane highway of mainstream music appreciation, stopping for a quick cuppa at Dexy's Midnight Runners, lunch at Cyndi Lauper, afternoon tea and a biscuit at Bananarama, before pulling in for an overnight stay at Prince, while I flicked my indicator and veered off at the sign that said 'The Blues, via Various Ageing White-Boy English Bands', heading off over the hill on a long journey bound for Muddy Waters and John Lee Hooker.

Second, *Tattoo You* was my first nervous foray into the world of albums, as opposed to singles or chart compilations. The enormity of this cannot be overestimated. It was a devastatingly mature and risky decision forgoing *1981 Rocks On*, which was chock-full of songs I knew, like Kim Wilde's 'Kids In America' and Rick Springfield's 'Jessie's Girl', in favour of a whole album of unknown tracks by the one band. What if I didn't like any of the other songs?

As it turned out, I needn't have worried. Sure, it was a little strange at first hearing the same voice on every song, but I adapted, grew to love *Tattoo You*, and played it to death on my little black mono cassette player. 'Black Limousine' was about the first blues song I ever heard (well, the first song with a blues progression, anyway). And I almost dropped dead in shock when Keith's tattered voice mentioned 'tits and arse' on 'Little T & A'. (I had no idea what T & A stood for, of course.) It was all so deliciously naughty.

When I say I played it to death, I mean it. One fine day we were all in the car, bound for a family outing of some description. Against my better judgement, I had brought along the cassette recorder and it sat on my shoulder like a prototype ghettoblaster, with its little speaker pressed against my ear and the volume turned down to what I considered a reasonable level. The countryside went past in a blur while *Tattoo You* played in my ear. I was happy.

'Turn it down,' my father said over his shoulder.

'What?'

'Turn it down, please.'

'But I can hardly hear it now.'

'*We* can all hear it, and we don't want to,' my mother chimed in.

'But it *is* down. I've got it pressed up against my ear so just I can hear it.'

'You'll have my hand pressed up against your ear if you don't turn it down.'

With Dad giving me meaningful looks in the rear-view mirror, I fiddled with the volume knob. Or at least I made a show of fiddling with the volume knob. I don't know why kids feel duty-bound to try it on with parents in these situations, but I somehow thought I could win this minor skirmish by *miming* turning it down.

Not long afterwards: 'Right, that's it, turn the bloody thing off.'

'Aw, Mum –'

'We asked you to turn that racket down and we can still hear it, so now you can turn it *off*.'

We continued to argue. Eventually my mother twisted around in her seat and held out her hand. 'Right, give me the tape. Now!'

It amuses me somewhat now to remember that the song playing at the time was 'No Use In Crying', track four, side two. I pressed eject and Mum snatched the cassette, wound down her window and tossed it out of the car. Just like that. It sort of skidded in the gravel and disappeared into a patch of scrub.

We all agreed, Dad, Darren and I, that it had been something of an overreaction. Actually, that makes the situation sound much calmer than it was. The car was filled with babbling voices, protestations and wailing. I was apoplectic with rage. My mouth worked but I could only produce a strangled mewling sound. I was in the grip of that terrible, impotent frustration I often felt when the parents committed some atrocious act. The injustice of it all was overwhelming.

Mum was defiant. I begged Dad to turn back but he said it was too late now, we'd probably never find it, and anyway, it would more than likely be damaged. (A London radio station once conducted a survey to find out what type of music could be found on those fluttering brown loops of tape you always see by the side of the road. In other words, what was the most thrown-away music in the country? What music was so bad that it wasn't enough just not to play it, it had to be immediately dispensed with out of a moving vehicle? The answer was Phil Collins' *No Jacket Required*. I'm not sure that this story is true, but I certainly wouldn't argue with the findings.)

It would be almost six months before I could scrape up enough money to buy a replacement copy of *Tattoo You*. In the meantime my Stones fixation festered away just beneath the surface, threatening to explode into full-blown obsession.

I realise that I have explained *how* my Rolling Stones love affair began, but not *why*. The closest I can come to pinning it down is by saying that when I discovered the Stones they were different. They were new and exciting. That sounds ridiculous, I know, but history somehow worked backwards. I'd never heard of the Rolling Stones, so they were new and exciting to *me*. They were unlike anything else I was used to seeing on the telly or hearing on Taree's radio station. By the time I discovered that they were dinosaurs and desperately uncool, I was hooked and there was no turning back.

As time has passed, I've grown to love them, not in spite of but because of their faults. Listen to any of their live albums, or watch one of their concert videos – the band is often alarmingly loose and quite often botches intros and endings. Ron Wood's guitar solos are slap-happy and rife with bum notes. Several times Jagger shoots nervous glances at Keith and Charlie, looking for some clue as to what might happen next. Even Andy Johns, an engineer on some of their seminal albums, describes them as the worst band on the planet. 'But,' he says, 'when it happens, they are transformed almost instantly from this dreadful band into the Rolling Stones. It is almost magical.' And it's that recklessness that still appeals to me. Much of their charm lies in the very fact that you're not sure which band you're going to get, the worst garage band on Earth, or the Rolling Stones. You just never know. The unpredictability is refreshing, especially when stacked alongside the usual parade of homogenous MTV fodder.

Anyway, here's a little piece of backyard psychology for you. I think my mother actually did me a huge favour that Sunday afternoon. Had my copy of *Tattoo You* not wound up in the scrub, maybe – and this is pure speculation – just maybe I'd have gotten over the Stones. Perhaps I'd have played 'Start Me Up' until the mere sound of the opening riff made me physically ill and, thus fatigued, I'd have moved on to pastures new. Howard Jones, perhaps. Or Thomas Dolby. Nik Kershaw. Ultravox. Haircut 100. The Go-Go's. Maybe.

Mum, I love you.

Before Keith Richards, though, there was Adam Ant.

Bet you never thought you'd see those two names in the same sentence, did you? Unless perhaps that sentence ran along the lines of 'In the grip of a drunken rage, Keith Richards today rammed a rather large and very empty Yukon whisky bottle up Adam Ant's rectal passage.' But it's true – before I discovered the Rolling Stones, I was enamoured with Adam and the Ants. One of Adam's biggest hits, 'Prince Charming', contained the words 'ridicule is nothing to be scared of'. Let me just state unequivocally that that is unmitigated codswallop. I wish to be plain: ridicule is *everything* to be scared of. And I should know because I'm from Taree, the town where they built a Big Oyster. Sorry, that should be the Big Oyster. The definite article.

Back in the late 1980s, for reasons best left shrouded in the mists of time, the Taree council decided that what was needed to draw tourists and really put the place on the map was a Big Oyster. Up it went, despite the protests of sane people, on the northern outskirts of town – several tonnes of corrugated grey bivalve with an art gallery inside. An enormous concrete mollusc. It was, and is, without question the ugliest, single most ridiculous and sorry example in a long line of questionable Big things dotted along the east coast of this country. It is now also the emptiest. It has been abandoned, although I hear talk of it being turned into a car yard. The shell has been left, well, a shell. Weeds grow through cracks in the concrete carpark. The council thought people might come to mock but that they would stay to enjoy. In reality they came to mock, mocked heartily, and went somewhere else. The Big Oyster's only visitors nowadays seem to be former residents who are writing books and the odd second-rate comedian, for whom a massive mollusc is a rich vein of material.

Oversized oysters aside, Taree is a pretty place, although I didn't appreciate that fact when I lived there. When I was growing up, I imagined that Taree was the Aboriginal word for 'Fuck me dead, how boring is this place?' I was certain there was more life in a tramp's vest. But when you've been away for a while, you see the place afresh. It has a wide, picturesque river and its well-ordered, kerbed-and-guttered, three-bedroomed, brick-veneer suburbs and manicured gardens give way to dairy farmland – lush, verdant fields and hillsides dotted with rambling, falling-down farm buildings with smears of rust on their corrugated-iron roofs.

Not quite so rustic is the high school. It is an imposing chunk of red brick in the middle of town, a structure which bears more than a passing resemblance to a maximum-security prison. Behind its fortress-style walls is a large concrete quadrangle where generations of Manning Valley offspring have roughhoused, played handball, lined up for assemblies, held hands, and stolen first kisses. And it was there, one fine day during my first year, perched astride my black Globite schoolcase with my grey school socks hoisted to my knobbly knees, that I turned to my girlfriend and asked if I might borrow one of her best frilly blouses so I might attend the forthcoming school dance dressed as popstar Adam Ant. As ideas go, it turned out to be right up there with 'Hey, why don't we build a Big Oyster?' But I wasn't to know that at the time.

In 1981 punk still hadn't made it to Taree, which was something of a relief because it could be a pretty rough place as it was. However, the New Romantics did make it to town, and for a brief period, somewhere between John Lennon being gunned down and my seeing the Stones on *Countdown*, I fell victim to pre-packaged, vacuum-sealed, cynically marketed pop. In case you've forgotten who Adam and the Ants were, heaven forbid, let me fill you in. Adam Ant's real name is Stuart Goddard which, let's be frank, is not a swoon-inducing moniker, with apologies to any Stuart – or, indeed, Stewart – Goddards who might be reading this. The brains behind Adam and the Ants was Malcolm McLaren, the same Malcolm McLaren who was the brains behind the Sex Pistols, which proves that manufactured bands – Spice Girls, Bardot, Scandal'us, Steps, Five, et al. – are not a new phenomenon. Shite perhaps, but not new.

Malcolm had had great success with the Pistols, as has been well documented, so when the ambitious young Stu asked him to manage his band, he thought he'd try the opposite approach and see if he could wring any money out of Britain's youth that way. Adam and the Ants were the antithesis of punk. They looked like the result of a tryst between Errol Flynn and a tribe of Native Americans. They were pretty, flouncy, swashbuckling, voluminous-sleeved buccaneers with warpaint on their pouty faces and ribbons in their hair. They stormed the charts like pirates boarding a treasure-laden galleon, singing percussive, chanting songs designed to boost teenage self-esteem and their bank accounts in equal measure. Punk meant furious songs about anarchy and nihilism and discontent. Adam and the Ants rose above the mucus and nasal piercings to sing songs laden with positive, life-affirming messages about being true to oneself and finding the Apache warrior within, but mostly they were about saying no to alcohol and drugs, dressing in really nice clothes and paying close attention to personal hygiene. 'Ant-music', their first big hit, was a song purely about them having arrived on the scene, and contained a one-word chorus – 'ant-music' repeated over and over again – with the band grunting 'uh uh uh uh uh uh' in the background. I assume this was sup-posed to be the sound an ant might make. They sounded more like rutting geese. In fact, many of the tracks on their first album, *Kings of the Wild Frontier,* were littered with blood-curdling yells and cries and quite unusual yodelling, if indeed yodelling can ever be described as usual.

The band was also notable for boasting two drummers, for no discernible reason. Their fans were known as Antpeople. I, apparently, was an Antperson. But, as I say, it was only for a brief time. And it all came to an abrupt halt, like a stylus being ripped off spinning vinyl, on the night of the school dance.

If Carlene was startled by my asking to wear her clothes, she didn't let on. She played it very cool, in fact. She just asked what colour and I told her the blouse would have to be white. And because Adam Ant was in the middle of his Prince Charming period, it would be great if she had one with ruffles at the neck and cuffs. She confirmed that she was in fact in possession of such a garment and would be happy for me to borrow it. She was a good stick, Carlene.

Carlene was, from all accounts, my first girlfriend. I say

'from all accounts' because we never really spoke about it. We never kissed. We didn't even hold hands. I did try to put my arm around her one day, but my timing was all out and I wound up cuffing her on the back of the head. Our 'relationship' had been arranged by proxy. One day, I was accosted in A-block by one of Carlene's friends.

'Do you like Carlene?' she whispered conspiratorially.

'Who?'

She nodded over to a pleasant-looking girl with long, straight blonde hair and glasses, who was taking great care not to look in our direction. 'Car*lene*. You know.'

I didn't know. In fact, I couldn't remember ever setting eyes on her. 'Oh, Carlene. Yeah, sure, she's okay. Why?'

'She likes you,' the matchmaker purred. 'Wanna go with her?'

Go with her? Go with her where? The friend explained the general idea.

'Er, sure, I guess.' I didn't want to be impolite.

And that was it. It was a bit like an arranged marriage. Carlene and I would meet in the schoolground at lunchtimes, sit together on our schoolcases – our proximity to each other the only sign that we were 'going together' – and ignore each other adoringly. But I had designs on taking things to another level at the school dance.

School dances, or socials as they were known, were held in our cavernous assembly hall. A local DJ would set up large speakers on the stage and play records while a battery of lights flashed colourfully at us. Employing the hip patois of the era, the DJ would exhort eight hundred-odd students to 'get down, get rockin'!' We boys were wearing acid-washed jeans, pastel shirts, thin leather ties, and jackets with the sleeves bunched up at the elbows. Girls wore Madonna-style lace gloves *sans* fingers, wide white plastic belts and leg warmers. Often at the same time. Beneath the Queen's regal and disapproving stare, and amid a humid fug of cheap perfume and sweat, we writhed and twisted to 'Mickey', '99 Luft Baloons', 'Hungry Like The Wolf' and 'Wake Me Up Before You Go-Go'. Billy Idol's dancing style was immensely popular, all forearms and fists. We looked like Wonder Woman deflecting bullets with her magic bracelets. During Human League's 'Don't You Want Me', the girls took centre-stage, giving vaudevillian performances while miming the bits where the ex-cocktail waitress tells the guy she'd have made it with or without his help. When the Uncanny X-Men's 'Fifty Years' came on, we all threw our arms around each other, rocked from side to side, and promised never – ever, ever – to lose touch. We danced in packs; friends formed a circle and mimed the lyrics while generating meaningful eye contact with members of the opposite sex. You could almost see the hormones zipping around as the throng tried to lend new meaning to the term 'social intercourse'.

Socials were always clamorous, frenetic, tumultuous and emotional. Someone always wound up in tears, someone always ended up in a fight. Time was compressed. People fell in and out of love so many times it was a wonder they didn't suffer concussion. Entire relationships were hatched and buried within a three-hour period, sprouting, blossoming and wilting like time-lapse flowers in a wildlife documentary. Girls spent much of the night fending off their rabid dates. The boyfriends of girls who didn't spent the night urging their mates to smell their fingers. Teachers prowled the edge of the dancefloor, wondering if some of the boys were actually dancing or suffering seizures of some description.

Before I left the house, I felt the whole Adam Ant thing was going swimmingly. Carlene's blouse was a fairly good fit, and the ruffles were just right. Leather pants and knee-high boots were a bit thin on the ground at the local Kmart, so sharply ironed jeans and joggers completed the ensemble. Not perfect, granted, but from the waist up I was the real deal. I raided the sewing basket for some ribbons to tie in my hair and plastered a thick line of white zinc cream across my nose and cheeks. My mother let me use a little of her eyeshadow and eyeliner. (On the subject of fancy dress, I've often wondered at the depiction of these parties on TV or in movies. Everyone always looks so good. The costumes are absolutely first-rate. So realistic. That's because the characters' costumes have been lavishly designed by whoever has designed the rest of their movie wardrobe. In my experience, fancy-dress parties in the real world are predominantly pathetic, consisting of a motley assortment of Vegas-period Elvises and the odd sagging Superman outfit. Most costumes are homemade and only one step removed from truly horrible school dressups. As a nipper, a friend of mine needed a hedgehog costume for the school play, and his exasperated mother tied the front doormat to his back with nylon rope. Full marks for improvisation, but the sight of a bewildered hedgehog crawling around with WELCOME emblazoned across its back sparked uncontrollable and inappropriate gales of mirth in the school hall.)

It wasn't like that with me. I wanted to *be* Adam Ant. I'd pulled out all stops. My father caught sight of me wearing a blouse and makeup and promptly announced that he was too ashamed to be seen in public with me. I told him I was a banshee. He said, 'Boofhead, more like it,' and stated in no uncertain manner that he was not driving me to the social. I would have

58

to walk. I said I didn't care. I was an Antperson. An individual. I *would* walk. And off I set. Down the average, tree-lined streets, just your average, heavily made-up, blouse-bedecked boy walking tall in the name of all things Antish. Truth be told, I was quite chuffed with my father's reaction. I felt like a rebel. It would have been a bit of a let-down having him ruffle my hair and laugh and say, 'You look smashing, mate. You're gonna kill 'em.' No, his utter disgust was sweet music to my ears.

However, after several carhorns had been honked and various obscenities had been hurled at me from passing vehicles, I began to have doubts. I felt conspicuous and vulnerable. I caught glimpses of my reflection in shop windows and my reflection didn't look confident. I told myself to relax, that once I was in the middle of hundreds of kids all dressed up it wouldn't matter. Everyone would look stupid. Then, when I was only one block away from the school and safety, I ran into Craig McKenzie and his gang and I knew instantly that I'd made a horrible mistake.

McKenzie was two years older than me and a regular little Genghis Khan. Only, had you actually called him that, he'd have thought you were accusing him of being a Pakistani medium-pacer. He was the scourge of the quadrangle. A complete and utter bastard. One of a line of bastards, in fact. There were McKenzie boys peppered throughout nearly every form, each occupying a different level of delinquency. Craig wasn't the eldest, but he boxed well above weight when it came to brutal idiocy. And somehow, even though I didn't even know him, I managed to annoy him. At school he found it impossible to pass me in the hall without inflicting injury of some description. McKenzie's idea of fancy dress was to wear a shirt instead of a singlet. The fact that he'd just come across me wearing a frilly blouse and makeup was enough to make him believe there was a God, and that the Almighty had delivered unto him an excellent excuse for some pre-social anti-social behaviour.

The gang surrounded me. One of them leant on my shoulder in a chummy fashion which I suspected wasn't all that chummy, and my guts churned. McKenzie eyeballed me silently for a few lingering seconds. He had a flair for the dramatic, I'll give him that. He was a weird-looking character, too. His features all seemed to be jostling for position in the centre of his freckled face. Nose, eyes, mouth all crowding together as if his ears had just farted. I thought it best not to mention it.

'Nice farkin' blouse,' he sneered. 'Whadarya sposeta be?' I could detect the sweet, cloying smell of alcohol on his breath, and suspected that he and his cronies had been down to the riverbank for a quick tipple or seven.

'Adam Ant,' I answered. I knew that wasn't the best response but it was the truth, and it sure beat 'Give us a kiss, big boy, and I'll tell you.'

''E's a fuckin' poofta, that Adam Ant,' one of the others chipped in.

'Prince-fuckin'-Charming fairy,' said another, displaying a gift for eloquence.

'He sucks cock,' someone behind me rejoined.

'Yeah,' said McKenzie. 'So I guess that makes you a cock-sucking poofta as well.'

I didn't have time to ponder that peculiar brand of logic. My life should have flashed before my eyes, but I was only thirteen and perhaps my brain decided it wasn't worth the effort.

I honestly can't remember much of what happened next, or how long it lasted, so other than 'It hurt' there's not much I can say, really. One minute I was standing there and the next I was on the ground, curled up with my arms over my head to protect me from the blur of feet and fists. The blows were punctuated with verbal attacks, so that each punch or kick coincided with a 'POOFta!' or a 'FagGOT!', and other equally charming terms of endearment. McKenzie's parting gestures were a bourbon-flavoured gob of spit in my face and a steel-capped toe in the perineum, which was simply agonising.

By the time I'd staggered to the social, I looked less like Adam Ant, and more like a sodden old prostitute after a hard night. The white zinc line was smeared across my cheeks, the hair-ribbons were unwound and dangling. Eyeliner, bulldozed by tears, carved a path down my face. I felt, and walked, as if someone were holding a bunsen burner to my nether regions. The blouse was torn and bloodied but I assumed Carlene wouldn't care. I imagined that, when she saw the state I was in, she would be distraught with concern; that she would rush up, hug me and generally make a big fuss. This thought actually cheered me up a bit. Maybe that prize twonk McKenzie had inadvertently done me a favour. My chances of sitting down for the next couple of days were zero, but my chances of pashing Carlene had suddenly sky-rocketed. That was how it worked on TV, right? The hero, battered but unbowed, always got to snog the girl.

Well, I was right about one thing. Carlene did make a fuss. No sooner had I entered the hall than I was approached by Paul Stanley, the lead singer from KISS. 'What *happened* to you?' Carlene asked from beneath her black curly wig.

As I briefly outlined my plight, her eyes widened in a most satisfactory manner. I noticed she was still wearing her glasses over her painted star, and felt a little surge inside. How could someone look so ridiculous yet at the same time maintain that air of sophistication? I could hardly wait to mingle lipgloss.

I stumbled to the end of the McKenzie tale and waited for Carlene to throw her arms around me. Instead she threw them up in the air. 'Look what you've done to my blouse!'

Maybe she hadn't heard me over the thumping music. 'But I just sai–'

'You've ruined it!'

'But Craig McKen–'

Carlene had tears in her eyes. 'My nanna gave me that for Christmas.'

'But Carlene, it wasn't my fault. I didn't go out and deliberately get myself beaten up, did I? What about me?' I pleaded, unconsciously echoing Moving Pictures' teen-angst smash hit.

Carlene wasn't listening. Her face had screwed up into an expression that was distinctly not adoring, nor sympathetic. 'You're gonna pay for that bloody top, you bastard.' And with that she turned and stalked off to rejoin Gene, Peter and Ace, all of whom had sprouted breasts and were jiggling them to great effect as 'Centerfold', by the J. Geils Band, blasted out.

Thus was the curtain rung down on my inaugural intersex relationship. Pop music had drawn a rapier and inflicted its first wounds on me – carved little nicks in my psyche. I'd had a rude awakening. Music could get you into trouble. In this town it wasn't always a good idea to wear your musical allegiances on your frilly sleeve. (I read recently how, before Queen became famous, Freddie Mercury walked into a bar full of miners in the north of England wearing black nailpolish and a fur coat. I assume he was also wearing pants of some description, they didn't say. In light of my Adam Ant debacle, Freddie's courage amazes me. Of course, the article failed to mention whether Freddie had seven shades of shite beaten out of him.)

From now on, I would have to be a little more guarded about advertising where my tastes lay.

More importantly though, and this is what *really* hurt, Adam Ant had indirectly cost me both the price of a blouse and any chance I had of kissing Carlene Allwood, and that was something I just could not forgive. Dandy highwayman, be buggered. Apache, my arse. As I stood there with my testicles throbbing in time with the bass from the speakers, I decided that, all things considered, I no longer wanted to be an Antperson.

So I was left with this to ponder: if liking the New Romantics was apt to result in the glinting point of a geometry compass puncturing my buttock, what style of music could be considered safe? What genre was deemed okay in a middling country town? The answer, I soon discovered, was four-on-the-floor, good old-fashioned, working-class, testosterone-injected, beer-fuelled, tight-jeaned, is-that-a-cucumber-taped-to-his-thigh Australian pub rock. If a band hadn't played the local RSL, then forget it. Cold Chisel (Chisel), Midnight Oil (the Oils), the Angels (no nickname), Hoodoo Gurus (the Gurus) and the Radiators (the Rads) passed muster. To a lesser extent, so did v. Spy v. Spy (the Spies) and Rose Tattoo (the Tatts). And of course supreme was AC/DC (AccaDacca).

These bands all forged a bond with regional youth. Their sound was hard and raw, unmistakably blue-collar. Blue-collar with axle-grease stains. Their raging guitars sounded like machinery in an industrial park – steel saws and grinders screaming and showering sparks. They sang about familiar places, familiar problems. Angry songs about the rape of the environment, the threat of nuclear war. They urged us to kick against society's restraints; they championed the plight of the working man, they nourished burgeoning political appetites. Mostly, though, they sang songs about getting laid. And that, my friends, was what we were really interested in.

We rarely, if ever, heard these bands on Taree's radio station, which had the admittedly impossible job of trying to please us young 'uns and older, conservative people-on-the-land at the same time, and so programmed a strange mix of Top Forty pop and country and western music. It wasn't unusual for Blondie and Gary Numan to be followed by Charlie Pride or Tammy Wynette or Kenny Rogers. Actually, two country songs from that era stick in my mind, largely because they tried so hard to tug the heartstrings that they ended up being comical. One was 'Teddy Bear', a thigh-slappingly funny song about a crippled boy who sits up at night chatting to truckdrivers on his CB radio using the call-sign Teddy Bear. At the end of the song, a whole convoy comes roaring in to visit young Master Bear, and one by one teary tattooed truckers hoist him into their cabs and take him for a ride. The other, 'IOU', was also a wet-your-pants howler. Over an ambling C&W tune, the narrator rattles off all the ways his dear old mother has helped him through the years, and how he can't possibly repay her for everything she's done to make him the person he is today. But he knows she will consider the debt paid in full with just four little words, 'Mom, I love you.' This was given a run nearly every Saturday morning during the wedding-dedications program, and I cried a sneaky tear every time.

Inexplicably, given our love for hard rock, we did go through a brief Dire Straits period, around the time of 'Money For Nothing', but Mark Knopfler's dusky mumble and twiddly guitar soon lost appeal, and the power chords reigned supreme once again. One friend considered booking himself in for psychiatric assessment when he found himself taking a liking to Redgum, a folky band long on fiddle, facial hair and broad Australian accents, and short on rock'n'roll cred. His passion was sparked by the band's surprise hit with the Vietnam War lament 'I Was Only Nineteen'. This friend confided in me because there was no-one else he could tell. He said that if there was anyone who could sympathise with being a musical outsider, it was me. But to be honest, even I struggled to come to grips with deviance on this scale. I don't know that he ever fully recovered.

The anthems of the day were a heady mix of three chunking chords and lyrics best appreciated through a thick hormonal fog, which, happily enough, we had in spades. They were veritable RSL club classics: 'Am I Ever Gonna See Your Face Again?' (No way, get fucked, fuck off! Oh, how we loved to scream that); 'Gimme Head' (Oh, how we'd have loved to scream that and receive an answer in the affirmative); 'You Shook Me All Night Long' (impossible to scream, as AC/DC's Brian Johnson has a vocal range which can only be imitated by whacking your testicles with a rubber mallet).

The basic rule of thumb was that as long as a band had a minimum of four members (v. Spy v. Spy excepted), wore a lot of black, and boasted only guitars and drums, it was okay. Reduce the members to two or three and throw in a synthesiser, or those hexagonal electronic drums that were the sound of the '80s, and you had a recipe for trouble. For God's sake, some of those bands coming out of the UK had no guitars at all. Not *one*. I was perplexed. How on earth could you air-guitar to a band that didn't boast so much as a single axe? As for clothes, you had bands like Kajagoogoo wearing drab, utilitarian beige coveralls and performing *barefoot*. Spandau Ballet were kitted out in kilts. Wham! wore tight little shorts and white sneakers in the video for 'Wake Me Up Before You Go-Go'. A popular move with the girls, maybe, but there's something desperately uncool about guys in bands baring their legs, regardless of how tanned, taut and depilated their thighs. Leather, denim or spandex only, please boys (unless you're Angus Young). Hair was growing more idiotic by the day – cuts were spikier, ends blonder, regrowth darker. Fringes were completely out of control, foreheads and brows engulfed by rampant, unchecked foliage. King of the dopey 'dos was the lead singer from A Flock of Seagulls, whose hair was sculpted into towering peaks either side of his head like peroxided wolverine ears.

Those skinny English boys with their painted faces and foofy hair might not have cut a lot of mustard with us boys – in fact, they constituted a direct threat to what being a bloke was all about – but unfortunately they were the bands all the girls loved. Simon Le Bon was arguably the pin-up spunk of the decade. George Michael's arse was much drooled over. The brothers Kemp from Spandau Ballet, Ultravox's Midge Ure . . . The list went on. You'd spend Sunday night scoffing incredulously at some synth-fingering knobhead with heavy eye makeup on *Countdown*, only to arrive at school the next day to hear the girls gushing that he was absolutely gorgeous. I think this was probably the first inkling we had that being a man might not be as straightforward as we first thought.

As far as I could make out, there were three distinct musical strands happening around this time. There was the pastel-pink *Countdown* strand, with its bent towards the Michael Jacksons, the Blancmanges and the Alison Moyets of this world. Running parallel to this was the Bloke Rock strand, with its overdrive guitars and frontmen who trashed the *Countdown* Awards on live telly. The third strand seemed to consist of me and my Fossil Rock. There I was, firmly rooted fifteen years in the past, suspended like an insect in amber, my head full of Stones, Who and Led Zeppelin songs.

The idea of these strands, each one as separate as the strings on a guitar, worked well in my mind, which craved clear and concise categories for everything, but functioned less well in reality. In truth, they weren't parallel at all. They did intertwine to some extent. For instance, it was with a sense of deep and profound shock that I learned of Mick Jagger's 1984 duet with Michael Jackson, on a single entitled, appropriately enough, 'State Of Shock'. My gast was flabbered. What was Mick thinking? How could he do this to me, after all we'd been through? What on earth must Keef be thinking? True, Jackson was unarguably the biggest pop star in the world at that time. However, to my way of thinking, his near-feature-length videos and cheesily choreographed casts of thousands symbolised all that had gone awry with pop music.

To be blunt, I loathed him. I mean to say, Jackson as outraged peacemaker in the video for 'Beat It'? Oh, please. How galling. I was cheering for one of the gangleaders to stick the corkscrew-curled, crotch-clutching Diana Ross doppelgänger. Except that they too possessed all the menace of a collection of Enid Blyton bedtime tales. One gangleader had that George Michael/Don Johnson carefully manicured three-day-growth look happening, and blow-waved hair. The other was dressed in a puffy white suit. With shoulder pads. And he sported a Freddie Mercury tash. The mere sight of Jackson, that red jacket and single white glove, his short trousers and white socks, the sound of his shy, girlish whisper and those little falsetto hoots and squeals, could drive me into a teenage rage. (Oh, how fickle the human heart. It was only a couple of years since my Adam

Ant affair, but now here I was pointing an accusing finger and yelling, 'Poofta!' at Jackson fans. Yessiree, the polished knee-high boot was on the other foot now.) And the thought that Jagger was scrabbling to find footing on the *Thriller* bandwagon – well, that depressed me more than any other single thing in my life at that time. Underwhelming exam results, chronic female rejection, a biblical outbreak of pimples across my chin and shoulders (that and the female rejection thing might have been linked, actually), St George copping another hiding – nothing else sank my spirits faster than Mick's infidelity.

Why couldn't he have left all that stomach-turning stuff to Paul McCartney, who had joined forces with Jackson to record the gag-triggering 'Say Say Say'? In my imagination, it was Jackson who begged Mick to take part, pestering him until Jagger relented just to get the aggravating Prince of Pop off his back. The one consolation, the thinnest sliver of silver linings on this purple-black thunderhead, was the fact that Jagger and Jackson (or the Two Micks, as a few radio jocks nauseatingly referred to them) weren't actually together when the song was recorded. Jagger recorded his vocals on one side of the world, and Jackson put down his on the other. The music was recorded in yet another studio. I clung to this sodden straw as the waves of disbelief and disappointment pummelled me. Since 'State Of Shock' was a cut-and-paste job, it couldn't strictly be thought of as a collaboration, could it? It wasn't the Two Micks at all. It was separate Micks, doing stuff at different times in different places. It didn't really count.

This was how I reasoned it out to the guys at school from the Bloke Rock brigade, who taunted me endlessly about the duet and who, secure in the knowledge that there was nothing more effective than an assault on someone's sexuality, accused the head Stone of bumjacking Jackson. All I wanted was for the song to vanish from the charts so life could slowly return to normal. But, stubborn bloody thing that it was, it wouldn't budge. I watched in horror as the song continued to climb, week after week. On Sundays I'd watch the *Countdown* Top Ten wrap-up and wince as each chart position passed and 'State Of Shock' failed to show up (I think it reached as high as five). Thankfully, there was no video clip owing to the splintered nature of the project, so the song was never played in full on telly.

It would be fair to say that my intense dismay could be safely filed away under 'O' for overreaction. I guess it goes to show what calamity-free, middle-class lives we led in safe old Taree in the early to mid-'80s. How relatively smooth and pain-free must have been my life that a collaboration between two pop stars should have vexed me so. But for an obsessive like me, following a band was like barracking for a footy team. You didn't flit from one to the other, liking a little bit of this and a little bit of that. You found one you really dug and you stuck with them through thick and thin, weathered the ups and downs. You nailed your colours to the mast and made a show of actively disliking other bands that appeared to be diametrically opposed to whatever it was you thought your band represented, even if they did churn out the odd annoyingly catchy tune. You collected and devoured every morsel of information, snipped articles from newspapers, shelled out for any souvenir and piece of memorabilia. The music itself was only the beginning. There were books to be had, posters, magazines, calendars, videos, badges, clothing, the lot. If they'd produced a Rolling Stones flag and scarf, I'd have bought those as well. Even though I couldn't read a single note of music and had no intention of learning,

I saved up and bought the Jagger/Richards musical companion because I *had* to own it. No question. I'd sit and stare for hours at page after page of musical hieroglyphics, even though they meant nothing to me, as if seeking some new insight.

So you see, I viewed Jagger's dalliance with Michael Jackson as a personal affront, a slap in the face. He had been sleeping with the enemy, in a manner of speaking. He'd been unfaithful.

I'm sorry, but I just do not understand those who claim no allegiances. They are the music-fan equivalent of Switzerland, neutral and passionless. People who, when asked what kind of music they like, shrug and reply, 'Oh, I don't know. A little bit of everything, I guess.' Or those who like songs, rather than bands, but never know the titles. 'You know, that song that goes *da da da da DA DA da da* – oh, *you* know, Triple M play it all the time.' This is complete anathema to me. What happened to these people? Have our lives been so different that music has somehow bypassed them yet run me down like a gravel-munching eighteen-wheeler? How stale and arid must be a world in which music is only this thing that happens in the background at parties, or just rattles out of the radio at work. How can they possibly subsist on a diet of half a dozen CDs, a paltry collection consisting of the latest chart compilation, Madonna's greatest hits, and maybe one or two movie soundtracks? Believe me, people do. I've seen it with my own eyes. Nothing betrays character faster than your CD collection. A quick look is all I need to pigeonhole a person. What have we here? Huey Lewis and the News? I see. Nice one. And Feargal Sharkey. Hmmm. Hanson's first album. What's that? They were quite good before their voices broke? Allriiiighty then. Back up slowly, don't make eye contact, grab your coat, that's it, nice and easy . . .

71

Many is the time I've come under fire for my zeal. 'You are a musical McCarthyist,' Paula said to me once, the morning after an alcohol-sodden dinner at a friend's place. 'A complete bloody Nazi.'

'What?' I asked, all wide-eyed hurt indignation. 'What are you talking about?'

'You know what I'm talking about.' She mimicked me. '"What's this? Soft Cell's greatest hits? Soft *Cell*? Bloody hell. How many hits did they have? Only one, that I can recall. Lookaddit, willya? There're twenty songs on here. Never heard any of 'em. Ho ho ho, what a joke." You were so rude I just couldn't believe it. I was so embarrassed.'

Through the bilious haze of my hangover, a memory blurped to the surface like a sulphurous bubble in a mud pool, and I winced. I'm holding the CD in the air triumphantly, cackling like a crow, waving a half-empty wineglass in the other hand. Then I remembered the other things I said. The bit about how they knew we were coming over and had plenty of time to hide that little gem. I remembered turning back to the CD rack and making a great show of scanning the titles, all the while slurring on. 'What other classics you got tucked away in here, eh? Come on, the Captain and Tennille must be lurking somewhere. How about it, you got a little Muskrat Lurve for me? Or Bronski Beat?' It seemed side-splittingly funny at the time. In the cold light of day it wasn't quite so amusing.

'I don't like it when you're like that,' Paula said, giving me that I'm-serious-about-this look. 'Other people are allowed to have their own tastes. How would you like it if they came round and bagged your CDs, hmm? Only that would never happen, would it? Because your taste in music is above reproach. You with your four hundred Stones CDs and your Van Morrison and Bob Dylan and your Tom-bloody-Waits. You're the arbiter of good taste. Well, I think you should phone and apologise.'

I agreed with her wholeheartedly because, of course, she was dead right. I would phone and say sorry for my appalling behaviour. I knew I was way out of line. But the deep, dark truth of the matter remained, and nothing I could say would change that. While I might apologise for voicing my views so vociferously, the views themselves would remain unaltered.

Still, at Paula's insistence, I've stopped rating people by the contents of their CD racks. No more shallow, vacuous value judgements from me. At least, not till I've had a quick shufty at their bookcase as well.

When I was in my teens, I invested so much in music – nearly every waking moment and every red cent of my meagre pocket money. (My brother and I each received the grand sum of two dollars a week, in return for which we were expected to make our beds, wash the dishes and water the garden. Mowing the lawn earned one of us a two-dollar bonus every fortnight.) Even back then, it took *weeks* to save enough to buy new music. Here we go, down the well-trodden 'when I were a lad' path. I might not have had to rise early to milk cows or walk ten miles to school barefoot every day, but I did have to make sacrifices. Being addicted to rock meant having to forgo many other fancies. I hated walking into a newsagent's or corner store, with their mocking counters of confectionery and racks of potato chips. Not to mention books and movies. Both were out of the question if I hoped to have *Exile on Main Street* in the tape deck before I turned twenty-one.

Each week Dad, with mock solemnity, handed over our slave

wages, a single green note, intoning like a priest, 'This hopefully will teach you the value of money,' to which I would reply, 'Well, I've already learned that the value of this ain't much, Dad. Any chance of a raise?' He would respond, 'Look after the pennies son, and the pounds will look after themselves. Besides, what do you expect for making your bloody bed and throwing the hose around a bit?'

I would immediately deposit my moolah in the safe box that doubled as my socks and undies drawer, then I'd try to forget about it and ignore temptation. There it stayed until such time as I had accumulated enough to ferry to the local record shop – little more than a hole in the wall – where I would hand it to the man behind the counter in exchange for cassettes of aural gold.

Buying music was such an event back then, and I'm sure that the weeks-long build-up added to my appreciation when I finally clapped ears on my new purchase. Today I never have to experience that delicious tease of anticipation. Now, by and large, I walk into a store, buy a CD, take it home and play it. Sometimes I might buy two. During the particularly flush periods of my life – which have been as sporadic as good Richard Marx albums, which is to say never, really – I have even been known to buy as many as half a dozen CDs at once (so much for my parents instilling careful and responsible fiscal practices). When that happens, there are always cast-offs, always one or two I'm not *really* sure about. Nine times out of ten they receive one listen, if that, then it's into the rack with them, never to be withdrawn again. Then one day they find themselves in a cardboard box on their way to the second-hand music shop or the markets, where they fetch, on average, a dollar each.

Buying music in bulk is such a decadent and risky practice;

it makes me feel somehow lazy, or lacking in acumen. Above all, it lacks the pinpoint focus of buying music back when I was a teenager; that narrow, laser-beam intensity I once applied to album selection. Choosing music was like mounting a military campaign. As I loved Fossil Rock, I seemed to spend most of my time in the record store leafing through back catalogues. My store stocked latest releases and compilations, but seemed to have nothing more than two or three years old. It had more Wang Chung than Stones in stock. (This is fact. I checked. And it's something I still do today when I walk into a music store. It's how I gauge them. They must have the full complement of Stones titles in order to cut my particular brand of mustard. If they've got, say, the Alan Parsons Project's *Eye in the Sky* but not *Let it Bleed*, then it's tools down and I exit shaking my head and tut-tutting.)

Time and again the beefy, balding proprietor would slide the bulky ringbinder across the counter to me and I would look up 'Rolling Stones, the', and drink the titles with my eyes. There were so many, it seemed I would never have enough time or money to buy them all. I pictured myself as a wizened old man, groaning on my death-bed and holding out a gnarled hand in desperation. 'He's trying to say something,' my grown children say, leaning close. 'What is it, Dad? Tell us. What can we do? Can we get you something?'

'Please . . .' I wheeze my dying wish. 'Please, can someone get their hands on a copy of *Get Yer Ya-Yas Out*?'

Sometimes I'd ask the owner for advice. After all, he was old. Thirty-something at least. He must know these albums. I didn't deem it possible that someone his age might not be completely *au fait* with the Stones' repertoire. And actually, he was some help. Once, after I'd spent a full half-hour staring at the catalogue, torn between ordering *Sticky Fingers* or *Goat's Head Soup*, he came over. 'Sticky Fingers is the one you want, mate. Has "Brown Sugar" on it. And "Wild Horses". Lotsa good stuff. *Goat's Head Soup*'s shit mostly, apart from "Angie", of course. *Sticky*'s got a cool sleeve too. Andy Warhol did it. It's got a close-up of a pair of jeans with the crotch, you know, and the zip's real. You can undo it, and on the inner sleeve, right, it's the same shot, only the guy's just there in his undies.'

That settled it. I'd never heard of Andy Warhol, but it didn't matter. The title reeked of sex, and the sleeve sounded sniggeringly naughty as well. I had to have it. And I knew that, regardless of what the owner thought, I would get *Goat's Head Soup* one day. (As it turned out, he was right. *Goat's Head Soup* is mostly shit. Not that I thought that when I bought it at fifteen. Then it was another solid collection of Stones genius to be added to the little shelf on my bedhead.) Of course, what the guy neglected to mention was that in purchasing the cassette version of *Sticky Fingers* I would not be privy to the full Warhol/zip/underpants experience. It was just a photo of the album sleeve, and thus disappointingly two-dimensional.

It took a few weeks for orders to arrive. When they did, the shop rang to let you know. Sometimes I still hadn't raked together enough cash, but I would nevertheless go in the following morning just to have a look. I'd leap off the schoolbus in the main street, dash along the footpath dodging blue-rinsed, floral-frocked pensioners, and stammeringly ask the music store proprietor if I could view my new arrival. Come the day when I could afford to walk out with it, school passed monumentally slowly. Entire mountain ranges could be thrown up and eroded while I sat through a double period of maths. At lunch, sitting by myself, I'd prise the little white paper bag from my school case, carefully peel back the sticky tape and behold the new addition.

Once I had finally burst through the front door that afternoon with a perfunctory 'Hiya' to Mum, my hands would tremble as I fed the cassette into the player and snapped it shut. I'd jab the play button, then endure the interminable hiss of tape, the chirpy little bleeps announcing the music was about to begin, until finally some new chords would be plunged into my brain. I'd lapse into a smiling stupor lying on my bed, letting each track seep into my pores. I played every new cassette repeatedly, devouring it until I'd memorised all the lyrics, until I knew where every drum roll and cymbal spash was placed, until the geography of each track was familiar terrain, so that my air-guitaring could be note-perfect. Only then, with the lustre slightly dulled, could it be ejected and one of my older tapes reinstated.

A bizarre affliction from which I suffer is repeat buying. The other week I walked into a second-hand CD shop and bought the Stones' *Undercover* for the fifth time. I have owned it once on cassette, once on vinyl and thrice on CD. *Three times*. I bought the cassette when the album was released in 1983, and even though I didn't own a turntable I bought the vinyl version as well because I wanted to see if the inner sleeve artwork varied at all from the cassette. Why I have bought the CD three times even I struggle to comprehend. Twice I suddenly decided it was a Stones offering I could live without and tossed it in the box of rejects bound for the markets. Then, some time later, I saw it in a shop, picked it up, decided that 'Tie You Up (The Pain of Love)' and 'Undercover Of The Night' were indispensable and bought it again. I took it home, played it, remembered how awful 'Feel On Baby' and 'Too Much Blood' are, and how much

'It Must Be Hell' is just a rip-off of 'Soul Survivor' from *Exile*, and relegated it to the neglected regions of the CD rack.

In my fifteenth year I walked around with a Stones T-shirt virtually glued to my frame, its front emblazoned with the famous lascivious lips and lolling tongue. I railed against what I described at the time as 'synthesised, soulless muzak churned out by the cynical corporate machine'. (Just goes to show that the more things change . . .) I used the word 'rapacious' a lot. I must have picked it up somewhere and thought it sounded hard and sort of clever at the same time, so music companies were all suddenly 'rapacious', or 'wallowing in their plastic rapacity'.

At school I revelled in my role as musical pariah. I paraded around the quadrangle and through the corridors loudly singing snatches of Stones songs that were carefully calculated to annoy and shock (and maybe, just maybe, impress). A little part of me was also arrogant enough to think that I might actually educate someone. That I could convert them. I honestly thought that one or two kids, who up until now might be labouring under the delusion that Marilyn or Wa Wa Nee were the be-all and end-all of music, might hear me singing about that slave owner whipping the women around midnight in 'Brown Sugar' and want to know more. I know you'll find this hard to believe, but they never did. Not once. Quite the opposite, in fact. The other kids were mystified by my fascination for what they considered ancient history. It earned me a certain notoriety, which I could not possibly have attained in any other avenue of my far too run-of-the-mill life. I wasn't a rebel by nature, only by musical selection.

This was very exciting. I was weird. I was the kid who loved 'all that old shit', and I played up to it relentlessly. To further position myself as somehow different or interesting, I took a stance against all the 'new shit'. And I mean *every*thing. I was scathing about all current music. With a Billy Idol sneer fixed to my face, I mercilessly bagged people for liking Culture Club or the Hooters or A-Ha, bands I considered to be without a skerrick of merit. It was extremely tiring keeping up all this blanket negativity, and sometimes I'd catch myself humming 'Do You Really Want To Hurt Me?', or singing 'Take On Me' under my breath when no-one was around.

My only serious competition in this field of Cranky Yet Knowledgeable Pop Music Fan came in the unprepossessing, sack-uniformed silhouette of Rhiannon Buchanan, a vegetarian who gained schoolyard fame on two fronts – her daily lunchtime ritual involving the peeling, slicing and devouring of raw potatoes, and for being Taree's foremost expert on the Beatles. And so the age-old argument was played out yet again. The Beatles or the Stones. The Stones or the Beatles. Right there in the concrete confines of the Taree High School quadrangle, twenty years after the rest of the world ceased to care, Rhiannon Buchanan and I staged our own running battle over who was better – the Fab Four or the Filthy Five.

It is a battle I still have with people to this very day. And it is an argument which, for Stones fans, is unwinnable. Yet each time it's brought up I groan, reach for my chain-mail and head off into battle. And each time, I return with my own severed head under my arm. I'm like a punch-drunk fighter, flailing away ineffectually while my opponent simply stands there keeping me at bay with their palm on my forehead. In an objective argument, Lennon and co. must always win out. All the statistics back the Beatles. Most number ones, biggest-selling albums;

you name it, the Beatles have the edge. Even people who know bugger all about music will tell you the Beatles were the biggest band in history. So any argument has to switch to a subjective level and I end up saying things like, 'Yes, but the Stones broke the mould. They bucked the Establishment. Even John Lennon conformed and wore a suit and tie onstage. It was the Stones who rebelled, both image-wise and lyrically, and *really* started rock music as we know it. I mean, even *grand*mothers liked the Beatles back then, right – and why wouldn't they, with crap like "When I'm 64?" Now, on the other hand, the Stones wrote "Satisfaction" and the entire world ran for cover. There, nuff said.'

Rhiannon Buchanan was able to effectively parry that thrust. She popped another sliver of glistening white, uncooked tater in her mouth, crunched thoughtfully for a while, pushed her glasses up her nose with her knife, and said. 'Well, if the Stones were such great songwriters, how come Lennon and McCartney had to write one of their first singles?'

I was so stunned I couldn't even rib her about the speck of potato on the bridge of her glasses. I didn't believe her. I *couldn't* believe her. She had to be mistaken. But when I got home, there it was, on the inner sleeve of *Rolled Gold*, right next to 'I Wanna Be Your Man', in parentheses, the dreaded Lennon/McCartney credit. I was shocked to my very core. A cold sweat prickled my brow. Convex became concave. My world had shifted on its axis.

I tried to avoid Rhiannon the following day, but she hunted me down in the library. I was skulking among the volumes of the World Book Encyclopedia, the one place I was confident no-one would look. 'Well, was I right?' she asked with one eyebrow raised and a knowing grin. I could only nod mutely.

'The Stones couldn't write a song to save themselves at that stage,' she went on with a pronounced lecturing tone. 'They just rehashed old stuff. The Beatles had already written about a gazillion hits, so they took "I Wanna Be Your Man" over to Jagger and Richards and gave it to them. Felt sorry for 'em, obviously.'

I had no comeback. Well, no music-related comeback. Belatedly I did rattle off some devastatingly cutting riposte about ingesting raw spuds, and something uproariously funny about her parents' iffy sense of rhyme, but by then Rhiannon was halfway out the door. I wonder what happened to her. Looking back, I think I could have easily fallen in love.

ᗡ

George Harrison died two days ago, and the person who fills my thoughts is Rhiannon Buchanan. This is a strange phenomenon. A famous musician dies and as I watch the endless television stories and read the tributes, I keep seeing the bespectacled face of a girl I haven't spoken to in fifteen years.

I'm wondering how she is. I'm wondering if she's distraught, sobbing inconsolably at the demise of another of her idols. I find myself conjuring up scenarios, trying to picture her maybe sitting behind a big desk in some law firm or architects' office, telling her PA to hold all calls as she slumps, head on her arms, and cries. Excessive, strenuous fandom can do this to you. It delivers fame by association. The Beatles and Rhiannon Buchanan are inextricably linked in my mind. Whenever I see a photo of the Fab Four, Rhiannon might just as well be standing there next to them.

Extrapolating from this point, I think it's probably safe to assume that the Rolling Stones and I might be similarly linked in the minds of people who have known me, however superficially, over the years. If my theory is correct, then Rhiannon

Buchanan might have recently read an article about how big a flop Mick Jagger's latest solo album has been (only nine hundred and fifty-four units shifted in the UK on the first days of its release), and might not she be thinking, Well, well, well. I wonder if Anthony's seen this. Betcha he's bought it. It's sort of nice to think that a certain percentage of the population will have watched a recent Jagger profile on *60 Minutes* and thought of me. It might have been only a fleeting thought. It might have even been a thought along the lines of, Wonder what happened to that dickwit? But nevertheless, for that brief moment, I would have been foremost in their minds because I was the guy who was nuts about the Rolling Stones.

Harrison's death prompted Paula to ask me, 'What will you do when Mick or Keith dies? Will you cry?'

I had tears in my eyes at the thought. 'Like a baby. I will bawl like a baby for a period of some weeks, probably.'

So Rhiannon, two things. First, yes I did buy the Jagger CD – out of loyalty, not in the expectation of it being any good – and it is pretty crappy. Second, I know George Harrison's death affected millions but I extend my sympathy to you in particular. After all, to my way of thinking, you're weren't just a Beatles fan. You were *the* Beatles fan.

There were things I just didn't understand about the crazy, mixed-up universe I lived in then. At the top of this lengthy list was the fact that my parents bought my brother a drum kit. This had me utterly perplexed. Every time I thought about it I found myself shaking my head. There was Gordon, who hated rock music with something amounting to religious zeal, and Leila, who was allergic to clutter and noise, allowing Darren to bring a couple of hundred dollars worth of bulky, used, grey-shelled drums and drum-related paraphernalia into his bedroom. Not only that, they *paid* for it. It beggared belief.

Darren, bless his cotton socks, had displayed much early drumming potential. One Christmas when he was about four, Santa left him a plastic toy drum kit, which he hit with little plastic sticks. Then one day, in an uncanny imitation of Keith Moon, he put his foot through the dinky snare drum, and that was that. A couple of years later, while air-drumming to a song on the radio, he toppled backwards off the green vinyl pouffe he was sitting on and crashed spectacularly into the china cabinet, shattering several of our parents' crystal wedding gifts. Miraculously he escaped injury from the broken glass, which meant he was in tip-top physical condition to deal with the corporal punishment Leila administered shortly thereafter.

Over the years, Darren taught himself to play a whole array of instruments, becoming annoyingly proficient in all of them.

Unlike me, he had a large reservoir of patience and a quiet determination. Perhaps I should add natural talent. Much of the time that I was hamming it up with the tennis racquet Darren spent in the next room poring over learn-to-play-guitar manuals. When he first lugged those antiquated drums home, though, his determination was anything but quiet. He pounded the hides with such force I could actually feel my eardrums quivering. But it was good pounding, it has to be said. A strong sense of timing was evident. There was cadence aplenty. It was quite astonishing; he just sat down and started playing as if it were second nature. The only thing he was lacking, as far as I could make out, was subtlety.

Anyway, things soon reverted to type. Gordon and Leila tolerated Darren's enthused walloping for – oh, it must have been forty-five, fifty seconds before the novelty wore off and laws were passed. A drum curfew was imposed, effective immediately. Darren could only play between the hours of 10am and 5pm, which of course ruled out playing during the school week. And he would have to put some form of padding on the skins to muffle the noise. He was never, repeat, *never* to play unpadded drums.

Old flannelette sheets were gathered and thrown over the kit, to be hastily whipped off whenever our parents left us alone in the house. The car wouldn't have time to disappear up the street before Darren was at it like Animal from *The Muppet Show*. Illicit sessions like this always began with a deranged burst to let off steam, and in the aftermath of one of these eruptions it was not uncommon to find splinters of drumstick lying about his room like shrapnel. They never lasted long, thankfully. Five minutes later, when the smoke had cleared and he had it out of his system, Darren would settle down to some serious playing.

When he practised, Darren wore headphones plugged into a clapped-out cassette player and drummed along to his favourite bands – usually some heavy-metal outfit with a surfeit of hair and a dirth of talent. The raging guitars being piped directly into his head dampened the noise he was making, so to him it sounded as though he were drumming on the track. To anyone else, it sounded like heavy artillery.

His drumming was a clarion call for other kids. He'd no sooner start than our front lawn would be awash with boys on bikes, attracted by the percussive thunder rolling over suburbia. Interestingly there were never any girls. Just boys, all possessed by that boyish fascination for hitting stuff. They all wanted to have a go but Darren rarely let them. The chance to let fly came along all too rarely and he wasn't about to waste it letting Eddie Wilcox from number seven bash away like an epileptic carpenter. So the boys had to make do with being Darren's first audience, and they turned up faithfully, congregating under his bedroom window and nodding along in time with the beat.

Inevitably, Mum and Dad found out about Darren's sneaky assaults, courtesy of an unsigned protest slipped into our letter-box like a ransom note. In our quiet corner of town this constituted a scandal. My father's face darkened, his jowls quivered, and his lips worked against each other. Out came the laughingly named Board of Education, a wooden paddle bearing a cartoon depicting a black-gowned headmaster administering corporal punishment to two bare-bottomed urchins. The Board of Education even came with a wrist strap so it wouldn't fly off during zealous disciplinary action. Suffice to say, that single sheet of curt correspondence provoked despondence in my younger sibling.

Occasionally, and I mean very occasionally, there was

sanctioned drumming *sans* padding when Darren would be allowed to play unsheeted with our parents still in the house. These times normally coincided with Leila vacuuming or Gordon mowing the lawn. One such morning the phone rang. How Mum heard it over the cacophony remains a mystery. On the other end of the line was an anonymous woman who informed my mother in cracked and faltering tones that she could stand Darren's drumming no longer. Her nerves were in a bad way, she said, and if Darren did not desist immediately she would be left with no other option than to call the police.

I was abuzz. Was this our anonymous note-leaver? Perhaps not. After all, Darren had made many enemies since the day the drums came home in the back seat of our brown Kingswood. At any rate, we never found out. The mysterious caller with the frayed nerves refused to give her name, but she said she lived some streets away and could still hear the drumming quite clearly.

Darren greeted this latest complaint with a withering flurry that threatened to flake plaster. He then snapped a drumstick in half in a fit of pique and stormed off on his BMX, chucking furious monos as he vanished up the street.

But he was to receive support from an unlikely quarter. Leila, overcome by a surge of familial indignation, phoned the local constabulary herself and inquired as to what level of noise was considered acceptable in the middle of the morning. The officer to whom she spoke wasn't certain, and after consultation with his colleagues declared that they would have to come out and judge for themselves.

The next day, a police car pulled up out the front of our house. Two friendly officers met Darren and were escorted into his bedroom to check out the offending kit. They made for a strange and exciting sight, these hulking uniformed men with their holsters and guns in my brother's room. One of them looked especially strange when he sat down at the kit – after asking Darren's permission, of course – and had a bit of a play. He was just trying to put everyone at ease, I guess, this burly, disjointed marionette whose strings seemed to be tangled. He simply could not make his feet and arms work with each other. As soon as his left hand got something happening, his foot forgot what to do.

The officers spoke to my mother and said they would go out and sit in their patrol car while Darren 'got stuck in'. They told my brother not to hold anything back because they were there, to just do what he'd normally do. So Darren got down to business, pelting the skins with his usual venom, while the policemen sat listening intently.

After about three minutes they came back inside. 'Yep, that was certainly pretty loud,' drummer-boy told my mother insightfully. Then he quickly added, 'Oh, he's good, Mrs Griffis, no fear of that. He can play, all right.'

'I didn't ask you out here for a critique,' my mother replied tartly. Darren and I hovered in the background, wincing. 'Is the noise level okay for this time of day or not?'

'Well, I reckon it might be a tad too loud.'

'Of course it sounds loud if you're right outside the front door,' Leila said. 'This woman who complained says she lives a few streets from here. Why don't you go park a couple of blocks away and have a listen? See what you think then.'

The policemen agreed to give that a go and see what happened. Darren gave them a couple of minutes to relocate, then let fly again. When the officers returned, they said that the drumming could indeed be heard clearly several streets away.

The time of day or the proficiency of the drumming didn't enter into it. Darren would have to keep it down.

'Sorry 'bout that, Ringo. See ya, good luck,' the drumming officer farewelled my glowering brother.

'You're good, mate, I'll give ya the drum,' the other joked. 'Might see you playing at the RSL one day, eh?' He looked, just for a moment, as if he might be going to ruffle Darren's hair, but he saw my brother's expression and thought better of it.

With his playing heavily curtailed, Darren turned his attention instead to 'improving' his kit. Over the next few months he made an endless array of intricate modifications and additions. Deciding the grey shells were a bit drab, he painstakingly removed the metal rims from all the drums and wrapped the shells in bright red contact. It bubbled and creased a little, but Darren was well pleased with the overall effect. Then he started to expand the kit, adding a bewildering number of percussion pieces. The existing stands started to sprout arms which were soon festooned with triangles, shakers, blocks of wood, anything that might make a sound when struck. Items dangled from clothes pegs like bats from branches. He spent hours sprawled on his bed ogling catalogue photos of chromium odds and ends with the same excitement the rest of us reserved for *Penthouse*.

In later years, when Darren played in bands, he'd be so concerned about including all the impressive flashy bits that he sometimes forgot to bring the essentials. On more than one occasion he fronted up to a gig minus his drumsticks. Once he even forgot to pack the bass drum pedal. 'No worries,' he assured the rest of us. 'I'll just kick it.'

Darren wasn't the only one to get up to mischief during parental outings. I too had fish to fry.

Mum and Dad owned a sensational 'stereogram', as they insisted on calling it, though it looked less like a device for playing music than a drinks cabinet with built-in speakers. But boy, what a sound. Deep, rich and full, it was unlike anything I'd ever heard. The bass sent a tremor through your vital organs. The guitar was so crisp you thought you might be able to snap bits off. Vocals cut through like a bandsaw. The playing of rock-'n'roll records on it, especially if there were no grown-ups around to supervise, was expressly forbidden. And so naturally, whenever Mum and Dad left the house, I made a beeline for it, albums clutched under my arm.

The stereogram hunkered moodily in the lounge room, a squat oblong about the size and shape of a sarcophagus supported by four legs. It was all dark timber with swirly grain running through it, and it radiated seriousness in waves. Believe me, this was not a stereogram to be trifled with. It always seemed to me that it had been constructed specifically to play Mozart, Beethoven, Tchaikovsky, Elvis Presley, Neil Diamond – *Hot August Night* seemed to have been standard issue in the '70s – Engelbert Humperdinck and Demis Roussos. (There was nothing funnier than singing 'My Friend The Wind' in a warbly falsetto, just prior to letting rip with a well-rounded fart.) It seemed to not want its time wasted with the likes of the Rolling Stones or Led Zeppelin, though that was obviously parental conditioning rather than any specific feelings on the part of the stereogram.

Now that I think about it, one or two incongruous albums did slip into my parents' collection, sneaking in under the radar in 1976. Bryan Ferry's *Let's Stick Together* was one, and Rod

Stewart's *A Night on the Town* was the other. My mother bought both solely on the strength of their smash singles, the title track on the former and 'Tonight's The Night' on the latter. At the tender age of seven, I completely missed the fact that Rod was trying to talk a woman into bed. As the song fades out, you can hear the woman murmuring and moaning. 'I think she's asking him if she can have a glass of water,' I once observed after several close listens, and felt vaguely stupid when my parents went into paroxysms of laughter.

Mother, the wily fox, craftily constructed an obstacle course which we had to negotiate if we wanted to get at the stereo-gram. It was an alarm system made of knick-knacks. On the wooden lid, which concealed the turntable and controls, she placed a large lace doily upon which she arranged a collection of ornaments and photos. These had to be removed. That was the easy part. The tricky bit was making sure they went back in *exactly* the correct position. This was a trap for young play-ers. Tentatively, as if defusing a bomb, I'd lift off each ornament and place it on the floor in its corresponding position, so that eventually the configuration was replicated on the carpet. Right down to the distances between each ornament – Leila had a sharp eye for detail and I couldn't afford to be sloppy.

This piece of intricate counterespionage could take anything up to five minutes, but it was worth it because, my God, this stereo was a beautiful piece of sound engineering. You could hear every nuance, every little fill. It was like listening in 3D. Sounds were distinctly separated, laid over the top of each other – somehow there seemed to be *space* behind each instru-ment. I discovered, to my inestimable delight, that different things happened in each speaker. If I sat in front of one I could hear a certain guitar part, while a few feet away something different was coming out of the other. Ah, so *that's* what stereo was all about. Sheer bliss.

And so it was that the normally sedate Griffis household exploded every time we were home alone. Upstairs Darren drummed himself into a lather, pausing only to practise twirling the drumsticks between his fingers, like he'd seen drummers do on TV. Downstairs I turned the volume up to drown out his racket and danced around the lounge room, my acrobatics often causing the stylus to skip across the record like a pebble across a pond. I once took a flying leap off the couch onto my knees, and the needle left 'Respectable' (*Some Girls*, the Rolling Stones, 1978, side 2, track 2) and landed midway through 'Beast Of Burden', a song and a half later. I'm not certain, but that could well be some sort of record. So to speak.

It probably goes without saying that I treated my vinyl appallingly. I can't explain why, being a music lover, I never cultivated the reverential mannerisms you normally associate with record devotees. You'd never catch me with a record poised between palms, holding it up to the light, flipping it over dexterously, checking for specks, or blowing on it to remove dust. I never possessed an anti-static cleaning cloth. Sheesh, they were lucky if they made it back into their plastic sleeves half the time. I broke every rule of record care several times a day. I gripped them between thumb and forefinger. In my haste to hear a track, I'd toss them around like frisbees, whipping them off the turntable before they'd finished spinning. I'd leave them lying flat instead of stacked upright in neat rows, bookcase-style. Occasionally one or two might unwittingly be exposed to direct sunlight for a few hours and gain a slight wonk as a result. No matter. The music still played and that was all I cared about.

Like a lot of music buffs, many of my friends have now turned their backs on the crystal clarity of the compact disc, opting for a return to what they like to call the raw honesty of vinyl. I'm not sure if this is some sort of fashionable luddite backlash, an attempt to mark themselves as serious fans who are in some way superior to the rest of the music-consuming public, or simply a severe attack of nostalgia. Perhaps it's all three. Vinylophiles seem to be infatuated with the *ceremony* of playing records. For them it's a sensual experience. The unsheathing, the careful slipping of the record from its sleeve, the placing of it on the turntable, seeing the glinting silver nub poke through the hole in the middle, the gentle manipulation of the arm. They adore the crackle as you put stylus to vinyl, the thin hiss that overlays the music – and I can well appreciate all that, to a degree. However, when they start claiming that vinyl sounds *better* than a CD, and I don't mean subjectively, I mean *qualitatively*, well, that's where we part company.

But in my friends' sepia-tinted imaginations, vinyl is aural gold. And so, a decade or so after they ditched their records and went out and bought everything on CD, they now spend their weekends trawling hip inner-city record shops and markets and car-boot sales, trying to repurchase vinyl versions of Echo and the Bunnymen, and Lloyd Cole and the Commotions, and they cheerily shell out three or four times as much for them as they did originally. To sort of quote Lou Reed, someone, somewhere, is laughing till they wet their pants.

I had another pop music fantasy I loved to indulge but, given the Adam Ant experience, I decided that I had to do it alone. This usually meant when I was home from school sick. Dad and

Darren would leave early in the morning but I had to wait until about eleven to get rid of Leila. She would fuss over me throughout the morning, then, after I'd given her numerous assurances that my ailment wasn't about to carry me off the second she left the house, she'd finally tear herself away and go off to work as a waitress at the bistro of the RSL club. With Mother out of the way, I'd leap from my sick-bed and make straight for my parents' boudoir.

Recently I'd scraped together enough shekels to buy a book called *The Rolling Stones: In Their Own Words*, one of a series of tomes featuring quotes from various rock luminaries like Led Zeppelin, the Who and David Bowie on numerous far-ranging subjects. ('All I'm really interested in is history and comparative religion.' – Mick Jagger. Oh, *how* mature.) Anyway, one of the photos shows Mick in full flight during a concert in 1975. The camera has captured him in mid-leap. He is sinewy and svelte like a large cat, frozen a few feet above the stage, legs splayed, sweat flung out from his long hair, the droplets twinkling like a miniature galaxy against the blackness. He is wearing what looks like a denim jumpsuit, unbuttoned to pubic-hair level. It is a great rock'n'roll photo, capturing the essence of a Stones show.

But what *really* excited me was the fact that my mother owned a jumpsuit that was almost identical to Mick's. She no longer wore it (in fact, I could not recall her ever wearing it), but it was still there, tucked away in her wardrobe. When I was twelve I was quite svelte myself – even skinny, some might say – and I had no trouble wriggling into it. Mum's jumpsuit wasn't denim, however. I don't know what material it was, but it was scratchy and coarse like hessian. And hot. The material didn't breathe at all, and sweat prickled even as I heaved the suit up over my thin shoulders. It had a zip at the front, which I left undone so that a few wisps of pubic hair frothed out. I only had a few wisps in those days, so they needed a bit of encouragement.

I'd also discovered an old wig that Leila had consigned to a laundry cupboard. It was blonde and big and flicked, like all good '70s hair, and it perched at a rakish angle on a crude styrofoam head that I christened Donna, after my latest schoolyard crush. Upon discovering the rudimentary cranium, the first thing I did was grab a texta and give Donna enormous eyes, a perky little nose and pursed lips. The second thing I did was practise my pashing technique on the foam face, with only vaguely satisfying results. The third thing I did was try on the wig. It completely covered my own hair, which pleased me beyond words. Leila was a frustrated hairdresser and insisted on lining up her two boys for homestyle trims on Sunday afternoons.

'I'm not handing over eight bloody dollars each for haircuts,' she'd growl as she dragged a kitchen chair out to the backyard.

For a cape she tucked a frayed old towel into our T-shirts. She didn't use the fabled bowl on our heads but we lobbied for it for some time. Trust me, it would have been sweet relief. Mother fashioned the meanest fringe in the Western hemisphere. She'd run the scissors straight across my forehead, stand back to study her handiwork, judge it to be crooked and commence the evening-up process, going back and forth until I was left with a fringe shorter than a Corey Hart greatest-hits album. ('Had your eyebrows lowered?' was the familiar Monday morning refrain.) The rest of my hair fell – well, perhaps collapsed is a better word – about my ears in uneven chunks. I suppose you'd call it a page-boy cut, loosely speaking. At any rate, Darren and I spent much of our pre-pubescent lives looking like ardent Prince Valiant fans.

The wig, however, provided me with the look I never had. The fake hair swept past my eyes to a satisfactory extent, and its length at the back allowed for dynamic tossing and more effective headbanging. Dressed in Mum's jumpsuit, wig on, I'd hit 'play', stand in front of the mirror and try to emulate Mick Jagger in that photo – leaping athletically into the air, legs like a wishbone, swishing the wig back and forth while miming the lyrics, pouting and looking generally insolent, all at the same time.

You have to understand that I regarded this, and all my other imaginary rock'n'roll antics, not as games or entertaining diversions – or cross-dressing, or as a stage I was going through – but as serious job training. I was, by any clinical standards, obsessed with music. By the time I hit my early teens, it was all I cared about. It filled my life. Entire weekends were swallowed by it. There was *Countdown*, of course. My memories of that program are numerous and seem to stretch back to a time when I can recall very little else, such was its impact.

For instance, I can remember virtually nothing else about 1975, yet I can still see Bon Scott on stage dressed as a gap-toothed, tattooed schoolgirl, complete with felt-tip freckles and blonde Heidi plaits. Over the next few years there was pretty-boy Mark Holden wearing a white sports coat and tossing pink carnations into the squealing crowd. He was actually dragged offstage and was lucky not to be torn limb from limb. (This never seems to happen any more. Have we become too cool and blasé to storm stages?) I remember John Paul Young hosting the show regularly and being called Squeak, and Australian Crawl's James Reyne singing 'Beautiful People' with his broken arm in a cast. I remember ABBA's 'Fernando' monopolising the number one spot seemingly forever (fourteen weeks, actually), and 'Mull Of Kintyre' for seemingly longer than that. I remember reading in *TV Week* that the then Doctor Who, Tom Baker, was touring Australia and was scheduled to host *Countdown* that Sunday. I worked myself into a lather during the week, and by 6pm on the Sabbath I was almost vomiting with excitement. I kept waiting for the TARDIS to materialise behind Molly during Humdrum. It never did. The Doc didn't show. Only a rumour, apparently. Then again, what would a Time Lord know about pop music? No less than His Royal Highness the Prince of Wales, I guess, who did front up only to have a gabbling, stuttering Molly ask, 'How's your mum?'

'You mean Her Majesty the Queen?' Charles admonished. Top stuff. Riotous television.

In the '80s the ABC followed up *Countdown*'s phenomenal success with *Rage*, on Saturday mornings, the famous theme music with its yelling and screaming sparking annoyance and excitement in equal measure. *Beatbox* followed, with its social conscience and outrageously curly-haired reporter who roamed the streets sticking his microphone under the collective nose of Australia's youth. On *Beatbox* the music clips were selected to complement the topic of the week – drugs, unemployment, the nuclear arms race – and they became a classic soundtrack of teenage angst and disenchantment. Then came *Rock Arena*, hosted by a woman called Suzanne Dowling, who had a long nose, a severe, jet-black 'do and a fringe on a par with mine. This show dealt mainly with the independent scene – none of your formulaic, teenybopper Top Forty bands here, thank you very much – and provided exposure for more obscure and interesting Australian groups like the Go-Betweens.

My Saturday televisual musicfest was interrupted at 3pm when Aunty crossed to the Rugby League Match of the Day, with Alan Marks. If the Dragons happened to be playing, it was entirely possible that I would spend a full eight or nine hours in the lounge room staring at the box. If they weren't, then it was off to my room for more intensive training, preparing for my inevitable and impending career as a rock'n'roll deity. Come 6pm, I'd be back in front of the telly for the repeat of *Countdown* from the previous Sunday. I just never grew tired of music. For the first time in my life I had discovered something that could capture and hold my attention for hours on end.

I soaked it all up like the proverbial sponge. Rock music trivia filtered into my brain seemingly by osmosis. I found that, without any effort at all, I could pluck names, dates, bands, lyrics, song and album titles out of thin air. I could rattle off the links between different artists, the bands they had been in previously, whole timelines and musical family trees. I even absorbed information about bands I didn't like. I can't explain how, it all just lodged in my head. It was as if I were a medium, channelling information from some ethereal sonic realm. Sadly, the same could not be said for quadratic equations or the periodic table. When it came to those subjects, my brain was suddenly teflon-coated, a fact which drove my father to Despair, stopping off at Distraction along the way. It didn't worry me; Dad might not have been able to see it, but all the signs were pointing to a future in which myself and music were inextricably linked. All I had to do was work out exactly how the ties would bind. This was the tricky bit. I couldn't actually play an instrument (apart from a smattering of drums), and besides, my rapidly evolving ego dictated that I would have to be a lead singer. Never mind whether I could carry a tune or not.

Disappointingly, the school careers advisor didn't have a glossy pamphlet with 'Rock Star' emblazoned on it, so he wasn't any help whatsoever. The irony is that today you *can* go off and study popular music at various institutions. You'll sometimes hear Jimmy Barnes on the radio telling you in his electric-razor brogue how tough the music biz can be and how much easier you'll find it if you do such-and-such a course and get yourself a certificate. Workshops, clinics, seminars. Sign up for a twelve-week songwriting course. Don't forget to register for deejaying lessons. Enrol now for an intensive overview of the music business, all the ins and outs. And by ins and outs, we're talking about the sound rogering you will assuredly receive from record company executives.

Call me a curmudgeon – or just plain jealous – but surely there's something fundamentally wrong when popular music becomes part of a solid curriculum, something to be taught and learned like geography. Rock music was born out of rebellion. It is, by its very nature, anti-academia. It is raw, primitive, subversive. Rock music never had its socks pulled up, its shirt was always untucked. Its shoes were never polished and its tie was always askew. It stole the little kids' lunch money and was regularly sent home. At its malign best, rock delights in its own delinquency. In many of the biggest bands there is a whiff of desperation. They had to break big because some of their members didn't have alternative career options outside a correctional centre.

I know these are generalisations but, darn it all, I like dumb rock. Talk to me not of concept albums, of seven-minute burblings and soundscapes, of *virtuosity*. Don't start me on the subject of pretentious English bands consciously trying to be inaccessible, refusing to write anything that might conceivably be released as a single, and slowly disappearing up their own fundaments. Give me two guitars, bass, drums, vocals. Keyboards? Take 'em or leave 'em. Give me two minutes – three, tops – get in there, hammer out a catchy riff and get it over and done with. I want urgency, heat, verse and chorus, a nice middle bit. Simple, maybe, but beautiful *because* of its simplicity. Pop music fails at precisely the point where it starts to take itself too seriously.

There's something sterile about courses churning out drones who will, in all probability, vanish into gloomy studios to embark on careers of concerted computer noodling and sampling. What are these people to do if they want to rebel? Storm off and become doctors or lawyers? Will aspiring roadies soon be able to master the difficult art of lead-coiling at TAFE? Or will they take short, intensive time-management courses, with the emphasis on how to snatch sleep on patches of beer-soaked carpet behind drum risers during gigs? And who do you employ to teach these courses? Faded stars of yesteryear? I imagine Angry Anderson up in front of Screech 101: 'Right, everyone, settle down, we've a lot to get through today. On your desks you'll find tumblers of Jack Daniels. I want you to gargle these for a full thirty seconds, and down the hatch. *Then* we'll see if we can't startle a few canines.' Or Australia's first lady of soul, Renee Geyer, taking Advanced Star Turns and Tantrums, a course frequently interrupted by the lecturer storming out. And Brian Mannix's groundbreaking tutorial Leather and Singlets would be standing room only. Not unlike his pants.

Does this mean people will start fronting up to band auditions waving diplomas? I have an image of someone sitting in a formal interview. 'Yes, Bruce. Well, the boys and I have studied your CV carefully and we're most impressed. Your credentials are impeccable. Bachelor of Bass Guitar, excellent. Honours in Hotel-Room Trashing – TVs out windows, no problem. I see here special mention has been made of your ability to get drunk and pass out stark naked on a pool table with your tackle dangling in a corner pocket. Great stuff. And Pete here was particularly taken with your first-class honours in Vomit-Choking. Only one question remains. Do you own a van?'

Suffice to say, I had no recourse to such academic avenues. There would be no institutional leg-up for me. If I was going to be a rock star, I'd have to do it the old-fashioned way.

Having said that, the sure-fire path to rock'n'roll riches wasn't immediately clear to me. As I grew older, other areas of my life started to crowd in and I became distracted. It's generally agreed that adolescence is a difficult time. One of confusion, contradictions and inexplicable mood swings. One when you discover, to your great joy, that genitals are capable of much more than urinary waste evacuation. It was also about this time that I came to the deeply saddening realisation that my parents, in whom I had invested so much trust, were in fact human and very fallible – that they didn't always have the answers to life's problems. In our house, however, not having answers didn't stop them asking some very pertinent questions.

'Anthony, are you masturbating?'

My mother pronounces the word 'master-baiting', so initially I'm not sure if she is accusing me of some other misdemeanour. Her look dispels that notion. I feel my face flare up like a stovetop element. I'm stunned, as much by her timing as her pronunciation. There we are, my mother, my brother and myself, in our pyjamas watching *A Country Practice*. Not a lot on *that* program to spark thoughts of self-love, I'd have thought, especially with Fatso the wombat trundling across the screen. And, for God's sake, *Darren* is there. Why would she ask a question like that with him sitting there, his face a mixture of horror and delight?

Time freezes as I seek the correct answer. Well, not the correct answer. The correct answer is 'Pretty much nonstop, Mum. Wearing it down to the bone, actually, now you mention it.' I mean the answer that will expedite my extraction from this excruciating situation. Perhaps I should coolly reply, 'What's master-baiting, Mum?' and toss it back to her. Try and put her off. But no, that will only prolong the agony. What's worse, Leila isn't backwards in coming forwards, and might well reply, 'You know, son, wanking, pulling, spanking the monkey, having a slap, jerking off, giving Yul Brynner a high five, strangling the goose . . .' which would just kill me. Good grief, it was bad enough that she knew the word 'masturbating', more or less. And so I marshal my forces – or at least the forces that haven't broken rank and run screaming for the hills – and calmly say, 'No, never.' Not terribly convincing, but it's the best I can manage at such short notice. Very soon afterwards, I remember I've overlooked some urgent homework and try with all my might not to run to my room.

Leila never broached the subject again, and I never found out in what context she'd framed her question. Maybe she'd just received a personally signed thankyou letter from the managing director of Kleenex because, truth be told, at this time masturbation was running neck and neck with rock music. They jostled each other, fighting for pole position in my life. And masturbation was in front by a short half-head. I took rock aside, had a quiet word in its ear, tried to explain that I still loved it, that my feelings were still very strong, but that I needed a bit of space so I could get to know my new friend better, someone I'd known my whole life but was starting to see in a new light. We'd still get together, I said, I could never break that bond. It's just that my plans for world rock domination were on hold, just for a while.

But pop music is a harsh mistress. She started playing tricks, tarting herself up all sexy-like to try and confuse me. Cheetah appeared on *Countdown* singing 'Spend The Night' and everything went pear-shaped. Cheetah – two women, one blonde, the other dark – wore spray-on jeans and gave the distinct impression that if the man in the song didn't get a wriggle on they would just as happily spend the night with each other. I don't remember if Cheetah had any other hits, but for a short time they were the subject of many an enjoyable interlude in my mind. Then there was *Solid Gold*, a cheesy American version of *Countdown*, memorable only for the Solid Gold Dancers, a troupe of buxom, big-haired women who wore gold leotards and bodysuits while performing little choreographed numbers during the Top Ten countdown.

The cream of the crop, though, was *The Kenny Everett Video Show*, 6pm weeknights. Amid Kenny's mad antics and parade of daft characters there was Hot Gossip, a group of dancers who caused a great stir in conservative circles and underpants alike. I sweated bullets waiting for their spot, which was called The Naughty Bit. In his introduction Kenny prepared his legion of hormone-charged viewers by leering close to the camera, whispering lecherously and rolling his eyes as wisps of dry ice cascaded over his collar. The Hot Gossip dancers looked as if they were kitted out by a kinky London fetish emporium. Suspenders, fishnet stockings, corsets, tight and shiny PVC, stilettos, and the briefest panties textiles allowed at the time. They writhed, grinded, pouted and high-kicked along to current pop hits and the collective groans of millions of boys.

For your edification, and at the risk of laying bare my peculiar tastes, here are my top five sure-fire, stiffy-inducing video clips from the '80s.

1. **'Girls On Film', Duran Duran**
   The director's cut – rarely shown, but nevertheless a hands-down, lay-down misère. Lingerie models having pillow fights never failed to get the feathers flying.

2. **'Babooshka', Kate Bush**
   Wild hair, gold body-paint and sword-brandishing. What more could one want?

3. **'California Girls', David Lee Roth**
   Diamond Dave takes time out from snorting coke off hookers' butts to consort with a bevy of oiled bikini babes on Venice Beach. Cheap, nasty and clichéd. Loved it.

4. **'Shiny Shiny', Haysi Fantayzee**
   Thought my memory might be cheating on this one, but I happened to catch it on Pay TV recently and the girl is seriously beautiful. Sculpted cheekbones, full lips; gorgeous, sexy eyes. The fact that she's wearing sheer black pantyhose and what looks to be a red rubber chastity belt doesn't hurt either.

5. **'Tired Of Toein' The Line', Rocky Burnette**
   I know, I know, a bit left field, this one. It's from 1980 and I have a vague recollection of being moved by Rocky's 'band', which consisted of attractive girls in tight, glittery tracksuits shaking their bums, tossing their long hair and pretending to play trombone in a none too convincing fashion. At the end of the clip Rocky, in fireman attire, hoses them down one by one in what I'd imagine is the biggest metaphorical money shot ever committed to film.

I'd also single out for special mention 'Centerfold' (J. Geils Band). Girls in big white sweatshirts and very little else clutching schoolbooks to their bosoms and doing cartwheels in a classroom. Good stuff. The Eurogliders' 'We Will Together', which was set on a beach, is a surprising inclusion but I stand by it. Grace Knight is an absolute revelation in dreads and a striped, high-cut one-piece swimsuit, but the whole thing is brought undone by Bernie Lynch, who also spends much of the video cavorting in his swimming attire, to wit, a pair of dick-stickers. Made it difficult to maintain the rage, that. The Angels' 'Sticky Little Bitch', perhaps not surprisingly given the title, boasted half a dozen saucy-looking vixens in black leather. The clip for 'Walk The Dinosaur', a ditzy funk song by Was (Not Was), featured Cro-Magnon women in caveperson attire – brief chamois skins and undies. I disliked the song, and its grasp of prehistory was obviously shaky, but it still found its way onto my black-label collection of vids taped from *Rage*. Other female stars like the trio from Bananarama, the two girls from Human League and Debbie Harry were spunkrats pure and simple, but they never revealed enough skin to really do much damage.

Whether or not you agree with my list, one thing is certain. It pales in comparison with the brazen sexual japery on display in today's videos. If there's one thing the current crop know how to do, it's fill a screen with an extraordinary assortment of booty. Of both sexes. They revel in it. Have a look at Lou Bega's 'Mambo No. 5', or Crazy Town, or anything by Destiny's Child. A recent number one, an ode to the G-string called 'Thong Song' by Sisqó, takes David Lee Roth's theme and sends it into orbit, culminating with black girls clad in white G-strings writhing in the dark under ultraviolet lights. All you can see is luminescent orange lipstick and narrow glowing triangles. The politics might be questionable but I just give thanks that I am not a teenager today. I'd explode.

As it turned out, I was lucky in being able to broker a truce between music and masturbation. I discovered that the two could exist side by side, and 'latest release' started to take on a whole new meaning.

∩

My mother, I was to discover, had other weapons of mass distraction in her arsenal.

I am slouched deep in my cinema seat, hoping no-one will recognise me. The movie theatre smells like old sandshoes. Mine, quite possibly. On the huge screen an enormous, well-rounded and fully conceived female bottom is wiggling pneumatically. The woman's taut thighs pump rhythmically. Quite a few of her other body parts are on the move as well, and some of the close-ups spark a slightly queasy sensation in the pit of my stomach. Tiny blossoms of hormonal fireworks detonate in my anatomical no-man's-land.

But there is another sensation, one which is curdling all this delicious naughtiness. That sensation can best be described as acute embarrassment. I am embarrassed not because I'm watching an extraordinarily sexy woman writhing and twisting on the screen, but because my mother is right there beside me, dancing. And it isn't a dream. In the middle of the cinema my mother, one of the most private and shy people I've ever known, is on her feet, clapping, swinging her hips and singing 'Flashdance . . . What A Feeling' along with Irene Cara. In the movie Jennifer Beals is doing that dance routine that forms the movie's climax. I don't mind admitting it was the basis of one or two of my own. Our Jennifer, all dark permed hair, leotard and leg warmers, is giving her all, gradually breaking through to that table of po-faced judges. Oh yes, there she goes, hunched over in a shaft of sunlight. Dust motes float dramatically. Look out,

106

here comes that enormous dive over the camera. A somersault and she's up, twirling and pointing at each of the panel in turn. And they're loving it. Feet are tapping, craggy faces breaking into smiles as Jen makes the stuffed shirts rediscover the innocent delight of a good knees-up. Hooray! Her ballet dream is assured. No more arc-welding and pole-dancing for our heroine. It's goodbye shapeless overalls and protective headgear, hello fame and fortune.

My mother wanted to see *Flashdance* because she loved the theme song, which the local radio station played on high rotation. I just didn't realise she'd want to see it with *me*. *Flashdance* wasn't that sort of movie. It was a group movie, a teen flick, the sort you went to see with your friends. Like *The Breakfast Club*, or *Pretty in Pink*, or *Footloose*. A movie the guys all went to so they could get an eyeful of Miss Sex-on-Celluloid 1983 and go, 'Phhwooar!' during the strip-club scenes. (*Fleshdance*, we called it.) When, one wet afternoon, Leila asked me if I wanted to go with her, I was too shocked to think of a reason why not. Had she said to me, 'Oh, and by the way, when that song comes on over the really good sound system, I probably won't be able to stop myself dancing and making an exhibition of myself,' I might have tried harder to wriggle out of it.

The thing that surprised me most, apart from Leila's spontaneous outpouring of enjoyment, was that my mother rarely went to the movies. She always claimed she didn't have the patience to sit through an entire film. 'I can't help it,' she often said. 'My mind starts wandering. Before long I'm thinking about everything I could be doing back at home.' *Flashdance*, apparently, was the exception. Although, strictly speaking, she didn't sit through the bloody thing, did she? As she bopped away, oblivious to the turning heads and incredulous looks – perfectly noticeable even in the dark – I sunk lower and willed my own spontaneous combustion.

'Come on, Anthony,' Leila hissed several times, slapping me on the shoulder. 'Come on, get up and have a dance. This is fantastic, isn't it?' Her face was alive, her elbows pumping.

I heard tittering a few rows back. No, Mother, this isn't fantastic. Quite the opposite, in fact. This is rapidly turning into the worst day of my life.

There is no embarrassment like teenage embarrassment. You are so self-conscious, so utterly self-absorbed, so completely caught up in trying to mould an image to fit your perception of yourself. And your own mother goes and brings it all crashing down in the space of one song. Unbelievable.

As the credits started to roll, I scarpered to the toilet and stayed in a cubicle until I was sure the crowd had dispersed. Only then did I emerge and meet Mum in the carpark.

Flashdance set the pattern for my mother's movie viewing. She liked anything with a poppy, commercial soundtrack and lots of bodies in motion. By the time *Dirty Dancing* hit cinema screens a few years later, I had thankfully left home and was well out of harm's way. 'I've Had The Time Of My Life' was the big hit from that movie. God, I hated that song. Needless to say, Leila loved it, although I don't know if she repeated her impromptu live performance in the cinema. 'That Patrick Swayze is a hunk,' she often commented afterwards. 'He can leave his shoes under my bed any day.'

That's strange, I thought. I used to get in trouble for leaving my own shoes under mine.

Nineteen eighty-four was a watershed year. I fell in love, and found the stains difficult to remove. And – infinitely more momentous in some ways – I saw my first live gig. It was a special under-eighteens show at the local RSL (or the Rissole, as we loved to call it), and if memory serves me correctly there were three bands on the bill. They were all local outfits. When I say local, I think the 'headline' act might have travelled the hour or so down the Pacific Highway from Port Macquarie. That was enough to make them seem as exotic as a lost Amazon tribe. Funnily enough, the second band on the bill, GEN-R8, was the band I would join in a couple of years. I don't want to go into too much detail just yet about this particular group, except to say that the members of GEN-R8 were all hovering in their very late teens and seemed so utterly fabulous and out of reach. I would never have believed that I could even be friends with them, let alone be onstage with them.

Judging by the girls' reaction, GEN-R8 were everything that we Year 10 males could only dream of being. They weren't schoolboys, for a start. They drove their own cars. They drank with impunity at the bar (and sometimes onstage). They wore tight black jeans, studded belts and earrings. Their mullets were long and meticulously maintained. Their parents apparently never told them what time they had to be home. The lead singer – my predecessor, as things transpired – not only sang, but played lead guitar and keyboards as well (though not at the same time). Infinitely more annoying than his musical proficiency, however, was the fact that he was also a gym junkie and boasted quite improbable shoulders and arms. Consequently he was loath to wear a shirt onstage, and when he clutched the microphone, his bicep looked as if it would split like a piece of overripe fruit. When I eventually replaced him, the band lost not only a lead guitarist and keyboardist, but a potential Australasian body-building champion.

As it happens, I don't remember much about GEN-R8's slot that night. The band I'd come to see was first up. I don't recall its name – Nuclear Winter, or something along those lines, I think. What was important was that its members hailed from my school. This was their first gig and it seemed that the entire student population had turned up to see them. I cannot over-state the excitement that percolated around the quadrangle in the lead-up to this night. The group's five members were the subject of much hushed and reverent discussion wherever they went. Of the lead singer, I recall only greasy blond hair with an outrageous Michael Hutchence fringe, Jaggeresque lips and jughandle ears. His black jeans were moulded to his crotch and stovepiped their way down his long legs. The silver studs in his belt glinted in the coloured stage lights.

During songs he was frenetic, throwing himself all over the stage in a painfully self-conscious manner. I suspect he was try-ing to meld all his favourite frontmen's moves into one, creating a rock'n'roll version of Frankenstein's monster that lurched and spun and windmilled and pulled faces. He was part Peter Garrett, part Doc Neeson, part David Lee Roth. Perhaps he thought this could well be his first and last chance in front of a crowd (an astute assumption, as things turned out), and wanted to try out everything he'd been practising in his bedroom. The result was a lead singer who behaved the way he *thought* lead singers were supposed to behave. In between numbers he stood at the mic stand looking bewildered and uncomfortable. He had nothing in his arsenal in the way of crowd banter, and the spaces between songs felt glacial. I swear one or two of the breaks were longer than the songs themselves. Then, after a few experimental plunking bass notes and a hastily convened conference during which the key of the next number was mutually agreed upon, the band stumbled into yet another Midnight Oil cover and he relaunched himself like an impeccably coiffed missile across the RSL stage.

Nuclear Winter, or whatever they were called, had only enough material for about thirty minutes and when the singer, who by this time had a white towel draped around his neck in true sweaty rock-star style, raised his arms in salute and said, 'Thanks, Taree. See youse later!' the few hundred students went ballistic. To top it all off – and I still can't believe this next bit – the Human Fringe twirled the towel above his head like a lasso and flung it out into the crowd. Now, it is conceivable – just – that he was being ironic, but I have a niggling feeling that he was completely serious. And I stood there, my face a fetching shade of envy-green, listening to the girls around me squeal about how spunky the band members were, gripping my glass of Coke with such force I thought it might shatter. I was desperately jealous. Insanely jealous. Completely consumed. More than anything, I wanted to be up there. I wanted to be that singer. I craved to be the focus of all that attention. I was sure I could do it, probably a whole lot better. I was a better singer, no argument – well, not in my mind, at any rate. *Much* better. If that mob could get it together enough to play at the Rissole – our equivalent of Wembley – then surely I could muster something.

In a peculiar, totally illogical way I felt somehow cheated. As if all that hard work in my bedroom had been for nothing. Where was the recognition for the hundreds of hours I'd put in, memorising lyrics, honing and refining my skills?

The other bands came on and did their sets. In a classic case of metaphorical genital-comparison, each band felt obliged to have bigger gear than the one before – larger amps, a bigger drumkit, more lights, more instruments, more hair, more attitude. The drummer in the headline band even had the band's name – the Skumbagz – painted on his bass drum in a jagged black font. The capital 'S' and the 'z' were lightning bolts. How unremittingly cool was that? You knew you weren't dealing with any short-term, fly-by-night, flash-in-the-pan group when they had their name on the bass drum. It lent the whole thing an air of permanence, of credibility. It told us that the Skumbagz were in it for the long haul. (As if a few letters daubed in black acrylic could keep a band together!)

Funnily enough, I didn't feel any jealousy watching the Skumbagz's lead singer. I quickly recognised that he was in a different class altogether, a whole other league. For a start, he reserved some of his energy for actually singing, as opposed to leaping, and when he sang he employed a certain mic technique, holding it slightly away from his gob during the screamy bits so that his voice didn't distort, and pulling it in close for the softer parts – unlike his Nuclear Winter counterpart, who I think spent much of the time fellating the mic. The Skumbagz's screecher also posed with one white-sandshoed foot propped on his foldback wedge and his crotch thrust forward, a supremely confident gesture and one which I immediately filed away for future experimentation. At one point between songs he sidled up to the rhythm guitarist and said, in a 20 000-watt rasp, 'Les, I had no idea Taree had so many hot chicks. Whaddya reckon?' Les leered and grinned. Female larynxes almost disintegrated. This guy obviously knew his shit, and I doffed my cap to him.

The other thing that struck me was the similarity of material. The Oils, the Angels, AC/DC, INXS, the Models, the Machinations, Talking Heads, Radio Birdman – each band covered the same ground. Unlike the others, however, the Skumbagz road-tested a handful of originals, which were met with less enthusiasm but nevertheless reinforced the impression that they were serious musos.

It's difficult to put into words the excitement of losing my live-show virginity that night. It was unlike any other musical experience I'd ever had. So rapt was I in drinking in every little detail, I can remember absolutely nothing else about the night. Not a single solitary thing. Who did I go with? What did we do beforehand? How did we get there? I've no idea. It's all static. Somehow I was just *there*. This was a world – nay, a universe – away from our school socials. It was the real deal. If our assembly hall seemed cavernous, then the gloomy RSL auditorium was like a cathedral. Instead of incense, the faintly sweet smell of stale beer and old cigarette smoke permeated everything. Even that was exciting. So *this* was what real rock-'n'roll smelled like. I was captivated by the sight of the front-of-house speakers, hulking black boxes on either side of the stage which gave off gusts of sound even when there was nothing happening – just amplified air, the live mics picking up crowd noise and feeding it back in metallic whispers. Even looking at the empty stage, with the silver microphone stands and drums reflecting tiny starbursts of light, excited me.

It was the anticipation. Over the years I have grown to

love all the pre-gig noodling about almost as much as the show itself. More, sometimes. Noodling about speaks of potential, potential not always realised when a band actually starts playing. It's the same with albums. I have a penchant for recordings with that live feel. Studio chat, count-ins, fart-arsing about, general preamble, I love it all. (The all-time best album for this type of extraneous material is Muddy Waters' *Hard Again*. Every track starts with Muddy chatting to Johnny Winter. It even has stuff at the end of songs, Muddy cackling and saying, 'Well, got that sonofabitch down,' and Johnny cackling and replying, 'Yep, that's *that* pain in the ass out of the way.')

That night, I felt butterflies in my stomach when I saw the unkempt, bearded bloke in the checked flannie take his place at the mixing desk, sit his schooner of Old down carefully, and start pressing buttons and pushing sliders, a sure sign that things were about to get under way. I loved how the crowd whistled and yelled when darkened figures scampered out of the wings onto the stage. I loved the loud electric pop and crackle as leads were plugged into guitars. The preliminary thwacks and thumps on the drums, the little warm-up rolls, the way the word 'Skumbagz' fizzed and shivered when the drummer stamped on the bass drum pedal. I soaked up every nervous test lick, each sparking, self-conscious experimental note. The amplified squeak of fingers sliding along a fretboard. I adored (that's the only word for it) the way the rhythm guitarist struck a chord then twiddled the knobs on the face of his gleaming red Stratocaster so that the volume suddenly leaped up.

And the really great thing about that night was that I was able to wallow in this rock minutiae not once, but three times. My friends must have thought I'd slipped into a trance.

I shouldered my way through the crowd so I could stand as close as possible to the PA. I couldn't get enough volume into my head. That was another thing I noticed – the sound was somehow different, too. The music played at our socials was loud but *clean*. The chart hits were produced and polished, with all the edges smoothed down for easy consumption. This sound was louder, and raw. No-one had taken the aural sander to it, and there were little rough bits you could snag your ears on.

When I emerged at 11:30 with my hair sweat-plastered across my forehead, a stupid grin smeared on my face and a high-pitched whine in my ears, Dad was sitting in the car listening to classical music on the radio and looking out over the darkened river. 'How was it?' he asked. His voice seemed muffled.

'Good, ta,' I said, letting my cool veneer slip momentarily and positively bubbling over with teenage enthusiasm.

'Bit loud, wasn't it?' Dad started both the car and the familiar rant of parents down the ages. 'Why does it have to be so bloody noisy?'

'It's a live band, Dad. It's always loud when it's live.'

'Yeah, I know that. But Jesus, I could hear it out here in the car. Crystal clear. Bloody terrible. I can't imagine what it must have been like in there. How are your ears?'

'All right.' To me, my voice sounded as if I were speaking through an empty toilet-paper roll.

'Bloody ridiculous. I don't know why it has to be up so loud. Too many more of those concerts and you'll do yourself a mischief. Damage your hearing for sure and certain.'

If you'd mentioned tinnitus to me at that time, I'd have thought you were talking about a fungal growth between your toes. And besides, I was fifteen. I was invincible. I didn't bother trying to explain to my father that music has to be loud because just hearing it is not enough. You have to be able to *feel* it. It has to pummel you. It has to get inside you and vibrate your vitals. He wouldn't have understood, anyway. Slade's frizzy-haired, muttonchop-sideburned lead singer Noddy Holder might already have been relegated to the yellowing pages of music history, but he still best summed up my commitment to rock music: 'Till deaf do us part.'

It was Alison McKechnie who introduced me to U2. I wasn't much taken with Bono, but I liked her enormously. Alison lived in Sydney and spent the Christmas holidays with a mutual friend who, as luck would have it, lived just around the corner from me. She was all sleek city sophistication, or what I imagined sophistication to be. Her father Graeme was an academic and something of a champion chess-player. He'd also been captain of the Australian debating team. I didn't know Australia *had* a national debating team. Her mother Patricia sang folk music in a band which had actually recorded a couple of albums. Now, this *did* impress me. The sum total of her audience might have been four stoned hippies and an aged labrador, but that didn't matter. She had recorded. She had been in a studio. Big points there.

Alison attended an exclusive school for young ladies where she notched up excellent exam results with affected nonchalance. She played piano and saxophone. She had one sibling, a precocious brother named Tarquin or Rupert or something, who at the tender age of five or six was already learning to play the violin. This wasn't sophistication so much as unbridled smart-arsedry on a monstrous scale.

I met Alison on the beach. She was dusky-brown and dripping wet from the surf. Our mutual friend Yoni made the introductions in a voice which suggested she was growing tired of introducing her friend to drooling boys. Alison smiled and I noticed a small gap between her front teeth. Her eyes were mahogany. A handful of small caramel freckles were scattered across the bridge of her nose. The sides of her head had been shorn, *à la* Alannah Currie from the Thompson Twins, and the stubble there was dark. The rest was chemical blonde and permed to within an inch of its life, curling forward in tight ringlets. Her bikini was light blue and alarmingly high cut. I was immediately smitten, and took myself off home for a good lie down with a cold compact on my fevered brow.

Over the next few weeks, I concocted all sorts of excuses to see Alison. I was truly pathetic. Several times a day I slapped my forehead and cursed myself for not hanging out more with Yoni. She'd been living around the corner for years and I'd never been round. Not once. Now that the object of my crush was living there, barely three hundred metres away, I was finding hopelessly transparent reasons to pay daily visits. 'Oh, just passing and saw your paper on the lawn. Thought I'd drop it in for you.' Alison didn't seem to mind. She encouraged me, in fact. Yoni's parents tried to throw me off the scent a few times. 'Sorry, Anthony,' they would say, 'we're all going out today for a barbecue.'

'Right, I'll just pop home and see if Mum's got any sausages in the freezer.'

'No, a *family* barbecue.'

'Oh . . . right. How are you off for tomato sauce? I can bring extra.'

'Anthony, bugger off.'

Alison seemed so worldly-wise, so intelligent, so wonderfully cynical. And, best of all, she knew about music. In fact, she was scarily knowledgeable. Like me, she professed to loathe all that 'Top Forty crap'. She talked instead of bands I'd never heard of. Strange names kept cropping up. Psychedelic Furs, U2, the Pogues, Joy Division and New Order. 'Joy Division and New Order are the same band actually, 'cept for the lead singer who committed suicide,' Alison informed me, in a tone that suggested committing suicide was an infinitely cool and romantic thing to do.

When we had the chance, we'd lie on the beach and deep-fry ourselves – there was the smell of hot skin, sun-warmed lycra and tanning oil. We'd loll around reeking of coconut while I paid rapt attention to my new soulmate. I drank in her nut-brown curves and her wisdom. I was a horny Eliza Doolittle to Alison's Professor Higgins.

Alison was a musical snob. She was one of those people, and I have met many, who pride themselves on 'discovering' bands, who think it important to hear someone before the rest of the world. (I myself am guilty of this in the case of Oasis and their first album, *Definitely Maybe*. I still like to think that I was the first person in Australia to own this CD. I bought it on a trip to the UK in 1994 and its arrival back home in my luggage predates its Australian release by a few months. For some time afterwards, I invited friends around, put on Oasis, and basked in their keen interest. 'What's this?' asked one chum, notorious for liking only obscure bands. 'Oh, a little something I picked up in London. They're called Oasis. You'll be hearing a lot more about them, I reckon.') For Alison, it was also important to be well and truly over a band just as everyone else was cottoning onto them. You had to stay one step ahead of the pack.

Thus it was that she proclaimed U2 to be already on the down-hill slide with the release of the album *War*. 'Yeah, they're going all commercial,' she insisted. 'I much prefer their older stuff.'

I didn't know enough at the time to say, '*Older* stuff? Jesus Christ, they've only been around about three years.' They hadn't even got around to recording 'Pride (In The Name Of Love)'. One can only wonder at what she made of *Zooropa*. I just tried to look clever and nodded in lovelorn agreement.

Alison had brought a couple of tapes with her from Sydney, and I listened to 'Sunday Bloody Sunday' and 'Gloria' and 'New Year's Day' and 'I Will Follow' over and over, drilling them into my head, making myself like them so that Alison would like me. She, on the other hand, couldn't quite get a handle on my Stones passion and politely declined when I offered her the loan of one of my cassettes, but she did give me points for at least seeking out something different. And Alison was much impressed by my level of commitment, something she commented on when I brought her back to our house and showed her the dozens of posters stuck haphazardly on my bedroom walls. We were sitting on my bed talking about music, trying to impress each other, when my mother's voice rang out.

'Anthony! Where are you?'

'In here,' I called back.

'Well, get out here, the pair of you. Now.'

My stomach churned. I had a sneaking suspicion I knew what this was going to be about. But surely Mum wouldn't embarrass me in front of Alison. Surely Leila would let her get clear of the house before she started. Surely.

'You should know better than to take a girl into your bedroom.'

Oh no. Please, no. 'Mum, we were just talking. The bloody door was open and everything.'

'I don't care. You do *not* have girls alone in your bedroom.' Leila turned to Alison. 'What would your parents think?'

I felt ashamed and embarrassed beyond words. Nothing, Mum, they would think nothing. Her father's an academic, for fuck's sake. He *thinks* for a living. He wouldn't have room in his head for something so harmless and paltry. And he's a chess-player. Her mother's a folk singer. They are far too open-minded and liberal. They wouldn't let themselves be hemmed in by such outdated, country-backwater bullshit.

Alison shrugged and confirmed my line of thinking. 'I don't think they'd mind, actually, Mrs Griffis.'

'Is that so? Well, they bloody well should mind. I'll tell you something, Miss Kafoops, it's not going to happen in my house, right? You can stay out here with the rest of the family or you can go back to Yoni's. Whichever you prefer.'

I couldn't believe what was happening. My mother was treating Alison like a hussy, offering ultimatums to a woman of questionable morals. Even though we'd done absolutely nothing, I felt as if we'd been discovered road-testing the Kama Sutra. I suppose there was also an unspoken subtext, one that meant my parents knew I knew all about sex. Why else would they be worried about me having a girl alone in my room? Well, I now knew that they knew that I knew. What's more, my mother had a point. I can't pretend that the sight of Alison sitting on my bed didn't spark thoughts of us rolling around on it with our limbs entwined. I also felt strangely detached, as if I'd left my body and was watching a drama being played out between strangers.

Surprisingly enough, Alison chose to leave shortly after this exchange. She didn't seem the least bit fazed by events. In fact, she seemed to find the whole thing faintly amusing. On her way out she gave me a sympathetic smile and squeezed my hand. It was if she'd given me an electric shock.

Once again, my mother's squally disposition actually worked in my favour. The 'incident', as it came to be known, helped bring Alison and me closer together. We felt as though we'd shared something, that we'd been through an ordeal and come out the other end relatively unscathed. We walked along the empty beach hand in hand. Conditions were perfect for windswept teenage infatuation. The afternoon was leaden and blustery. Alison wore an enormous sweatshirt, like the one Jennifer Beals wore on the *Flashdance* poster, and it kept slipping off one brown shoulder to reveal a white bra strap, something she didn't try to conceal. Against her deep tan, the strap looked so white it was almost blue. The wind drove a light sea spray into our faces. Alison waved away my constant apologies.

'Look, don't worry about it. It's perfectly obvious that your mum feels threatened by another female presence.'

'Huh?' I attempted to send a smooth pebble skimming across the water. It careered into the shallow foam and sank.

'Of course. Try and see it from her point of view. There she is, the sole female influence in your life for what, fifteen years? Then suddenly you walk in not with one of your mates, but with a girl. It's just starting to dawn on her that her little boy's growing up. And when she's confronted with the hard evidence, i.e., me, well, she's bound to feel a little confused and hostile, isn't she? It's perfectly natural.'

'You reckon?' Alison's maturity and insight was staggering. 'You seem to know a lot about it.'

'Sure, I've read heaps. I tell you, your mum's a classic case. Anyway, I don't mind. Believe me, I understand.' Her voice suddenly changed. 'And trust me, if she wasn't happy about me being in your bedroom, she'd go troppo over what I'm going to do next.'

I felt like my heart was trying to work its way into my throat and throttle me. The blood roared in my ears. I had to say something, anything, so that this moment didn't dissolve. 'Yeah, and what's that?' my larynx squeezed out.

'Come here,' Alison said, and kissed me. Just like that. My God, this girl knew her mind. She stopped walking, turned to me and leaned in with her eyes closed, her mouth open, and her head tilted to one side. She's done this before, I thought, and dove straight in. Our lips met and my circuitry shorted. This was *very* different to kissing Donna, the foam head in the laundry. There was a vague sense of – how should I put it? – *combat*. A feeling that Alison's tongue was trying to wrestle mine, trying to control it. It had a fair job on its hands too, because mine was flapping around like a trapped bird. When it started to rain, we ran under the awning of the deserted kiosk, sank down against the Peter's ice-cream sign, and began some earnest, Olympic-qualifying pashing. We were all teeth and tongues.

I couldn't believe it. I was kissing a girl from Sydney! My stocks were about to go through the roof. I suspected that Alison would tell Yoni every detail, and I could bank on Yoni telling everyone else. My reputation back at school would be assured. I would be an official long-distance lover, carrying on a torrid affair with some mysterious stranger from the big smoke. Well, as torrid as you could expect when you were separated by five hundred-odd kilometres of bitumen. I worked all this out while we were still locked together like Siamese twins joined at the lips. Afterwards, my jaw ached from having held my mouth open for so long.

In the days immediately following the clandestine kiosk clinch, excitement would bubble up at strange and unexpected times. I might be reading, mowing the lawn, or washing the Kingswood, and a little tremor would ripple through me. Sometimes it was all I could do not to jump up and down, clapping my hands. From then on, whenever I strapped on the air guitar, my rock'n'roll fantasy suddenly shifted focus. Hordes of screaming girls still offered outstretched hands for me to touch as I ran across the stage, but now Alison was there. Not in the crowd, she was too special for that. She stood in the wings, laminated backstage pass around her neck, and looked on adoringly, getting off on the music and my genius. At certain times I would glance across and Alison would beam at me and nod her approval. I might wink back. Just a little moment shared amid the maelstrom. Sometimes she joined me onstage, like Linda McCartney, to play keyboards or some big, greasy sax. The crowd would go wild when I called for her to come out.

When Alison went back to Sydney, we had to have our final ardent pashing session the day before she left, because on her last night Yoni's family was taking her out for a farewell tea at the Chinese restaurant. She promised to make up a compilation tape of all her favourite songs and send it to me, so that my musical education could continue by correspondence. She asked me if I would ring. I said probably not because we weren't allowed to make long-distance calls unless it was an emergency, and although I considered her leaving to be an all-hands-on-deck, klaxon-blaring red alert, I doubted my parents would view it as having quite the same import.

After she'd gone, I was morose and mooched around the house in a delicious, aching funk. I was forlorn, moody and melodramatic; Hamlet in a hamlet. Yoni quickly tired of me hanging around talking endlessly about her friend, and mimed vomiting. I started to love songs I normally detested. I lay on my bed and listened to bloated ballads. 'Time After Time' could suddenly make me teary. 'It Started With A Kiss' was the greatest song ever written.

Barely a week after Alison had returned home, I spent my accumulated pocket money not on a cassette of the Stones' *Emotional Rescue* as planned, but on a box of chocolates, which I gift-wrapped, complete with curly ribbon and soppy card, and posted to Sydney. Another week went by, and Alison finally called. I felt as though I were going to be physically ill as I grabbed the phone from my father.

'I got the chocolates,' Alison said. 'Thank you.'

There was something wrong. She didn't sound as overwhelmed as I might have hoped.

'Were they okay?'

'Yeah, no, they were great. A little melted, but otherwise great.'

'Melted?'

'Well, what did you think would happen when you sent a box of chocolates in the mail?' She didn't actually say 'you fucking imbecile', but it dangled there at the end of the sentence. 'It's February. What do you think chocolate does when it's in the back of a truck in thirty-degree heat for a couple of days? And the bloody box had been squashed. When I opened it, I got chocolate all over the place. Patricia and Graeme had the shits something chronic.'

If I'd thought about it for a nanosecond, I might have realised the pitfalls associated with sending cocoa-based products via Australia Post. If I'd thought about it for a fraction longer, I might have realised the pitfalls associated with a long-distance relationship, something Alison was now pointing out to me clearly, concisely and logically. Emotion didn't enter into it.

Her father's debating skills had obviously rubbed off on her. There were phrases like 'nicest boy I've ever met' and 'I had a wonderful time', but there was always a 'but' tacked on the end of them. By the time I replaced the receiver, I was single again. Alison wasn't nasty about it, just pragmatic, as women tend to be in these situations. It would never work, she said. It was a summer romance. It was foolish to expect any more. She'd thought I was smart enough to realise that too.

Well, obviously not. A squashed box of Dairy Milk Assorted was lumpy evidence of that. The classic 'Can we still be friends?' line got a guernsey as well. Alison's parting words were: 'Don't hate me, Anthony. Good luck with exams this year. See you next Christmas, yeah? We'll have a great time.'

Feeling like a complete dork, I fumed. We'll see, missy, I thought to myself. I mightn't be just hanging around next Christmas. A year was a long time, there might be someone else by then. When it came to Alison and the Great Cadbury's Fiasco, I would have to develop a hard centre.

I stalked back to my room, dug out my tape of AC/DC's *Dirty Deeds Done Dirt Cheap*, plugged in my headphones, and rocked out with a vengeance to 'Squealer' and 'Problem Child', throwing myself around my bedroom like someone taken leave of their senses.

She never did send me the compilation tape. I was relieved, to be honest. What sort of name was the Edge, anyway? Plonker.

Heading into 1985 I was in need of some love aid, but I had to make do with Live Aid instead. Its sheer, mind-numbing size was enough to wipe all thoughts of the opposite sex from my mind. For a weekend, at any rate.

This stupendous charity concert, which raised around $140 million for starving Ethiopians, was without question *the* rock music event of the '80s. It was the brainchild of that notable wanker Bob Geldof. I do not use the term 'wanker' in a derogatory sense. In his autobiography Sir Bob says that, during periods of chronic unemployment – pre-Boomtown Rats success – he filled his days by lying in bed masturbating, because there was simply nothing else to do. Hence his wanking was notable. His admission sparked, among my circle of friends, the euphemistic phrases 'going the Geldof' or 'having a Geldof'.

Anyway, all that is beside the point. Although you could say Geldof displayed deft prick-handling skills *vis-à-vis* convincing the world's biggest pop stars to take part in Live Aid. Delicate massaging was surely the order of the day.

The world had seen nothing like it. The greatest acts of the era – most of whom I detested out of sheer bloody-mindedness – on two stages, one at Wembley and the other at JFK Stadium in Philadelphia, with live feeds between the venues. A whole weekend of nonstop music watched by more than one and a half billion people worldwide. Remarkable then, given its import, that I remember very little about it. I have murky memories of Bob himself doing a couple of numbers, and Queen, who were sensational, and (for some strange reason) the Hooters.

About the same time that countless roadies were wheeling enormous crates of equipment up and down ramps in London, I was in my pyjamas wondering how I could avoid missing the biggest rock event in history. See, we didn't own a VCR at that time, and permission for all-night viewing was neither expected nor forthcoming, so Darren and I had no choice but to go to bed and pray that nothing too exciting would happen on those stages while Australia was enveloped in darkness.

As luck would have it, while I was unconscious Led Zeppelin reformed (albeit with Phil Collins on drums), as did the Who (*bugger*!). On the other hand, the Stones did not play together because Mick and Keith were feuding at the time. Instead Mick did a well-received solo spot and two duets – a live version of 'It's Only Rock'n'Roll' with Tina Turner, during which he ripped off her leather skirt to reveal a brief black leotard, and a hammy video with David Bowie in which the pair reworked Martha and the Vandellas' 'Dancing In The Street' and mocked each other good-naturedly.

Unfortunately international time- and datelines conspired to make me a victim of a cruel fate. In other words, I was wide awake when Keith Richards and Ron Wood joined Bob Dylan on stage for the finale in Philly. Looking tiny and frail on the vast stage, this trio of bedraggled deros mumbled, bumbled and stumbled through a clutch of patently unrehearsed Dylan numbers. They clung to their acoustics and stared about them as if they'd just woken up, cigarettes drooping from bottom lips. Dylan's steel-wool syllables scoured the warm night air, and it soon became apparent that Keef and Ronnie only half knew the song list.

The applause could be nothing other than vast, but there was something missing. You could sense the crowd urging them on, willing them to suddenly snap out of their torpor and assume the exalted mantle of Rock Gods. But they were too busy looking at each other, trying to work out what was going to happen next. Just when it seemed things could get no worse – short of Richards actually falling off the stage in a stupor – Dylan voiced the opinion that some of the money being raised should go to struggling American farmers instead of starving African waifs. It was a sentiment that did not go down well with the crowd, and certainly not with Bob Geldof.

I watched this folly unfold with the air of a disappointed parent. I was hoping the two Stones would be far better behaved. Instead they'd embarrassed me, really let me down. Why couldn't they be more like Mick? Jagger at least always knew how to rise to an occasion. I never thought I'd be in a position to say this, but I was actually relieved when Lionel Richie came on and led everyone through an arm-linking, sway-altogether version of 'We Are The World'. That, my friends, is how truly awful it was.

So my lasting impression of Live Aid is not one of staggering altruism or global togetherness; it isn't one of Bob Geldof being borne aloft on the shoulders of Paul McCartney and Pete Townshend, the crowd roaring and the future knight of the realm beaming with success. It's of three wasted figures teetering around at the front of a stage in front of a billowing curtain, sounding absolutely woeful and looking in worse condition than the people they were supposedly raising money to help.

'Er, hi everyone. We're Horizon. Welcome along to the Manning Valley Christian Youth Centre. Yeah!' These are the first words I utter as frontman for a real band at a real gig.

To my left, on the cramped ledge which masquerades as a stage, the guitarist – a guy called Jeremy whom I've met only once before – plunges straight into the opening riff from 'Satisfaction' and out in front, under the fizzing white glare of the strip-fluoro lighting, jaws drop. Those jaws belong to devout Manning Valley Christians who have, this very evening, gathered together in a drafty red-brick box with other like-minded Christians and their impeccably attired offspring, there to lift up their hearts to the Lord and let their children have fun away from the harmful influences which have spread like a cancer through this increasingly secular world of ours. One of those influences, needless to say, is the devil's music, as practised by Messrs Jagger and his ilk. Not an ideal choice then, kicking off the evening with 'Satisfaction'. Something of a bold gambit, you might think.

Well, let me just say it was a choice born of desperation. There was no desire to offend, we weren't daring the Almighty to send fire and brimstone raining down upon us from on high. It wasn't my fault. Good grief, it wasn't even my *band*. At the start of this surreal evening I was an innocent bystander, an observer, no more.

It was typical, I suppose, that my first foray into the heady world of rock'n'roll would happen purely by accident – not serendipity, note, but accident – and involve me performing with a band I didn't know in front of two dozen eleven-year-olds and their outraged parents at a Christian Fellowship knees-up. How did it come to pass? There was no-one directly to blame. Events, as they have a habit of doing, conspired to place me there on that stage. To misquote an old saying, some men have mediocrity thrust upon them. Indirectly, however, there was a culprit, someone at whom the finger of blame could be pointed in a clear and distinctly unwavering fashion.

My brother.

It all started a few weeks after the Alison affair melted away in a gooey, chocolatey mess. Even more galling than the fact that I had just been dropped, and the fact that, owing to my reckless confectionery purchase, it would be another month or so before I could afford to buy *Emotional Rescue*, was that Darren suddenly found himself in a band. A real band. With real musicians. Fan-bloody-tastic. That just topped it off nicely. You take your eye off the ball for a second, just a *second*, and your little brother ducks in under the radar and pinches your rightful place. Jealousy didn't even come close to describing how I felt. I was furious with myself. How could I have wasted so much time on a *girl*? I'd spent half the summer foofing around like some Byronic moron, skipping through metaphorical mead-ows and plucking petals from daisies, and meanwhile Darren was taking care of business big time.

The band was called Horizon and its members were all students. Darren's inclusion was by pure chance. One day, as Horizon's keyboardist and bassist cycled past our place, they heard my brother giving the skins some tough love. They listened for a while, had a brief conference on the footpath, knocked on the door, introduced themselves, took one look at the kit and offered Darren the gig on the spot. Now, it's a fact that good drummers are hard to find. Schoolboy drummers who own their own kit are as rare as rocking-horse excrement. I'm fairly sure it was Darren's gear that secured him the gig. The fact that he could actually play was a bonus.

My brother accepted without hesitation. So excited was he, he forgot to ask the Horizon lads what sort of material they were intending to play. 'Who cares?' he shrugged. 'They're a band without a drummer, I'm a drummer with no band.' He was immediately transformed. I watched him go from regular, sporadically aggravating sibling to totally insufferable prick in world-record time. When a rehearsal was called, he loaded the drums into our parents' car with an infuriating air of importance and gave smirking waves from behind stacks of chrome as the car disappeared round the corner.

When he returned, it was all I could do not to rush from my bedroom and accost him with questions. Curiosity was devouring me alive, but I had to feign lack of interest. Grinding my teeth, I remained in languid repose on my bed, pretending to be absorbed in a music mag. Eventually he came to me.

'How'd it go?' I forced myself to keep flipping pages.

'Yeah, good.' Something in his tone made me look up. His brow was furrowed.

'What's up? Are they crap?' I asked hopefully.

'No, it's not that. They're really good.' My heart sank. 'They've got great gear and everything . . .'

'What's the singer like?' I braced myself.

'Not great. His voice is too deep, hasn't got the range.'

Good. Good. 'Well, what's the problem?'

Darren paused. He was obviously struggling. 'It's the stuff they want to play.'

I pounced. 'Hah! I knew it. They're doing bloody Culture Club, shit like that.'

'Nah, nothin' like that. 'S just that I've never heard any of it before.'

What? A schoolboy covers band not playing the Angels or the Oils? In Taree? What was the world coming to?

'You ever heard of a band called Petra?'

I shook my head.

'What about Stryper?'

Stryper. That name rang a bell. An image was floating up from the Stygian depths of my mind. American hair metal band, spandex à gogo. They all wore black and yellow, looked like frizzed and teased bumblebees. More importantly, I seemed to recall that their name stood for Salvation Through Redemption Yielding Peace, Encouragement and Righteousness, and that they spent a lot of time throwing bibles into the crowd.

'Oh my God, you're not telling me they play *Christian* rock, are you?'

Darren nodded his head. 'The two songs we worked on today are called "Judas Kiss" and "Road To Zion". Our first gig's the Christian Youth Centre, three weeks' time.'

I could hardly contain my glee. However, my callous cheerfulness didn't last long. Once my initial hooting and derisive laughter subsided, the bald facts remained: Darren was still in a band, and that band was still about to play a fully-fledged gig. To an audience, presumably. Sobering thought. I was absolutely desperate to try my hand at singing, but my only outlet thus far had been playing Curly in the school production of *Oklahoma!* the previous year. I'd auditioned not because

I loved musicals, but because it was a chance to perform in front of an audience, and, being a showpony, I wasn't about to miss out on my chance of whatever glory went along with that. I suppose, too, that my being cast confirmed I wasn't completely tone deaf. Once again, though, my wardrobe caused a few ripples. The costume designer had dredged up a pink cowboy shirt with white tassles across the chest. *Pink?* What were they trying to do to me? As if a macho, bow-legged bloke like Curly would be caught dead in a pink shirt! They also gave me a hot-red bandanna to tie around my neck. Pink and red together? Was this person on drugs? Why not just give me a pair of leather chaps with the arse cut out of them?

Schoolboy rock groups were few and far between in Taree. In fact, until Darren joined Horizon, I didn't know a single solitary person who was in a band, or even interested in being in one. That was the perplexing thing. You had someone like Jenny Cromer, who played a frighteningly high standard of organ at local eisteddfods. Watching her hands flutter over the two-tiered keyboard and her feet bounce from pedal to pedal during 'Una Paloma Blanca' was an experience not to be missed, but she was only interested in solo work. I was beginning to think that joining a band was as mysterious and difficult as gaining entry into a secret guild, but now I saw that my brother had unwittingly opened the door for me. There was a sliver of light. Desperate times called for desperate measures, and I was left with no option. It didn't matter if I had to sing the Hallelujah chorus, I would have to somehow wheedle my way into Horizon.

♪

'This is my brother Anthony. He's helping me out with the drums.'

I had infiltrated a Horizon rehearsal by adopting a cunning

disguise – I became a roadie. There was no choice. I asked Darren if I could tag along for a look and listen. He said no. He said it was his band and I could bloody well go and find my own band. 'Why would you be interested?' he asked, quite reasonably. 'You were laughing at us last week.' So I tried a different tack and offered to lug his drums if he let me come along.

He thought about it for a moment. 'Okay, but you gotta take all of them, right? Everything. I'm not touching even a stand. You lug 'em in. You set 'em up. Then you pack 'em up again at the end. Okay?'

Sure, there was much tongue-biting and pride-swallowing involved, but it was worth it just to get a peek inside the Aladdin's cave that was Damien Hedler's garage. Guitars, amps, keyboards, microphone stands, coiled leads – all the trappings were laid out before me on the oil-stained concrete floor. Darren chatted with the rest of the band while I tripped back and forth from the car, hefting his hardware. He stood, hands on hips, loving every second as I sweated and grunted.

'Just over there, thanks,' he said, nodding towards a rancid piece of carpet. 'That's my spot. Hey, careful with that ride cymbal, mate.'

Fighting the urge to hurl the cymbal at his head, I wrestled with the drums, slowly erecting telescopic stands and flicking wingnuts tight, while trying at the same time to take in everything else around me. The other members of Horizon looked like your regular, run-of-the-mill teenagers. T-shirts, jeans, trainers. Hair at various stages of mulletdom. I'm not sure what I thought they'd look like. I suppose, given what Darren had told me, I expected to walk in on a room of Buddy Holly look-alikes. In a word, I thought they'd be nerdier. Their conversation covered normal topics too – exams, sport, girls – and it was peppered with the usual range of expletives. No talk of God. No mention of Jesus Christ Our Saviour. No-one had produced a bible, or tried to convert me. Yet.

'Oi, headjob,' the keyboardist – Gavin, I think his name was – called out to Damien Hedler. 'Your parents left yet?'

'Yeah, 'bout half an hour ago.'

'Beaudy.' Gavin fished a packet of cigarettes out of his back-pack and lit up. Something told me no-one would try to give me religion today. Immediately one or two of the others dropped what they were doing and lit up as well. They clutched their smokes between finger and thumb, a pincer grip, with the lit ends facing back towards their palms. They tilted their heads and exhaled towards the ceiling, where the blue smoke wafted around the tools and old bikes hanging there. I declined the offer of my own ciggie and continued attaching Darren's bass drum pedal. Darren also declined, though that could have been for my benefit.

The other non-smoker was the lead guitarist. I could tell, even then, that he was the lead guitarist because he was the quiet, moody-looking guy sitting off to one side, running a rag over his guitar and playing a few licks while the others faffed about. His name was Jeremy and he didn't say much. He just hunched over, hair flopping in his eyes, watching his fingers move up and down the fretboard as if he were studying a rare variety of insect crawling along a branch. I looked on for a minute, then it dawned on me that I knew the tune he was playing.

'"Behind Blue Eyes"?' I ventured.

Jeremy stopped playing and turned to me. A look of surprise scudded across his face. 'You know the Who?' he asked.

I shrugged, nonchalance personified. 'A bit, yeah.' Pressing home my advantage, I rattled off half a dozen song and album titles like a fighter delivering a flurry of blows.

Jeremy jerked back as if physically struck. His surly features split into a grin. 'I don't believe it,' he said, and started peeling off snatches of other Who songs while I joined in on restrained, self-conscious vocals. Suddenly energised, Jeremy stood up and now I could see that the front of his shirt had a picture of Pete Townshend on it and the words 'Hope I Die Before I Get Old'. He plugged into his amp and nodded towards a microphone clamped on its stand waiting for action.

I could hardly believe it. Feeling nervous and excited, I grabbed hold of it, started singing, realised it wasn't turned on, felt stupid, fiddled about trying to find the little black switch, found it, flicked it, started singing again, and I could immediately hear a voice coming from somewhere else. My voice, yet not my voice. My voice with a slightly thin, daleky overtone to it. All treble, no bass. But then I was coming through the crappiest amp in that garage. I was a ventriloquist, opening my mouth and singing over here but with the sound coming out of the little black box on the upside-down milk crate behind me. I was also acutely aware of the microphone – it's smooth cylindrical shape, its coolness, the feel of the bulbous grilled head against my lips, the sharp smell of the metal.

I looked at Jeremy and realised that he did in fact bear an uncanny resemblance to Pete Townshend. Especially when he played guitar. He had him down pat, in fact. All the moves – legs akimbo, shifting weight forwards and back, windmilling chords, pumping the neck of his guitar as if trying to shake every last decibel from it. I knew obsession when I saw it. I knew how to recognise it. We were the same, this Jeremy character and I. Same cause, same effect, definitely the same symptoms. I could just see him at home in front of a mirror, putting himself through his paces, trying to be as much like his rock'n'roll hero as possible. I simply couldn't believe that I'd found another person who was so obviously completely nuts over a long-lived '60s rock band. And if he loved the Who, I concluded excitedly, then surely he must love the Stones as well. Had to. I mean, *I* loved both. Stood to reason.

We played all of 'Behind Blue Eyes' without stopping or making a mistake. Jeremy separated the quietly plucked bits from the loudly strummed bits by stepping on a pedal. I was stunned by the effect this had. Suddenly his guitar's tone leaped from acoustic to snarling electric. I withstood the urge to grab the mic off its stand and whirl it around my head, Roger Daltrey-style, but I couldn't resist trialling a few mic-stand manoeuvres and lunged forwards, forcing the stand down like a submissive dancing partner. Felt good.

When the final chord finished ricocheting around the garage, Jeremy and I grinned at each other, and I looked at the band. They appeared stunned, cigarette stubs still smouldering between their fingers. Yeah, right, mighty impressed, I thought, then noticed that they were not in fact looking at me, but at something over my shoulder. Some time during our impromptu performance, Horizon's lead singer had walked in, and he was standing there staring at me.

The rest of the rehearsal I spend sitting on a bike in the corner of the garage, rolling gently back and forth, staying very quiet, very out of the way. A weird mix of emotions churns inside me. I feel slightly embarrassed, the same way I've felt when I've been sprung with the tennis racquet in my bedroom. But the overwhelming feeling is one of excitement. I've done it. At last, I've laid my hands on a real microphone and sung a rock song. And it was good. Well, at least it *felt* good. Jeremy certainly seemed to enjoy it. And I have to admit, I'm feeling a tad confused. If this guy can play all that Who stuff, what on earth is he doing playing God rock? For that matter, why are any of them playing it? None of them seem to have a religious bent, yet here they are, trotting out turgid sonic psalms. (There can be no question that our civilisation's cultural nadir has been reached when the pious reach for guitars and cans of hairspray.)

Horizon obviously believe that, even at close quarters, each instrument must be played as though they're trying to reach the furthest rows of a seething stadium. Perhaps they're trying to ensure that God hears them. In the confines of the Hedler garage, a structure built with scant consideration for acoustics, the noise is so loud that after a while you realise you're squinting, a reflex action to try and stop your eyeballs popping from their sockets. Every song quickly collapses into a molten mass. Echoes rebound upon echoes, until the whole thing gives way under the sheer weight of the sound.

Midway through one number, Gavin looks up from the keyboards like someone emerging from sleep, realising that he has somehow fallen an entire bar behind. Only he notices. Darren's arms gleam as he flails away, oblivious to everything else. The lead singer, Simon, who eyed me suspiciously and grunted when we were introduced, hasn't paid me the slightest bit of attention since. He is alarmingly tall and tanned and well built for a fifteen-year-old, a legacy of his surf-club summers, and he has short blond hair and a pimple-pocked chin. His voice is like Nick Cave's, only without the light and happiness. It's a nasal baritone that often cracks hilariously mid-note. Out of his larynx every song sounds like a dirge, regardless of its tempo or lyrics. With eyes squeezed shut, he yells into the microphone, trying to hear himself over the cacophony. I can make out the odd word or phrase – 'tell Satan to go to hell', 'rock of ages', things like that, but mostly he sounds like an announcer coming over the PA on a railway platform. Totally unintelligible, basically.

This is my first taste of the Band Rehearsal, something that will become all too familiar over the next few years. Let's be clear about this, rehearsals are 9 per cent rehearsing and 91 per cent dicking about. I'm not sure whether any members of bands other than lead singers ever realise this, but it is thrown into sharp relief for us, and the reason for our awareness is quite simple. We possess no instrument with which to dick about, so are forced to wait until all the preliminary musical throat-clearing has subsided before we can do anything. I shudder to think how much of my life has been frittered away waiting for a band to get its collective shit together. Einstein explained how much of our universe works, and one of the last things he discovered, but didn't get time to jot down, was this: a guitarist, in possession of a guitar, will play. No force of physics can prevent them from strumming, plucking and generally mucking around. Ditto drummers. Just try giving a drummer a pair of sticks and then asking them not to use them. They simply don't understand the request. They stare at you like quizzical puppies, heads tilted at a slight angle. 'Why me no play? I have sticks in hands and drums in front.'

It's different for singers. We don't stand there at the microphone practising scales, crooning, 'Doh re mi fa so la te doh' at an enormous wattage. But when a guitarist throws that strap over his shoulder, it's as if he's pulling some sort of invisible shield down over himself, or activating a cloaking device. He seems convinced that he's in his own private, soundproofed world.

You'll have one guitarist cranking out 'Smoke On The Water', while the other is practising a blues scale, squeezing in so many notes per second that the plectrum is on the verge of disintegrating in a little puff of smoke. Add to that the drummer practising para-diddles on the snare and the result is an ear-bleeding blancmange of noise.

The main problem, as far as I can make out, is that bands are mostly run by a democratic process, a cycle of 'Whadda-youreckon?'s and 'I dunno, whadda*you*reckon?'s, when what a band really needs to function smoothly is a totalitarian regime. A dictatorship. A band needs a leader, someone like an orches-tra conductor, someone not afraid to come in, clap their hands officiously and take control of proceedings. A person who's not backwards in coming forwards and saying, 'Right, well *that* was a piece of poodle shite, if ever I heard it. We're going to go from the top. Oh and Stu, if it's not too much trouble, can you make sure *all* your fingers are functioning for those chords, hmm?'

That certainly didn't happen at Horizon's rehearsal. Every one of their six songs broke down at some point. Some had dodgy starts that tripped and faltered, others had wobbly, stag-gered finishes, and a few had middle parts that were a bit shaky on their pegs as well. But when it was all over, they simply nod-ded at each other. 'Yeah, pretty happy with that,' Gavin noted, to a chorus of agreement.

'You sure you're ready for this gig?' I asked Darren as Dad drove us home.

'As we'll ever be, s'pose,' he grunted, staring out the window. A few moments silence.

'Did you like "Behind Blue Eyes"?' I ventured.

Darren turned to me. 'You're an interfering prick. Couldn't

help yourself, just had to muscle in on my show, didn't you? And piss Simon off into the bargain. Bastard.' Suddenly, totally unexpectedly, he grinned. 'But yep, it was pretty good.'

I could have stayed home. I didn't have to be there. I'm sure there was some school assignment I should have been doing. But I couldn't resist the temptation, I wanted to see my brother play live. I was three-quarters unqualified support and one-quarter sadistic anticipation. There was that little part of me that wanted to see the whole thing collapse in a screaming heap, a terrible thing to admit but true nonetheless.

I tagged along and helped Darren set up his kit. The hall was cold and functional. Bare floorboards, high brick walls, rows of narrow windows running just beneath the ceiling. Pimpled plastic chairs, a ghastly shade of orange, were stacked in banks around the edges of the room, each moulded bottom nestling in the lap of the one beneath. At one end the little stage jutted out from the wall. There was no curtain, no backstage area, no dressing room, just that bare stage. It was more a largish shelf than a stage, really. Owing to the chronic shortage of space, Darren was forced to send much of his kit back home with Dad. He kept his snare and bass drums, the high-hat cymbal and a crash cymbal. The bare bones. Muttering and har-rumphing, he erected the kit at the middle rear of the stage. It didn't take long.

The rest of Horizon showed up and the remainder of the stage was soon a clutter of amps, guitar stands, powerboards and tangled leads. There was barely room for any people. It would certainly have to be a restrained performance, I thought. There would be no rock gymnastics this evening. Like Rick

Brewster from the Angels, or Bill Wyman, they would have to just stand in one spot and play.

People started trickling in. Most of them looked to be in their late twenties, early thirties, which of course seemed terribly old at the time. The children were all miniature carbon copies of their progenitors. Clean-cut, scrubbed and smiling. After a little while, a squat, middle-aged man with a comb-over and ruddy jowls approached the stage. He wore a short-sleeved, blue-checked shirt tucked into a pair of sharply pressed black trousers. He beamed at us in an avuncular fashion.

'How are you, boys? All ready for the big show?' His forearms were all knotted muscle and completely devoid of hair. I noticed this because he had a nervous habit of rubbing his hands together constantly as he spoke, as if warming them over an open fire. 'Thanks for playing for us tonight.' *(rub rub rub)* 'We're all really looking forward to it.' *(rub rub rub)*

'Yep, Mr Nancarrow, should be a good night. Hope you enjoy it,' replied Damien.

'Jolly good, then. Well, I'll let you get on.' *(clasp rub rub)* 'Oh, just thought I'd let you know, I do a pretty mean "Love Me Tender".' Chuckling to himself, Mr Nancarrow walked off.

About ten minutes before the band was due to start, as Damien and Gavin stole secretive puffs around the back of the centre, Jeremy realised the band was missing one vital component. A singer. Everyone was so nervous, so wrapped up in their own concerns, it had taken that long for anyone to notice that Simon hadn't shown. They had seen neither hide nor hair of him all day. Theories as to his whereabouts were bandied about. It was generally agreed that, seeing as it was Simon who'd organised for the band to play in public for the first time on this auspicious occasion, it wasn't all that likely that he'd forget to turn up.

The truth behind his mysterious disappearance was incalculably more horrifying. A frantic phone call revealed that Simon had been grounded for the evening as punishment for punching his sister on the arm during an argument. No amount of begging and pleading could sway his mother, who was apologetic but adamant that her son would have to learn his lesson, and that his sound personal development was infinitely more important than 'some band thingy', as she put it.

When Jeremy returned from the phone booth down the street, hands plunged deep in his pockets, he melodramatically kicked a plastic milk crate across the stage, the sound echoing around the half-empty hall. Heads jerked around. Ignoring the startled looks, he relayed the news in angry whispers. There was a brief, astonished pause.

'Well, fuckin' . . . *fuck*,' Damien hissed, which quite eloquently summed up everyone's feeling on the subject.

'Great. Some rock band,' said Darren. 'Well, bugger it, we'll just cancel. Just get on the mic and say, "Sorry, ladies and gentlemen, Horizon can't perform tonight because the lead singer's been sent to his room."'

'What are you going to do?' I asked Jeremy.

'Well, there's always Mr Nancarrow. He seemed pretty keen,' Gavin said.

Jeremy ignored him. 'Just as well you showed up,' he said to me without missing a beat. 'You'll have to do it.'

It took a second for his words to sink in. '*Me?*' I gabbled. 'I can't . . . No way . . .'

'Come on, hero,' Darren said. 'It's your big chance.'

'But I don't know the bloody *songs*, do I? I've only heard them once. I can't possibly do it. One of you will have to sing. You guys must know the words.'

There was a moment's pause as they exchanged glances. 'Well, not as such, actually,' Damien confessed. 'Doing the religious rock was Simon's idea. His older brother's in the Christian surfers, and he plays Petra and all that shit at home all the time. Simon's been brainwashed, he thinks it's great. We reckon it's mostly crap, but we wanna play and he's the only one of us who can sing – well, sorta. So we just go along with it.'

'Let me get this straight. *None* of you know any of the lyrics?'

Shrugs all round.

'Well, why the fuck would you imagine *I'd* know them, if you don't?'

'Look, hang on. I didn't mean we'd play the religious stuff,' Jeremy cut in, and suddenly the others were staring at him with the same bemused expression as me. 'Well, obviously we can't, not without bloody Simon, the dickhead. So,' he gave me a look, 'we'll just have to play something else.'

🎧

Which didn't work. Well, 'didn't work' isn't really strong enough, we were in the realms of dismal failure here. It was a stupid decision. We should have been honest; we should have taken up Darren's suggestion and told the truth. Instead we chose the 'show must go on' path and embarked on a rock folly. When all was said and done, the boys just wanted to play. There being precious few opportunities in town for a band of schoolboys, you didn't walk away from a chance to play, no matter how small the gig or how ill-prepared the material. I confess I was excited about being up there, even at such short notice. I'd wanted in, and here I was. I knew in my heart it wasn't going to be great, but beggars couldn't be choosers.

I don't know if any other band in the history of rock has

scrapped its entire songlist just before going on, but that's what we did. Out went 'Road To Zion' and 'Judas Kiss' and in came 'Satisfaction', 'Behind Blue Eyes' and 'My Generation'. Fine for Jeremy and me, and for Darren who knew the songs from years of being force-fed them at home. Gavin and Damien, on the other hand, had no idea and panicked. Jeremy told them not to worry, they were easy. He'd just call out the chords as we went along.

It has to be said we didn't have much going for us that night. Apart from the fundamental problem of never having played the material, not to mention its inherent inappropriateness – it was akin to the Seekers playing for a particularly bad-tempered chapter of the Hell's Angels – we had no PA. Instead of a blended mix, each amplifier blurted out huge, raw, squelchy dobs of sound which struck the stunned audience like buckets of mud. It was deafening. Jeremy spent most of the time with his back to the hall mouthing chords to Gavin and Damien, who wore expressions of intense concentration mingled with terror. Their trepidation was evident. The bass notes were that fraction of a second late, the keyboards uneasy and wavering. Not that 'Satisfaction' works that well with keyboards anyway. Gavin certainly had his work cut out for him. Darren, meanwhile, struggled to keep the whole mess together by hitting the drums harder and harder, as if to say to the rest of the band, 'THIS-IS-THE-TEM-PO-THIS-SONG-SHOULD-BE-PLAYED-AT.'

And me? I had a brilliant idea. I thought that if I was as over-the-top as possible, I could distract the audience and people might ignore what was happening behind me. So I did the only thing I could. I aped Mick Jagger. Hands on hips, pelvis thrust out, I strutted back and forth across the front of the stage, wagging my finger, wiggling my bum. I pulled out every Jaggeresque pose and move I could recall. Those that space allowed, at any rate. As for the actual singing, I honestly couldn't tell you. We had no foldback speakers, so I couldn't hear myself, and felt I had to scream to get over the top of the hullabaloo of guitars and drums.

Somehow 'Satisfaction' got faster and faster as we went along. As the end approached, Jeremy and Darren started giving everyone that look that musos give each other when they want to end a song – a look which makes you wonder if they're about to sneeze. The eyebrows raise, the mouth and eyes open wide, the chin rises higher and higher as the song builds to a crescendo. Gavin obviously missed all this subtle facial communication, because when the song ended with a judder, he didn't. Half a bar later he sheepishly withdrew his fingers from the keyboard and silence settled over the hall like a sheet.

'Thank you,' I said, even though no-one had applauded. I put that down to the fact that there was hardly anyone left in the room. The adults had evacuated and were clustered outside like office workers taking part in a fire drill. Inside, a handful of children played chasies around the hall, yelling boisterously. Even they ignored us. Stoic in the face of overwhelming indifference, we launched straight into 'My Generation'. Halfway through, though, Mr Nancarrow appeared in front of us, his red face screwed up. He was waving his arms as if directing aircraft, obviously trying to attract our attention. It took a moment to notify Darren, who had his head down, hammering away, but eventually we ground to a halt.

'Fellas! Fellas, that'll do, eh? That's it. I think we've heard enough.' He didn't sound angry. More disappointed. Let down. 'It's not quite what Simon led us to believe it'd be,' he said. 'It's not the sort of music we want to hear.' There was a murmur of agreement from a few people who had wandered back inside.

'If you don't know any nice songs, then I suggest we just call it a night, okay?'

Mr Nancarrow looked at us. We looked at him. Jeremy embarked on an explanation for the sudden change of repertoire, but Mr Nancarrow shook his head and held up his palms. 'That's okay. It doesn't matter. Thanks anyway, boys,' he said, and walked away shaking his head.

If you believe that some events cast long shadows before them, then that should have been it. I should have popped that microphone back in its black vinyl pouch and zipped shut any thoughts I had about being a rock star or even playing in a band. Much of what happened that night at the Christian Youth Centre encapsulated my music career (and I use the term in the loosest possible fashion). The absence of preparation, the general apathy, the lack of decent equipment, the delusions of grandeur – it had all the hallmarks.

That aborted gig struck Horizon a mortal blow. With their enthusiasm dented and tarnished, Gavin and Damien drifted off to concentrate on other, more fruitful pursuits – namely surfing and girls. Darren shrugged his shoulders and went back to pretending to be Peter Criss in his bedroom. I thought this might open the way for Jeremy and me to work on some stuff, but he lapsed into a quintessential lead-guitarist sulk, and that, coupled with my parents putting the screws on me to knuckle down and focus on my schoolwork, brought the shutters clanging down.

Horizon was an unmitigated disaster, but with a life span of precisely one and a half songs, it might well hold the record for the shortest-lived band in the history of popular music. Or unpopular music, as the case may be.

About the same time as the boys from Horizon were playing God's cavalry in Damien Hedler's garage, our town was invaded, and no amount of railing against Satan in song could protect us against the forces of darkness.

It began innocently enough. One morning, a chill wind blew up out of nowhere, sending narrow ripples across the surface of the Manning River. The light dulled momentarily, as though a large cloud were passing across the face of the sun. An aluminium sandwich board out the front of the ice-creamery bearing the legend 'EUREKA CHOCADES $3.20!' toppled over with a tinny clatter. Men emerged from the TAB, clutched at their hats and threw their eyes skywards. The womenfolk gathered their cardigans closer about themselves and shivered. Mothers clucked and called children indoors. As quickly as it came, it was gone. The wind dropped to a zephyr, the sun shone brightly again, and people went about their business, the brief squall forgotten. Nobody suspected that our little town had been infiltrated.

Soon after this freak phenomenon, people started to notice a clapped-out Kombi burbling around the streets. In fact, it was difficult not to notice it. The riotous paintwork made heads turn and tongues wag. It almost forced you to squint. An orange sunset was splattered across its flanks. The sun, a crimson orb, was a fraction away from touching a violet ocean. Orange and yellow rays radiated out from the sun across a lilac sky. It was a professional airbrush job, quite possibly worth more than the vehicle it adorned. In the foreground the words 'The Marrakesh Express' were painted in flowery '60s script.

The owner of the Kombi rented an empty retail space and opened a second-hand record shop. This caused more whispers and chatter. The shop the mysterious stranger chose to rent was tucked away at the rear of an arcade; it was dingy and cramped, and the light inside appeared dim and stale, as if it too had been locked in when the door was closed however many years ago. The space had been vacant for some time because it was accepted wisdom among business people that being hidden like that was tantamount to committing retail suicide. The last occupant had opened a sewing and fabric shop and had gone out backwards soon after. It never seemed to occur to anyone that there might not have been a great demand for sewing and fabric.

At any rate, the owner of the Kombi wasn't perturbed. Then again, nothing appeared to ruffle Raffy Styles. Probably somewhere in his thirties, Raffy was almost as colourful as his mode of transport. Tall and gangly, he moved as if his arms and legs had been fashioned from twisted pipe-cleaners. A beaky nose protruded from his long, thin face. His hair defied gravity and rose off his scalp in matted clumps. Raffy's clothes were relics from a bygone era. Tie-dyed T-shirts and velvet trousers, worn in places like old carpet. To my knowledge he was never seen without a pinstripe vest, festooned with badges. Some had photos of rock stars on them, others slogans. Some boasted pictures of marijuana leaves and the words 'Legalise It', and 'A Friend With Weed is a Friend Indeed'.

Raffy named his shop after his van, although The Marrakesh Express was more an indoor market stall than a normal shop. The air was redolent with sickly sweet incense. Trestle tables swathed in rich Eastern fabrics groaned under the weight of tattered cardboard boxes – dozens of them – all filled with a treasure trove of hard-to-find (and some hard-to-believe-you'd-*want*-to-find) albums. The boxes were packed so tightly it was sometimes impossible to flick through their contents. There was no system, no alphabetical order, yet Raffy was nearly always able to lay his hands on whatever album you were look-ing for. The walls of the shop were decorated with creased posters featuring everything from obscure, early '70s bands sporting long straight hair and beards to fantastical New Age depictions of unicorns galloping across the infinite blackness of space with no visible means of purchase beneath their hooves.

Speaking of no visible means of purchase, it was never clear to us how Raffy stumped up for the rent each month. School-yard discussions concluded that he must have been living off some inheritance, making the earning of money redundant. It was clear Raffy would never make president of the Chamber of Commerce. He didn't seem to grasp the basics of sound busi-ness practice; i.e., the exchange of goods for legal tender. After a little time, The Marrakesh Express became more a library than an ongoing financial concern. If Raffy liked you, if he thought you were 'right into' music and worth educating to some extent, he would stock you up with albums and send you on your way. 'Just a loan, right?' he'd say, with the faintest trace of an English accent lending him an even more exotic air. 'Just for a cuppla days. 'Ave 'em back Thursdee.' Even as you were walking out the door, he'd be wedging 'anuvva l'il gem you should get into' under your arm.

I don't know how many of those loaned records made it back into their boxes, but if they didn't, it didn't affect Raffy's policy. Maybe it was actually quite a shrewd marketing plan.

Like jewellers who let women take home expensive trinkets for a trial period, safe in the knowledge that they won't be able to live without them after a few days, Raffy might have been working on the assumption that once you'd heard Fleetwood Mac (the early version with Peter Green, not the phenomenally commercially successful '70s lineup), you'd be left with no option other than to fork out, or else suffer chronic withdrawal symptoms.

I did shell out for a few albums. At two dollars a throw, they were a much cheaper option than ordering cassettes. Besides, I doubt whether I'd have been able to order some of the titles in Raffy's eclectic collection. He sent me home with an unbelievable pile of blues records slipping from under my arm. Howlin' Wolf, Muddy Waters, Albert King, John Lee Hooker. He even unearthed a couple of Stones-related rarities and bootlegs – the mystifying, poorly recorded, hardcore-fan-only muckabout, *Jamming with Edward*, and Bill Wyman's *Stone Alone* solo effort, to name two. I relieved him of the Faces' *A Nod is as Good as a Wink . . . to a Blind Horse*, and Roger Daltrey's solo album, *Ride a Rock Horse* (what was it with nags and album titles?), the cover of which showed the blond-maned Daltrey as a bare-chested, fist-pumping centaur, his airbrushed body morphing into that of a pure white steed. Raffy also palmed off a Hush album, *Get Rocked*, which included an unforgettably silly track entitled 'Nunchucka Man'.

On learning that I was becoming quite a connoisseur of AC/DC, Raffy beckoned me over to a box in the corner. Gingerly I joined him. Being at close quarters with Raffy was an experience in itself. The olfactory system quickly became overloaded with sensory data. Some exotic fragrance I couldn't place mingled with incense, unwashed hair, cigarettes, mothballs, stale sweat, and a top note of instant coffee and aged dental detritus issuing from his mouth. Raffy rifled through the box for a minute, exclaimed, 'Aha! Goddit,' and plucked out a dog-eared album by some band called Geordie.

'You know AC/DC's new singer, Brian Johnson?' he asked. Well, of *course* I did. Stupid question. I nodded.

'This was his first band. They were glam rock. Y'know, like Marc Bolan and T. Rex. Bit of a difference, yeah?'

There certainly was. At first I refused to believe the evidence of my own eyes, being used to seeing Johnson in his current guise as macho, black-jeaned, tweed-capped screamer. As far as I knew, he didn't have a past. He just sort of popped up out of nowhere to join one of the world's biggest rock bands. The photo on the Geordie album cover showed a Johnson from a different time. A different planet. A Johnson with long frizzy hair, makeup and black nailpolish. A Johnson wearing a sleeveless bodystocking adorned with black and white vertical stripes (the design of Johnson's beloved Newcastle United soccer team, Raffy informed me). I was dumbfounded. How could this *Rocky Horror* reject have been in the running to replace the immortal Bon Scott? The explanation, as told to me by Raffy, remains my all-time favourite rags-to-riches rock story. Are you sitting comfortably?

Once upon a time, during glam rock's heyday in the early '70s, Geordie was a moderately successful band in Newcastle-upon-Tyne, northern England. But when glam faded, Geordie was among the early casualties. Johnson hung up his bodystocking and, resigned to the fact that his brief tilt at pop stardom was over, went into the distinctly unglam business of vinyl roofing for cars. Thus life, and the production line, chugged along until Bon Scott's death in 1980, when a rabid AC/DC fan sent the band's management a tape of Johnson giving it a good lunging out the front of Geordie. Accompanying the tape was a letter in which the fan detailed why he thought Brian Johnson would be the perfect replacement for Scott. The next thing you know, an astonished Brian's on a train bound for London and a fateful meeting with the brothers Young. The rest, as they say in the classics, is history. Twenty-odd years down the track, Johnson is still playing the foil for Angus's ageing school delinquent, still bellowing at thousands of manic fans, and still salting down millions of dollars in royalties. How rich is he? He owns his own Formula One car and takes it for spins around his own private track. And you know what? He's never found out who sent in that tape of Geordie.

This is the story as related to me by Raffy Styles. I know I could probably access the Internet and find out if it's true but, to be honest, if it isn't I don't want to know. It's precisely the type of story that breathes life into every deflated rock dream. What I'm more interested in is what it was *like*, going on stage with AC/DC that first time. What was it like toughing it out in Tyneside one minute, convinced that your glory days, such as they were, had come and gone, and the next standing in the wings listening to the surge of the crowd, about to play the biggest gig of your life, about to sing your predecessor's songs and steeling yourself for the inevitable comparisons? How on earth did he stop himself from screaming, vomiting and fainting in quick succession?

Of course, after Raffy told me that tale I had to have the Geordie album. I had to know what Johnson's pre-Accadacca days were like. And the verdict? Well, let's just say he was one lucky, lucky bastard.

Amid the unremitting conformity of life in a stolid National

Party town, Raffy Styles seemed like a mangy wizard, a down-at-heel warlock who had all us kids spellbound. Music was always belting out of The Marrakesh Express, and the sound of it was like a cartoon smell, a smoky waft of scent that tapped us on the shoulder and turned into a beckoning finger. We were drawn, as if by invisible threads, to the centre of Raffy's web in the rear of that arcade. Before school, after school, lunchtimes, weekends, The Marrakesh Express was a favourite hangout. It was somewhere to go. Its burgeoning popularity caused ripples among the parental population, and those ripples radiated and gathered momentum, becoming swells of something akin to mass hysteria. What sort of baleful influence was this stranger exerting on their impressionable offspring? What else, apart from rock'n'roll, was he pedalling?

A pigeonhole was hastily constructed for Raffy, with the words 'Marijuana-inhaling, patchouli-soaked hippie' stamped on it. Neighbouring shop-owners, who equated incense with drugs, reported 'suspicious smells' emanating from Raffy's 'den of iniquity'. Others complained about the music 'blaring all day'. Still others reported seeing students frequenting Raffy's shop during school hours. Why didn't Raffy report this to the appropriate authorities? Why didn't he act like a responsible adult and send the truants back to school? What sort of misanthrope encouraged such behaviour? There were letters to the editor, with phrases like 'While I consider myself to be open-minded' and 'Now, I am not a prudish person, but . . .', penned by the demonstrably closed-minded and prudish. 'Riff-Raffy', some stubbies'n'thong-wearing pisshead in Fogg's pub called him, and it caught on. Rumours circulated. Raffy was a drug lord who'd moved in and taken over cultivation and distribution on the mid-north coast. He was a child molester; a depraved, perverted monster who lured schoolgirls into his lair and had sex with them in the tiny kitchenette at the rear of the shop. He hoisted his prey onto the little stainless-steel sink top, the cold metal leaving corrugations in the sullied flesh of young bottoms, and had them right there next to the electric jug and the clutter of dirty cups.

Any number of deep-seated fears and unfounded concerns were projected onto Raffy, who reacted to it all with a kind of weary resignation. The welcome our town gave him was neither new nor unexpected. To his credit, Raffy never responded to the vitriol, but let it wash over him like soap and water rarely did. He remained holed up in his trippy bunker, talking music with those kids who were still allowed to frequent The Marrakesh Express. I was not among their number, although I would still mount the odd covert operation and sneak in to say hello. I was embarrassed. I never knew quite what to say to Raffy, how to explain why I no longer came in every lunchtime. I'm sure he knew exactly why, but he never spoke about it. He'd just greet me normally and embark on some fresh musical story, or pull out a few new acquisitions that he thought vital to my education. But I no longer bought any records or accepted his offers of a loan, because there was no way I could be sure I'd be able to smuggle them home successfully.

Just for the record, so to speak, I don't doubt, and nor do I care, that Raffy enjoyed the odd spliff – his lapelwear certainly suggested as much – but I never saw him smoke and he certainly never tried to give me any. The only thing he pushed onto me was music, and I am eternally grateful to him for making the effort. He did show me an eye-popping German porn mag once, but I had picked up and riffled through similar publications in the local newsagent's a hundred times. As for the stuff about the girls, I can't say for sure. I wasn't privy to that particular part of Raffy's life, so what went on behind that bead curtain at the back of the shop, or in the interior of his kaleidoscopic Kombi, I know not. I do know that quite a few of the girls in my year found him attractive, his peculiar fug notwithstanding. He was different. And for a nubile seventeen-year-old, that was enough. He wore funky clothes and radiated rebellion. He had travelled and could tell tales of exotic places a world away from Taree. He knew nothing of football, or sport in general, and cared less. Why wouldn't they concentrate their budding feminine wiles on such a unique beast?

One day, little more than six months after Raffy's Kombi first rattled into town, I snuck down the arcade to say hello and The Marrakesh Express was gone. I couldn't believe it. We'd been away for a week on a family holiday – a mere seven days – and now I was confronted with a locked door and a large 'For Lease' sign once again propped in the window. Behind it, I could see the trestle tables still in position, but now they were naked, stripped of their boxes and their dusky pink, blue and gold dressings. Where the posters had been were now just the dirty grey marks of Blu-Tack. The bead curtain still dangled in the kitchenette doorway. I asked around, but no-one had seen Raffy before he left. No-one had spoken to him. No-one knew what prompted him to up sticks so quickly, although we could all make fairly shrewd guesses. For a few days afterwards, I kept my eyes peeled on the streets, but there was no flash of outlandish colour amid the usual parade of Holdens, Fords and Datsuns.

There wasn't a celebration, exactly. People didn't gather cheering in the streets or toss their hats in the air. There was no civic parade or anything like that, but with Raffy gone, the town perceptibly heaved a sigh of smug relief.

'Good riddance to bad luck,' a woman who had never met Raffy but who was well up to date on all the gossip said, her lips set in a straight, triumphant line, and I fumed.

If there was more to the Raffy Styles story, some solid proof of sordid deeds, something more substantial than innuendo and salacious speculation, I never heard or saw it. As far as I could see, his only crime was to look and act a little differently. Raffy Styles wasn't the devil's emissary, he was just a square peg in a town full of round holes. And arseholes.

To borrow from the late, great Muddy Waters, my mother went to the gypsy woman afore I were born. The gypsy woman gazed into her crystal ball and said, 'You got a boy-chile a-comin', he's gonna be a son of a gun.' Then she frowned and added, 'He's also gonna get his hair a-coloured and a-permed and wear a white tux to his high-school formal. And by the way, the boy-chile you got a-comin' after him is gonna take up breakdancin'.'

I don't know if you remember breakdancing. It started in New York in the late '70s, early '80s, and was, from all accounts, inspired by watching people suffer epileptic seizures. The term refers to the inherent physical dangers posed by suddenly throwing yourself on the floor and flopping around spasmodically. As was the case with most overseas fads, there was a slight delay in breakdancing making it to Australian shores. When it did arrive, Darren was waiting on the dock to greet it, and he suddenly started getting around in fleecy-lined tracksuits and dark sunglasses. Overnight he shelved the drumsticks and the KISS records and emerged wearing a cap backwards and an enormous gold chain, the provenance of which I can't be certain. He started listening to Rock Steady Crew. He and his friends – or his 'crew', as he called them – would go 'breakin''.

Breakin' involved getting together in public places with a portable cassette player, standing in a circle, and taking turns trying to spin on their backs like tracksuited turtles, or perform rotating headstands with their legs splayed like chopper blades. The others, meanwhile, sort of bobbed up and down on rubbery knees, making hand signals and gesturing at the solo performer, as much as to say, 'He's gonna break his neck if he doesn't watch it.' Most attempts were clumsy at best and downright suicidal at worst. The solo spots consisted mostly of backspins lasting less than one complete revolution, and a lot of saying, 'Hang on a sec, I'll just try that again.' Occasionally someone would pull off a successful move, and the others would suddenly become normal Australian kids again, dropping the hip-hop facade and jargon, and applauding. 'Good one, Rilesy!' Most stuck to the relative safety and ease of the 'popping' robotic moves, adopting a new pose with each beat, raising their hands and turning their heads to the side, that sort of thing.

Brotherly breakdancing bugged the bejesus out of me. I don't know exactly why. Maybe there was something pathetic about middle-class white kids in Australian suburbia carrying on as if they lived in south central LA or Harlem. It might have been the simple fact that Darren and his mates looked so utterly ridiculous trying to do it. I made him aware of my annoyance, which, needless to say, only ensured that he did it at every available moment. From his bedroom came the constant thumps of his body collapsing from a headstand position, the occasional clatter of his flailing legs striking drums and cymbals, and accompanying grunts and swearing. To really piss me off, he would burst into my room while I was studying/reading/sleeping/air-guitaring and start popping. He'd do that arm-waving move that looks like a ripple passing across your body. Something about the look he'd give me as he did it brought down the red mist.

'I'll pop your shoulder out of its fuckin' socket if you do that again,' I threatened.

For our father, who regularly complained about American culture being all-pervasive and who despaired of Aussie kids slavishly trying to do 'whatever the bloody Seppos do', this was almost the dizzy limit. 'That cap must've cut off the blood supply to your brain,' he said to my brother. 'If an American jumped off a bloody cliff, I suppose you'd throw yourself off as well?'

Darren, whose favourite TV shows were *BJ and the Bear*, *The Dukes of Hazzard* and *The A-Team*, considered his reply. 'Prob'ly,' he said.

'The Yanks have managed what the whole Roman Empire couldn't.' Dad embarked on a general lecture. ' A bloodless coup. They've taken over the whole bloody world without a shot being fired, all because you kids won't think for yourselves.'

'The Romans couldn't fire shots. They didn't have guns back then.'

Pause.

'If you're not out of my sight in three seconds flat, I'm gonna string you up by that bloody necklace.'

I say that it was almost the dizzy limit for Dad because I think the absolute dizzy limit was attained when I permed and blonded my mullet. This new hairstyle had come about only a few weeks after I'd worn a gleaming white tux to my high-school formal, and I think Dad was still reeling from that. I deliberately chose white because all the other boys chose black. Black with black tie and cummerbund. Black with red tie and cummerbund. Someone trying to be outlandish went with a blue tie and cummerbund. I walked into the formal-hire shop, flicked through the catalogue and pointed to an all-white number, complete with an ice-pink tie and cummerbund and white slip-on shoes.

'Are you sure that's really what you're after?' The man with the tape measure draped round his neck looked at me over the frames of his glasses.

'Why, has someone else already ordered it?'

'Ah, no, no, they haven't.' He studied me for a moment. 'Most of the boys are going with, er, traditional black.'

'Right. Well, I'll have the white then, ta very much.'

There's a photo, taken just before we set off that night. My mother, looking vivacious in red, stands smiling prettily, her arms interlocked with her two sons. On her right, I am trying to look serious and cool. Everything about me suggests that I'm acutely aware of the import of this moment, that this photo is recording one of the milestones in my life, a rite of passage. My final night as a school student. Shame, then, that I look like the result of a passionate tryst between Barry Manilow and Richard Clayderman. On the other side of my mother, Darren glowers at the camera like a moody rottweiler. He's still wearing his grimy school clothes and looks as if he's fresh from some scuffle. His expression suggests he wouldn't mind popping across the frame and giving me a right nutting for looking so poofy.

My date Robyn, resplendent in maroon waterwave taffeta that shimmered like spilt engine oil, swallowed her shock and put on a brave face. Her father didn't do such a good job of hiding his astonishment. 'Shit! It's an albino penguin,' he said, then caught his daughter's horrified look. 'Er, sorry. Well, you guys will certainly, er, stand out from the crowd tonight, won't you?'

Later, at the formal, which was held in the RSL auditorium, Robyn and I sang a duet we'd prepared especially for the occasion. A song for our fellow classmates. It was an abridged version of Bob Seger's 'We've Got Tonight', the significance of which eludes me. With a friend backing us on piano, we barely managed to warble our way through a couple of verses before the poignancy of the whole evening hit Robyn and she broke down in tears. Everyone exclaimed, 'Aaahhh,' and clapped. Some of the other girls were also crying and hugging each other as they realised a chapter of their lives was coming to a close. I stood there like a sadly attired Vegas crooner, mic in hand, looking out at the crowd, hugging Robyn and thinking, Bugger! We still had two verses to go.

At no stage was the perm planned. No sir, the perm was Lea's fault. Lea was a hairdresser who worked at the salon my mother went to. Lea, not to put too fine a point on it, was a spunk. I was infatuated with her. Her slim legs and pert backside were poured into black leggings. Her not insubstantial top half was clad in a blousy pastel-blue shirt cinched at the waist with a white plastic belt of ludicrous width. She had a mane of permed brunette hair and wore boiled-lolly earrings. She had dimples. God, I loved her. I never spoke to her, of course. That was out of the question. I'd just wander past the salon, try to ever-so-casually catch her eye, smile and wave. Sometimes it would take a few passes, because she might be out the back or fussing over a customer at the basin. But if she did see me, Lea always beamed back and waved her scissors.

I booked in for a cut, bravely asked that Lea administer it, and, once she got me in that chair, didn't ever want to leave. She sat me in front of the mirror and smiled at my reflection as she ran her fingers absently through my hair, discussing our plan of attack. She led me to the basin and washed my greasy locks. She massaged my scalp and it was the most excruciatingly sensual three minutes of my life. Thank heavens I had a black cape draped over me. Tenderly she wiped drool off my chin and led me back to the chair. We chatted. I can't remember any specific topic, but at some stage Lea must have uttered something along the lines of, 'You've got such lovely long hair. Be a shame to cut it all off. Why don't we perm it and maybe put some blond highlights in instead?' and I must have consented, because the next thing I knew she was rolling a perforated bathing cap over my head, prising strands through the little holes, and painting on an acrid, chemical-smelling mixture with what looked like a basting brush.

Over the next couple of hours I was her doll, a plaything. Looking at my reflection huddled beneath the dome of the dryer, tendrils of doubt, fear and regret unfurled at the corners of my mind, but they shrank like a snail's eyestalk each time I caught a glance of Lea's moulded buttocks in the mirror. The up side was that enduring all this palaver meant I got to spend some quality time with the object of my desire. Lea was so sunny and bright. I loved everything about her, the way she took appointments over the phone, the way she spoke to other customers. She had a spark. The considerable down side, however, was that I left the security of the salon looking like Robert Plant. Well, not so much Robert Plant, actually, because looking like Robert Plant would have been quite a good result. I looked more like 'Locomotion'-era Kylie Minogue.

I suspect that the salon door had barely swung shut behind me before everyone exploded in guffaws. Lea included, probably. Dear oh dear. I hadn't even asked her out. Now I'd never be able to muster the courage. Not even to walk past the salon. I just wouldn't be able to bear it. Too many painful memories.

My parents were beside themselves. There they stood, the four of them, doubled over with laughter, slapping their thighs, pointing at their fashion-challenged son, buckling at the knees, holding each other upright as the ferocity of their mirth threatened to topple them. They found the whole thing so funny, they forgot to be angry. I went to my room, and still I could hear them. At different times their laughter would subside into sighs, then suddenly splutter anew.

Later, I looked at myself in the bathroom mirror and it occurred to me that never again would it be necessary to employ Leila's old wig. I now had my very own blond headbanging locks. If nothing else, my hair was ready to rock and roll.

And the rest of me followed soon after. In something of a tumultuous few weeks, all my friends left town, bound for the
beer-sodden excitement of life in Sydney and university. There
was a seemingly never-ending round of goodbye shenanigans,
and before the cumulative hangover had even worn off, my
peers had all disappeared.

University held no appeal for me. Having been institution-
alised for the past twelve years, I was keen to try something
new. I entered the Taree job market and found employment not
once, but twice. In one guise I was the new cadet journalist on
the local newspaper. In another I was the lead singer of
GEN-R8, the band I'd seen at the RSL a few years before. This
was DC Comics stuff. Mild-mannered cub reporter by day, and
rock'n'roll demigod in the wee hours. I could hardly believe
how fast things were moving.

No need to tell you which position I was more excited about.
I considered the newspaper job to be the backstop, an entertaining little diversion that would keep the coffers topped up
while I concentrated on my music career. You could hardly
blame me, not when I spent my days typing tide reports. (It
probably shouldn't have taken me that long, but I was learning
to type at the same time, so everything I did took an age.) I'd had
to sit through a couple of rigorous interviews to get the cadet
position. In one of them I had to answer ten multiple-choice

questions designed to test applicants' local knowledge. I scored three. I can only assume I was the only one going for the job.

Getting the GEN-R8 gig was much easier. Then again, it has to be said there wasn't a whole lot of competition for the position of lead singer in a rock band. In our small town word had apparently filtered through to GEN-R8 that there was this young guy, fresh out of school, who could hold a note and who might be a suitable replacement for their singer – he of the bulging biceps, who'd recently pulled the plug and gone off to start his own 'project', with the aim of getting 'serious' about his music and doing more original compositions. He apparently told people that he felt stifled within the confines of GEN-R8 and was becoming frustrated creatively. He needed to branch out and explore other musical avenues. The other members weren't as keen on his original compositions as he obviously was, and were quite happy to continue down the commercially safe covers-band route. Thus came the parting of the ways.

This split made considerable waves in certain circles. GEN-R8 had been around for some time and had become a fixture on the north-coast pub and club circuit. They did have something you might loosely refer to as a following. Well, among people who were keen to hear Angels and Hoodoo Gurus songs performed by people other than the Angels and the Hoodoo Gurus, that is. Rest assured, there were plenty of rival bands keen to pick over the carcass, and divvy up the available Friday and Saturday night spots should GEN-R8 fall apart. The key to their survival was to get back on the road as soon as possible, before unsure publicans started looking elsewhere to fill their entertainment bookings sheets.

Enter me. On the day in question I was at the paper, wrestling with my first real story. Ironically it was a music-related piece, documenting the expected good turnout for a country hoedown to be held on Noel 'Poly' Everett's property the following weekend. Poly was my first interviewee. His wife came to the front desk and asked to speak to the journalist assigned to the story. She seemed somewhat taken aback by my hair, but recovered her wits and told me Noel was in the car. His legs were playing up a bit, and Mrs Everett asked if it was all right if we conducted the interview in their old ute. Which I dutifully did, clambering onto the red bench seat behind the steering wheel. 'So, Mr Everett –'

'Call me Poly, mate. Everyone calls me Poly.'

'Oh, right.' I wasn't used to this level of informality with an adult. 'So, er, Poly, expecting a good turnout on the weekend?'

'Yep. Always a good show, the hoedown.'

'Right, right. And, ah, you've been hoedowning for some years now?'

''Bout eight, I reckon.'

'That long, eh? Right, right. Excellent.'

We continued in this vein for some time. When I came to write the story later, I realised I had managed to avoid most of the basic questions. Little things like how, when, where, why. You know, the basic stuff all journalists are supposed to ask. 'Well, what *did* you bloody well find out?' the editor snapped at me. 'I can see the headline now: "PEOPLE DANCE SOMEWHERE". Sen-bloody-sational.'

Chastened, I phoned Poly and conducted a second, more in-depth interview. Later that day, I was single-fingeredly typing up Poly's story on an old typewriter when a call came through.

'That Andrew Griffin?'

'No. It's Anthony Griffis, actually.'

'Oh, sorry, mate. My name's Ian. I'm in the band GEN-R8. You know us, yeah?'

It was more a statement than a question.

'Look, mate,' Ian went on, 'I don't know if you're interested – and I'm not sayin' *we* are for sure – but you sing a bit, yeah?'

I was surprised. 'Out of the blue' is the phrase that springs to mind. 'Er, well, y'know I've done a bit. Mostly musicals, y'know, stuff like that.'

'You're into rock but, arncha?'

'Yeah, course.'

'Well, I don't know if you've heard, but our singer's just left. We need a new frontman and we need one quick. You interested in comin' on board?'

I could hardly believe my ears. Poor old Poly Everett's country knees-up was receding into the distance, shrinking to something insignificant in a far corner of my mind. Somehow I kept my cool.

'Might be,' I said.

'Okay. Let's get together this weekend. I'll get the boys round and we'll trial you on a cuppla songs, right?'

I found GEN-R8 and their entourage holed up in a rundown weatherboard house just beyond the railway line. Even as I pulled up in my newly acquired, third-hand, daffodil-yellow Datsun, I could hear the muffled thunk of a bass guitar and my stomach started cartwheeling.

Through the torn screen door I could make out a dim hallway with rooms branching off it. A full-blooded version of the *Peter Gunn* theme was pulsing out from behind the third door on the right. I knocked a couple of times to no avail, then called out. The music continued unabated, but a moment later a silhouette appeared at the far end of the hallway. When the silhouette opened the creaking door, it revealed itself to be an attractive woman in her early twenties. She had long, straight blonde hair and wore a white T-shirt and black jeans. Slouching against the door to keep it from slapping shut, she looked at me for a second, plucked the cigarette from her lips and exhaled.

'Hi. You Anthony?'

I responded in the affirmative.

'Gail,' she said simply. 'Come in, come in.' She turned and walked back down the hall.

The house smelled old and damp. The carpet was a dirty olive-green and threadbare. Horrific floral wallpaper peeled in limp despair. I caught a glimpse of a lumpy sofa direct from the early '70s, all burnt-orange upholstery and brown vinyl armrests. The rest of the sparse furnishings looked to have been knocked back by St Vincent de Paul's as well. Music and motoring magazines littered the floor. At the other end of the house I glimpsed a kitchen, where some people were clustered around a laminex table, drinking from steaming mugs. As I passed an open door I looked in and saw a largish woman, about the same age as Gail, strapped to one of those weight-loss machines with a vibrating belt that had been popular a decade or so before. The machine whirred, the belt thrummed like a plucked guitar string, and the woman jiggled. She stood there with her arms slightly raised, like someone perched on the end of a high-diving board, clutching a cigarette that trembled ash on the carpet.

'Oi!' Gail yelled to attract the woman's attention. 'Rhoda! This is Anthony. He might be the new singer.'

The woman glanced over her shoulder, saw us watching from the doorway, and laughed an embarrassed, vibrato-rich laugh. 'Oh, hi th-ere. I'm Rh-oh-da.' Then, 'Do-on-n't thi-i-nk this thi-i-ng will get an-n-y we-i-ight off, Gail. Mi-i-ght be a go-oo-od se-e-e-x to-oy-oy, b-u-ut. Bi-i-gg-est blo-oo-ody vi-i-bra-a-tor you've e-e-ver se-ee-en.' Laughing delightedly, she popped the cigarette between her lips.

GEN-R8 were crammed into a bedroom stockpiled with music gear. Amps, guitar cases, big black speakers, foldback wedges. Over in the far corner, almost obscured by a pile of sturdy silver cases, the drummer perched on his stool, his tanned, handsome face and mop of jet-black hair floating among a forest of cymbals. Standing knee-deep amid the chaos were two guitarists. When Gail opened the door it struck the bass player, who was standing directly behind it. At the same time we were struck by a blast of loud, humid air which reeked of perspiration.

'Ow! Wha' the . . . ?' The bassist grabbed the back of his head.

Gail made a big show of sympathy. 'Oh, diddums. Shall I kiss it better?' She puckered up and made as if to cradle his head, but he laughingly batted her hands away. 'Get off!'

Ian Every, Terry Dury and Dale Maddox made up the remaining three-quarters of GEN-R8. Ian – tall and rangy with acne-scarred cheeks, silver ear jewellery, a green T-shirt and grey marble-wash jeans – played rhythm guitar. Dale – shorter, stockier, with long black hair, black shirt, black jeans and black boots – played bass. Terry – lean, fit, muscular, with a sweat-darkened singlet and football shorts – walloped the skins. 'My mum reckons you can sing,' he said with a wide grin, shaking my hand in his slick paw.

I was taken aback. 'Your mum?'

'Claire Dury. Singing teacher. Saw you in one of those school musicals a while back. Says you were good.'

So *that's* how they'd heard about me. Despite my nervousness, I laughed. Of all the richly imagined rock scenarios I had dreamed up over the years, none ever revolved around someone's mezzo-soprano mother giving me the thumbs-up. Ian cut through the small talk, handing me a crumpled sheet of paper bearing a list of song titles. 'Know any of these?' he asked.

I studied the list. The usual suspects. Angels and Oils, with the odd classic like 'Wild Thing', 'Twist And Shout', 'You Really Got Me' and Dragon's 'April Sun In Cuba' sprinkled throughout. 'Most of 'em, I reckon. Some better than others,' I said.

'Well, pick a couple you do know.'

I chose the Angels' 'No Secrets', and 'You Really Got Me'.

'Bastard,' Ian said, laughing.

'What? What's wrong?' I asked, suddenly nervous again.

Dale explained. 'He's still trying to learn the lead break for "No Secrets". The last singer used to play lead, see. Now it's down to Ian to learn the breaks, for *all* the songs. It's a bitch, isn't it, mate?' he asked with an evil cackle, aiming a light punch at Ian's shoulder. Ian fended him off and tossed me a microphone. 'Okay, there you go, champ. Let's get on with it.'

'Why don't you bring in a lead guitarist?' I asked.

They all looked at me as if I'd suggested they incorporate a Rick Astley medley into their repertoire. 'Moolah, my friend,' Ian replied, rubbing his fingers together. 'Spondoolah, cash, rubles, payola. We get another guitar, we gotta split the readies five ways. Cheaper if I learn the lead breaks. Trust me, if any of us could sing, you wouldn't be here either. Right, "No Secrets", let's go.'

Terry clicked his sticks together four times to count us in, lifted one buttock, broke wind in a trumpeting fashion, and fell off his stool with laughter. Some time later, after we'd all regained our composure, he repeated the count-in and a taut, crisp version of 'No Secrets' immediately swamped the room. The sound spilled out of the door, down the hall and into the street, a decibel deluge. Once outside, it was swept away by the roar of passing freight trains.

Strangely, I don't remember a lot about the audition in terms of performance. I do remember thinking how smooth it felt, how tight they were. They really knew the material. Inside out and back to front. They could have played it in their sleep. Consequently, as a group, they gave off a slightly blasé vibe. I think I was probably still preoccupied by thoughts of money. Could it be possible that someone would actually pay me to sing rock'n'roll? It hadn't really occurred to me before. Well, I mean it had occurred to me, but I guess it just wasn't all that important. That's how much I wanted to perform. I wanted to sing for the sake of it, because I enjoyed it, so I could say that all the years of bedroom japery were worth it. Even after Ian had phoned me at work, money never entered my head. What a bonus, being in a band *and* being paid for it.

Ian didn't even attempt the lead break in 'No Secrets'. 'That's not important right now,' he said, we're here to listen to you.' I think they were impressed because I remembered the whispered bit at the end, the part where Doc Neeson asks what the time is. It was a little frill, an added extra, to show them I knew what I was on about. As 'You Really Got Me' ended in a stupendously loud crescendo of hissing cymbals and machine-gun guitar, I let loose a throaty howl, and a 'Yes!' on the final crunching chord. It's the little touches, you know, that make all the difference.

'All right!' Dale grinned, and I immediately relaxed.

'You'll do.' Ian threw me a little brown case, the kind I had when I was in primary school. I flipped the catches and inside were dozens of pages of scrawled lyrics. 'Get your head round those,' he said. 'We got gigs to do.'

'Good one.' Terry stood up from behind his kit. 'And fellas, have you noticed? He's got the hair to boot.'

A few days after I was anointed GEN-R8's new lead singer, Ian decided the name had to go. I didn't see why. They had been GEN-R8 for years. Everyone knew them as that; it was their *brand*, to borrow from consultant-speak. And besides, I wanted to be able to tell people I was in GEN-R8, not some band they'd never heard of. But being the new boy, I figured I should keep a low profile.

'Never liked the fuckin' name in the first place.' Ian squeezed the top off a stubby and sank back on the '70s sofa. Fresh from the bakery where he worked part-time, he was dressed all in white and lightly dusted in flour. 'It was the last singer's idea. He just wanted to have a name that sounded like INXS and U2. I reckon it's time for a change.'

Terry straddled an armrest, hands idly drumming a tattoo on the tired upholstery between his legs. Dale, clad in his customary black, flicked through a car mag and gave no sign of having heard a word that had been said.

Ian took another swig. 'Well, what – are you all mute or something? Whaddya reckon?'

'I dunno, mate. Everyone knows us as GEN-R8,' Terry ventured. *Yes!*

'But we're not the same band any more. Not now we've got old leather lungs over there on board.' He nodded at me. 'It's as good a time as any for a fresh start. Whaddya think about the Stalkers?'

'That sucks.' Dale didn't even raise his eyes from the magazine. 'Makes us sound like flashers or something.'

Ian wasn't perturbed. 'Okay then. What about . . . what about – stop that fucking drumming, willya, Dury? What about shortening it to the Stalks?'

'The Storks?' Terry misunderstood.

'Not Storks. *Stalks*. S-t-a-l-k-s. I like it. Sounds sorta phallic.'

'What about the Knobs? That's phallic,' said Dale.

And so the discussion went. Names were thrown up, names were shot down in flames, names were proferred just for laughs. Ridiculous names that surprised everyone by becoming possibilities. Said often enough though, any name loses its meaning. Even the most famous band names sound a little lame when detached from success. The Beatles? The Rolling Stones? Led Zeppelin? That day in the mouldering lounge room, we meandered along streams of consciousness which more often than not became trickles then dried up completely.

Nonoxynol-9 was one of Dale's favourites. 'It's the name of the spermicide they put in the tip of condoms. Sounds sorta cool.'

'Maddox, you're as mad as a meataxe,' said Ian.

Terry was scathing. 'No-one'll know what that means, you boofhead.' Then he reconsidered. ''Cept maybe some pharmacists. They'd probably know. But I don't think we get many pharmacists coming to our gigs.' He trailed off when he realised we were all staring at him.

'Well, *I* knew what it was.' Dale sounded a mite sulky. 'It's right there on the box.'

On we went. Nonoxynol-9 was out, but it inevitably led us on to the Condoms, the Rubbers, the Frenchies, the Erections, the Stiffys, and Protection.

'*The* Protection?' I asked. 'Or just Protection?'

Ian thought for a moment. 'Just Protection, on its own,' he said. 'It's stronger.'

'Nah. How about the Foreskins. We could wear turtle-neck pullovers onstage.' Terry was warming up. 'Hey, and we'd stretch the necks up so that only our eyes and the tops of our heads poked out. It'd be a good hook, guys. Get everyone talking.'

'Yeah, and what everyone would be saying is, What a bunch of fuckwits.' Ian sighed. 'Can we take this seriously, just for a minute?'

'How would I sing with the bottom half of my head stuck in the neck of a pullover?' I'd spotted the crimp in Terry's plan.

Before Terry could answer, Ian jumped in. 'Forget it. We are *not* calling the band the Foreskins. End of story.'

'Should we perhaps consider the possibility of a non-dick-related name?' Dale asked.

Thoughtful silence.

'Slugtank,' Ian said suddenly.

'*Slug*tank!' Terry exploded. 'Now who's not being serious?'

'It's a good name. Sounds tough.'

'What is a slugtank, anyway? Is there any such thing?' asked a bemused Dale.

'A tank you put slugs in, I would imagine,' I offered, not all that helpfully.

'Yeah, but do you mean the animal slugs? Or slugs from a slug gun? I mean, do you fire slugs *into* the tank? Y'know, like target practice or something?'

Ian grabbed another beer. 'You blokes are complete morons,' he said, shaking his head. 'There's no such thing as a bloody slugtank. It just came into my head.'

'Well,' said Terry, 'your mind is diseased. That's the stupid-est name I've ever heard.'

'We could just stay as GEN-R8,' I ventured tentatively.

Ian glared at me and I shrugged. 'Just a thought.'

'We're gonna leave here with a new fuckin' name if it kills us,' Ian growled, still eyeballing me intently.

In the end, after more than two hours of arguing, laughing and name-calling, it came down to a choice between the Remedy and Fourplay. The Remedy was my suggestion. Rose Tattoo had a song of the same name on their eponymous debut album and I'd always liked the way the word rolled off the tongue. It also had good associations, our rock music being the perfect remedy for a week of nine-to-five drudgery. But the others plumped for Fourplay. It had overt sexual connotations, yet, in a devastatingly witty piece of wordplay, it also alluded to how many people played in the band. Geddit?

'Right, Fourplay it is,' said Ian, and raised his fourth stubby to the ceiling in mock salute. 'Fuck off, GEN-R8. Here's to Fourplay.'

Ian phoned me three days later.

'No-one'll book us using the name Fourplay. They say it's too rude and the punters'll kick up a stink. I reckoned most of 'em wouldn't know what it means anyway, but they aren't having a bar of it. I'm not going through all that naming malarkey again, so I've made an executive decision. We're the Love Spuds. Right?'

'The Love Spuds?' I repeated, thinking I must have misheard.

'That's right. Whaddya think?'

I couldn't contain myself. 'You can't be serious. What about the Remedy? Why don't we just go with that?'

'Too late. I had to think of something on the spot and Love Spuds was the first name that came into my head. So that's what we are, mate. Like it or lump it.'

That was 1987. Two days ago, I spied a poster on a telegraph pole near my house: 'FRI NITE: FOURPLAY LIVE'. Oh, how society's mores had been rent asunder in those intervening years.

⌢

At the Spuds' first gig a week or so later, not even an outlandish name could save us from being completely upstaged by a masturbating dwarf. We were playing in a nightclub bearing the erroneously upmarket name of Jaxons-on-the-Park. Jaxons occupied the top floor of a nondescript brick building in the main street, across the road from the memorial clock and council-tended flower beds. The interior was equally nondescript. A bar ran the length of one wall, a low stage jutted out from the wall opposite. In between was a polished wooden dancefloor, the requisite expanse of sticky, foul-patterned carpet, a collection of functional tables, and chairs clad in mushroom-pink vinyl. The Love Spuds had secured the Friday night slot at this salubrious establishment. Midnight till 3am. We were to be paid three hundred and fifty dollars for the night, plus free drinks. Dale, Terry and I would receive eighty dollars each and Ian a hundred and ten, as he was still paying off the PA.

Dale and Terry had been equally appalled when Ian revealed our new name. Dale sulked as we set up, his face in a scowl. 'Love-fuckin'-Spuds,' he spat at one point from behind the amplifier he was lugging up the stairs. 'What a crock of shit.'

Tension simmered between him and Ian. They traded muttered insults while Terry and I hung back quietly, uncoiling leads and setting up mic stands. The band even had lights. Well, when I say lights, there were empty beetroot cans with globes lodged inside and coloured gels attached to the front with clothespegs.

There was a churning somewhere behind my breastbone

and I was thinking, This isn't how it's supposed to be. This was my first show, I was already nervous, and the friction between Ian and Dale was only adding to my discomfort. Didn't they understand what a big deal this was for me? Couldn't they appreciate that I'd spent a large portion of my life preparing for this momentous occasion? And a large portion of the previous week trialling different outfits for my debut? Would I go with stonewash jeans, T-shirt and denim jacket, or tight grey jeans with the tear just beneath the left buttock, red singlet and denim jacket? Or should I maybe ditch the denim jacket and go the T-shirt by itself? Or the singlet? In the end, I decided the singlet wasn't an option. Terry was bound to wear one and I wasn't going to try and compete with his brawny arms and shoulders. So I opted instead for a white T-shirt bearing the silhouette of a soldier saluting a flag with a dollar sign on it. I didn't see it as some awesomely cutting anti-capitalist statement, I just thought it looked kind of cool. After much agonising, I also plumped for the grey jeans, mainly because they were tighter. The resulting ensemble looked as if I'd given precisely no thought whatsoever to my wardrobe, but that wasn't the case. If Keith Richards could be described as 'elegantly wasted', then I would be 'meticulously dishevelled'.

In any case, my attack of pre-gig nerves made little or no impression on Dale and Ian. The former believed the odds of us achieving national fame and fortune had suddenly lengthened greatly, owing to Ian's rush of blood on the naming front. Although I agreed that the name was not what you might call inspired, I felt at pains to point out that record companies wouldn't exactly be knocking down the door to sign a band that regarded the Eagles' 'Already Gone' as one of its show-stoppers, so the fact we were encumbered with an idiotic moniker probably wouldn't, all things considered, make a great deal of difference.

It mightn't sound it, but the Jaxons gig was probably the best on offer around town. We started playing when the RSL closed. It disgorged its drunken contents, which then wobbled down the road to Jaxons, keen to imbibe and party some more. That meant that each week, the Love Spuds, née GEN-R8, were supplied with a crowd of ready-made revellers. There was no cool, stand-offish period at the start, the punters were lubricated, primed and infinitely forgiving. On that first night, I was amazed to see people spilling onto the dancefloor as soon as we took to the stage, the opening chords of 'April Sun In Cuba' acting like Pavlov's bell.

'Why "April Sun" first up?' I'd asked upon being shown the song list.

'Trust me,' Ian replied. 'Everyone loves that song. It's a sure-fire opener.'

And he was right. Before I'd even opened my mouth to embark on the first verse, the place was alive with writhing bodies.

That moment is etched in my memory. It was real. At last, it was real. And everything – our risible name, Ian and Dale's bickering, my own nervousness – dissolved. None of that mattered any more. What mattered was that I was finally up there, sucking in lungfuls of second-hand cigarette smoke, singing, posturing, tossing my hair around, feeling the sound, and, more importantly, feeling the response from the crowd. A *real* crowd, made of flesh and sweat and perfume and overdone makeup.

During our short breaks, a large screen descended from the ceiling over the stage and upon it were projected the latest video hits. I remember 'Beds Are Burning', 'Need You Tonight' and 'The Final Countdown' being played over and over. I and my fellow Spuds were sitting off to one side, conducting a post-mortem on the first set and generally agreeing that things were going quite well, considering it was the first gig back from a brief spell and with a new singer, when a very drunk dwarf took it upon himself to climb onto the stage and embark on an exhibition of self-love that sent Jaxons into an uproar.

No-one could say for sure what it was that motivated him to start masturbating in public. There was talk that it was a sick joke, that one of the bar staff had dared him to do it in return for a free beer, but that rumour was never substantiated. He was suddenly just there – larger than life, one is tempted to say – standing centre-stage, directly in front of the screen, belt undone, jeans loosened and bunched around his thighs, right hand kneading his unco-operative and dozing member. The music kept playing and he swayed in time to the beat. The video clip washed across him, Michael Hutchence flickering and distorted, while on his face he wore a strangely serene expression (the masturbator, that is, not Michael Hutchence). It was like a scene from some debauched, unfathomable European arthouse film.

There was a moment of shocked silence, a disbelieving pause, then the room erupted. Squeals, screams, gasps, cheers, hoots, wild applause. Out of the chorus of heckling, these quick-witted gems have stuck in my mind:

'Oh, so this is what they mean by dwarf tossing?'

'Oi, mate! Didn't I see you in that *Willy Wanka* movie?'

'Which one are you then? Horny?'

A girl standing nearby had a more scientific appraisal. 'Michelle,' she said, turning to her friend, 'do you reckon he's got a big dick? Or is it just an average-sized dick and it looks big because it's on a dwarf?'

This prompted me to look more closely. The dwarf's appendage, which appeared at last to be reacting to its owner's ministrations, did look somewhat prodigious. Any hopes of further examination were scuttled, however, by the arrival of two bouncers, who wrestled the man from the stage but who had less success removing the smiles from their faces. As the impromptu performer was being escorted from the building, the manager shouldered his way through the mayhem.

'For God's sake, get back on and play, willya?' he said in a panicked voice.

'Regular customer?' I asked.

'Yeah, un-fuckin'-fortunately. Little bastard's in here all the time, carryin' on. If he's not exposing himself, he's runnin' his hand up skirts. 'E's never done it onstage before, though. Should ban the little fucker. Anyway, get up there and take their bloody minds off it.'

'Well, that's going to be a hard act to follow,' I said to the crowd as Ian and Dale strapped on their guitars and tried to compose themselves. 'Will you please thank our support act – I think you'll agree, a nice set of love spuds indeed.'

The newspaper editor peered out at me from between his rampant muttonchop sideburns like a predator observing its prey from behind a clump of spinifex, and said, 'We need to target a younger demographic. Do you think you're up to handling your own weekly page? Double spread in Tuesday's edition covering, you know, rock music, young people – stuff like that.'

And so began my first brief foray into rock journalism. The prospect excited me. Not only would I be a part of the scene (i.e., in a band), a functioning cog in the clanking machine that was north-coast rock music, but I would now have invested in me the power to *control* that machine. To influence its direction from within in some way. Or so I thought. And before I'd produced so much as a single keystroke, I was well on the way to complete megalomania. From my lofty position as doyen of the decibels, I would decide who received coverage and who didn't. With a simple flurry of my fingertips, I would consign bands to the scrapheap. I would favour the broadsword over the stiletto, and do away with the Spuds' competition. I pictured myself as a controversial media figure whose opinion, whether you agreed or disagreed, loved or loathed it, would make unmissable copy.

The reality, of course, was somewhat different. For a start, I didn't get to write much copy. Certainly nothing in the way of reviews. Whenever a notable act came to town, the beefy, balding proprietor of the local music store – the very same who had once steered me away from *Goat's Head Soup* and towards *Sticky Fingers* – was asked to attend the concert and jot down a few of his thoughts, for inclusion in *my* section. 'Why him and not me?' I asked. Not unreasonably, I thought.

'Because he's known to be some sort of expert in the field. He runs a music store and his tastes have been refined over many years of listening to lots of different music. If I asked you to go along and review, say, Jon English or Doug Parkinson, you'd just think, There's a sad old bastard, and write your review according to your prejudice. Am I right?'

Indeed he was. Right on the money, in fact. 'But don't you want some attitude for this section?' I argued. 'Don't you want something, you know, with a bit of an edge to it? I mean, if it's youth you're after, you're not going to be reviewing Jon English or Doug Parkinson in the first place, are you?'

The editor snorted in triumph. 'See what I mean? A major musical act comes to town and you're telling me you wouldn't even acknowledge their presence.'

I went away confused. The paper, wanting more young readers, set up a section specifically for them, put their youngest and most eminently suitable staff member on the case, then immediately put them on a leash because they were too young and might choose to ignore the imminent arrival of Brian Cadd. How was that supposed to work?

What my superior also neglected to tell me was that my new duties, *vis-à-vis* having my finger on the pulse of the region's music, youth and 'stuff like that', did not replace my existing workload. They were an added burden.

'What sort of budget do you think we have here?' he asked when I pointed out that I was still having to cover the local court, do the police rounds, and type up reams of competition results from the local bowling clubs. 'Do you think I can afford to have someone who writes only about pop music? No bloody way. It's a good learning curve for you. Time management, son, time management.'

It wasn't long before the new weekly spread – christened, stultifyingly enough, Music Scene – became a difficult child, for which I bore responsibility. It was never satiated, always pulling on my shirt and whining, always needing attention. A double page takes some filling, and I was soon desperate. There were times when I prayed that Don Burrows or Chad Morgan would announce a nationwide tour. So much for incisive, cutting-edge prose examining youth culture. In no time I was resorting to any old press release I could lay my hands on, just to fill up those haunting columns of off-white. Travelling magician performing at Wingham Ex-Services? Beauty, in you go, mate. Local unknown singer/songwriter pens song for Bicentenary? Wouldn't want to look un-Australian now, would we? Half a page and a photo for you, my talentless but patriotic songbird. On one occasion, in an article about a Newcastle band coming to town, I included their entire playlist, in order of performance, including encores. I even seriously considered colouring-in competitions and spot-the-difference cartoons (music-related, of course).

There was some wheat among the chaff. For instance, I was able to conduct a handful of phone interviews with real stars on the eve of their arrival in town. Doc Neeson, Joe Camilleri and Ross Wilson each gave me quarter of an hour of their precious time. I was always hugely nervous about doing these interviews, awed by the prospect of chatting one-on-one with homegrown rock luminaries. I'm not quite sure, though, that I ever maximised those opportunities, given that I can remember asking each of them the hoary question, 'So what can audiences expect from an Angels/Black Sorrows/Ross Wilson show?'

'They can expect to get sweaty, drunk and hard-of-hearing,' was one deadpan reply.

I kicked off the Doc Neeson interview by telling him that, as chance would have it, I was singing in the band which would support the Angels at the Taree RSL. I imagined that having this common ground would break the ice, spark a conversation between empathetic musos. We were, after all, fellow frontmen with much to share. Doc's reply, *in toto*, was, 'Make sure you don't do any of our stuff.'

(That reminds me. I was standing at the counter in a crowded deli the other day, when an unasked-for plastic-wrapped blueberry muffin was plonked down in front of me. 'It's for the gentleman behind you,' the server explained. The gentleman to whom I passed the said muffin was none other than Doc Neeson. It was relatively early and he looked like a towering, anaemic vampire. 'Thank you.' He smiled briefly and drifted from the shop. Another opportunity to rub shoulders – well, shoulders and wrists – with rock royalty missed. But there you go, Angelophiles, your man loves a blueberry muffin.)

Each week Music Scene included the latest charts – Top Ten singles, albums, predictions – and only now, fifteen years later, I notice that, according to me, 'What Have I Done To Deserve This?' was performed not by the Pet Shop Boys in collaboration with Dusty Springfield, but by the Pet Shop Boys and Slim Dusty. Whether this was a slip-up made by a young journalist crumbling under the pressure of a looming deadline, or shoddy work on the part of a typesetter, or even some kind of subtle joke played by a subeditor, I cannot say for sure.

The very first edition of Music Scene, though, did not suffer from any desperation to simply fill its space. Being shiny and new, it had much attention lavished upon it and was carefully constructed and designed. It will come as no surprise that the first major article written for it detailed the arrival of a new band bearing an eyebrow-raising, vegetable-related name:

BAND RISES OUT OF GEN-R8'S ASHES

The Love Spuds have risen out of the ashes of GEN-R8 to play on the Manning entertainment scene. Three members of the band, Dale Maddox, Ian Every and Terry Dury remain, as does much of the material. However, there has been an injection of some harder material, as well as a return to the roots of rock'n'roll with some blues numbers.

Maddox and Every are the band's guitarists, with Dury on drums. The band's only new inclusion, Anthony Griffis, is the Spuds' vocalist. Every and Maddox have had experience in local bands. The latter was a member of both Sleezy Wonder and Pigs Fly Backwards before joining GEN-R8 three years ago.

Influences

He has been influenced by hard rock bands such as Status Quo, AC/DC, while Dury has found inspiration in Australian bands such as The Angels and Midnight Oil. Griffis cites the music of The Rolling Stones, The Who and blues by Muddy Waters as major influences, as well as the vocals of Bon Scott and Angry Anderson.

This diversity of tastes comes through in the band's material. The Love Spuds have strived for light and shade in their music. Songs range from the Beatles' *Let It Be* and Joe Jackson's *Is She Really Going Out With Him?*, through to The Angels' *Take A Long Line* and AC/DC's *Whole Lotta Rosie*. Interspersed among the better-known numbers are renditions of Muddy Waters' *Mannish Boy* and the Stones' *Honky Tonk Woman*. Also there is an enterprising '50s collection which includes *Johnny B Goode*, *Jailhouse Rock* and *Blue Suede Shoes*.

The band's main aim is to play good-time rock'n'roll. There

is nothing pretentious about The Love Spuds – their music is simply to have a good time by.

At present the band has a regular spot at Jaxons-on-the-Park, Taree, on Friday nights. This week they will be appearing at Gloucester Golf Club tomorrow night and the Wingham Hotel on Saturday night.

Okay, so I wouldn't have scored a job writing for *Rolling Stone* and I won't hold my breath waiting for it to be included in an anthology of rock writing, but I was still new to the game, and if nothing else I think you can probably detect my enthusiasm in the breathless phoenix analogy. It possesses what you might classify as a 'loose charm'. (Although, where was the subeditor when I needed him? 'Their music is simply to have a good time by'? Good grief.)

The rest of the band loved it. 'Ooohh, "pretentious", that's a big word,' Ian teased. 'You see that, boys, there's nothing *pretentious* about us.' And so it went for a few days. Every time someone said anything, on any topic, the reply was standard. 'Now, you're not being pre*tentious*, are you?'

I'd completely forgotten that we did a '50s medley. At the time I wasn't in favour, thinking it a bit naff, but Ian wanted to cover all bases – he was pragmatic, I'll give him that – and I have to admit, it worked. After all, is there anyone alive who doesn't know 'Jailhouse Rock'? I was surprised to see 'Let It Be'. That song is basically piano, and we didn't have a piano, or any other keyboards, so I don't quite recall how we pulled it off. And 'Whole Lotta Rosie' with only one guitar? We might have been many things, but unambitious was not one of them. What surprises me most, though, is that I seem to be intimating that 'Honky Tonk Woman' wasn't a well-known song. Why I, of all people, would suggest that is anyone's guess. Maybe I was suffering the effects of several years of anti-Stones browbeating.

I love the part where I list Dale's CV, as if anyone could possibly care that he'd done time previously in two other hopelessly plodding covers bands before winding up in GEN-R8. But the curriculum vitae always seemed to be a staple ingredient of the rock-group press release. Band photos were another essential publicity tool, and such was every group's burning desire to look cool and dark and tough and mysterious, the results were inevitably hilarious.

The Love Spuds weren't above trotting out the odd stereotype. One of our photos shows us studded along the facade of a decrepit brick building, sites of urban and industrial decay always being immensely popular with any two-bit rock band worth its salt. Run-down factories, abandoned warehouses, partly demolished buildings, tangled wire fences, signs declaring 'NO ENTRY', 'HIGH VOLTAGE', or 'BILL POSTERS WILL BE PROSECUTED' all provide fertile photo fodder. In our shot, Terry is framed in a blank window, smouldering annoyingly. The rest of us are leaning on the wall, adopting carefully choreographed poses of aggressive torpor and insolent expressions. Dale isn't even looking at the camera. He gazes off to one side, not interested enough to acknowledge the lens. Actually, chances are he was looking at another band, waiting just out of frame for us to wrap up so they could do their shoot. 'Won't be a sec, fellas. Just a couple more shots and she's all yours.'

The other photo session we did employed 'band *noir*', another tried and true method that has stood the test of time. Our four faces, set in solemn mode, emerge from inky darkness. Nothing else is visible. The lighting, coming directly from the side, is harsh and white and throws into sharp relief every pore, acne scar and mild deformity. Our floating visages resemble grainy photos of the lunar surface.

If there's anything sadder than a young covers band trying to look like the Doors, it's an old covers band trying to look like the Doors. Too many times, photos were skimmed onto my desk that should have given me a chilling glimpse into the future. In these photos the bands are up against a crumbling wall, or standing outside an electricity substation – the usual scenario – but the members have been around the block a few times. Their mullets are streaked with grey, the number of chins on show is more or less double the number of people present, the black rock garb has to stretch over paunches and doughy physiques. Their expressions are the same as ours – flinty-eyed disdain – but there is something else in those eyes. A hint of fatigue, perhaps? Or resignation? Whatever it is, it gives them away. Once upon a time, these guys believed in the rock'n'roll dream, but with their wives most likely waiting on the other side of the camera, bouncing children on their hips and exhorting their partners to hurry up or else Woolies will be closed, it's a little harder to look convincing.

I can say, with all honesty, that for a few months in 1987 I made more money playing music than I made working at my 'real' job. In fact, when I look back, I think that probably is my greatest musical achievement. I am proud of the fact that, for a flickering moment, jumping around on a stage screaming myself hoarse every weekend brought in more money than journalism. To be fair, I was only a D-grade cadet at the time, so the amount we're talking about is not what you might describe as princely. I took home a hundred and forty dollars a week, twenty of which disappeared straight into Mum's housekeeping purse by way of board. The Spuds were playing two and three nights a week, which meant I sometimes raked in almost double my salary, depending on the venue. That was a whopping, delirium-inducing amount of cash, in the hand, cheers and thanks for coming.

And what does a bright young fellow do with such a fortunate fiscal influx? Does he stash it away in the bank, saving frugally so he can one day do the smart thing and invest soundly in bricks and mortar? No, my friends, he does not. Instead he finds a wall, avails himself of its propinquity, and pisses it all up against it in a liberal fashion. That much at least is expected of a young rock dude with a bit of cash to flash.

In one of our stranger gigs, we were booked to play at my old high school, a place I had vacated only months before. This caused me a minor identity crisis. A lot of the students knew me. The teachers all knew me. I'd been a – mostly – well-behaved student. Now here I was trying to pass myself off as some low-down, dirty-assed rock mongrel. Which is difficult to do when you still feel compelled to address teachers as Mr and Mrs and are forced to field questions from the headmaster about how your new journalism career is progressing.

We were playing in the same hall in which Carlene Allwood had unceremoniously dumped me all those years before. As we performed, I watched the student body play out the very same scenarios from socials past. All the roles were filled. There were the couples pashing, the teachers pulling them apart, couples falling apart of their own accord, groups of people dancing in circles trying to impress one another, the heavies in the far corner skulking ominously and trying not to reveal their true drunken state. And, right up the front, a small posse of real enthusiasts, rock-music trainspotters like me, watching our every move intently with their heads jammed up against the speakers.

When we played 'Am I Ever Gonna See Your Face Again?', hundreds of students screamed back the famous refrain, as expected, and onstage I was suddenly joined by my form master. For a split second, a confused moment, I thought he'd come to join in. But no. Quite the contrary, in fact. Mid-verse, as I was trying to sing, he yelled in my ear, 'Stop this. Stop this song. NOW!'

I looked at him blankly, trying to fight my natural instinct to obey immediately. How could we just stop in the middle of the song?

'Stop it now, or I pull the plug,' he warned.

I gestured to the other Spuds, running a finger repeatedly across my throat, and they pulled out of the song with a little flourish, trying to save face. The packed hall booed when I explained the reason for the truncated rendition. Ian, Dale and Terry rolled their eyes at me, generally displeased at being censored in such a heavy fashion. It was quite a good little moment, actually. Once again, rock music was causing a frisson, sending tremors along conservative spines. But then, we are talking about schoolkids yelling, 'Get fucked, fuck off,' at the top of their lungs in a school hall, in front of dozens of teachers. Under those circumstances, causing an upset was always going to be like shooting fish in a barrel.

∩

At Ian's request I designed a poster for the band. Typically, the one I dashed off as a joke was the one selected. A cartoon potato – lumpy, misshapen, unwashed – emerged from a black circle, a lecherous grin splitting its rudimentary features. One arm was thrust into the foreground and a middle finger was raised in rude salute. To top it off, the words 'Love Spuds' curled around the top half of the circle, and 'Very A-Peelin'' edged their way around the bottom.

'Brilliant,' said Ian, who set about having the image printed on some T-shirts. 'We'll sell 'em at the gigs,' he enthused.

We sold a grand total of three, one each to a pair of staggeringly drunk punters in Gloucester, about eighty kilometres west of Taree, and one to Ian's cousin, a girl called Evol – 'love' spelled backwards – who came to all our gigs, no matter where we played.

'That'd be right,' Ian was heard to growl. 'We get one fully-fledged groupie and I'm bloody well related to her. Typical.'

'Yeah, but we're not,' Terry pointed out, grinning maliciously and waggling his eyebrows.

Ian aimed a finger in our direction. 'If any of you pigs so much as touches a hair on her head, I'll thump you.'

'Don't worry, mate, the hair on her *head* is quite safe,' Dale joked, and disappeared beneath a piledriving tackle from Ian.

It has been said that the only reason a guy ever picks up a guitar is in order to facilitate the acquiring of female attention. 'Playing licks means gettin' chicks,' is how I heard it expressed once. We all know that women are attracted to musos, for what I suppose are obvious reasons, but it always amazed me that girls could be so interested in a group of part-timers playing other people's songs. But they were. Putting Evol to one side for a moment, the Spuds did have some track record when it came to attracting the opposite sex. Not on a large scale or anything. We didn't have women mixing up bowls of plaster of Paris so they could make casts of our genitalia. I didn't get to stand on hotel balconies and select playthings from the crowd of screaming fans below, like I was choosing chicken breasts at a deli.

'No, not that one, *that* one, the one just behind, thank you.'
We were denied the pleasure of stripping submissives naked en route to some gig in our private Lear jet while the road crew played bongos in the aisle. But in our own humble way, the Love Spuds managed to keep the flame sputtering.

Dale was on sticky territory in this respect, because he and Gail were an item. A long-term item. A we've-been-going-together-since-we-were-thirteen item. Maybe they thought their partnership had been divined because their names rhymed, I don't know. Theirs was a tempestuous relationship, riddled with jealousy and mistrust. Most of which, it has to be said, came from Gail's direction. Full-Force Gail, we called her, though not to her face. She came to most of our gigs and eyed Dale like a hawk. She would sit and smoke and watch his eyes as he played. She drew invisible lines from his pupils to whichever girl she thought he was looking at. A large number of our shows ended with guitars and amps being smashed, but it wasn't our onstage theatrics, only Dale and Gail working through yet another misunderstanding. It all became very tedious. I lost count of the number of times Gail exited a room melodramatically, crying or being comforted by Rhoda.

It seems every group of people contains a couple like Dale and Gail. They bicker incessantly, and think their bickering is a sign that their relationship is poised at a more mature, sophisticated level than everyone else's; that they only fight because their feelings for each other are so deep. They have the 'storming off in tears' routine down to a fine art. Every argument is the end, for all time, never again. One or the other tricks you into taking sides, into being their confidante, and then, five minutes after you've said something disdainful about the absent party, they're back together, canoodling on the couch and being sickeningly loving. For poor Dale, every gig was an optic mine-field. One stray glance, real or imagined, one lingering look, and *bang*, he was being garrotted with a guitar string. Ian's advice to Dale was simple and typically straightforward. 'Fuck it. If you're gonna cop the punishment, you might as well do the crime.'

Gail needn't have worried, though, because Terry was the Spud all the girls loved. There was no getting around it, and it niggled the rest of us. He sat at the back of the stage, he was only half visible behind his kit, yet it was as if the rest of us were made of glass. On numerous occasions Terry sidled up to me at the end of the night and asked if I wouldn't mind pack-ing up his kit for him because some girl had had a quiet word in his ear, and, well, you know, best to strike while the iron's hot and all that. If she had to wait while he lugged out, he rea-soned, she might lose interest and go off with someone else. If I ummed and ahhed long enough, he would offer me part of his cut for the gig as a sweetener. And then he would vanish into the night with his arm around some spunk while I van-ished into the carpark with my arms around a black bass drum.

My own moment of groupie glory arrived during a sweaty Saturday night show at Jaxons. I spied in the throng a lithe blonde on the dancefloor. Actually, everyone had spied her. Her lean, tanned legs emerged from beneath an outrageously short and tight white dress, which I discovered later was made from the same material as wetsuits. Those legs tapered down and disappeared into white high-heels. A vinyl handbag, colour *blanc*, sat miraculously untrampled at her feet. Other women shot her venomous looks. Girlfriends sneered and slapped boyfriends who leered. Dale played that night with a blindfold, just to be on the safe side.

During a break, I was not a little surprised when the woman appeared beside me at the bar. I was enveloped in perfume and body heat. 'Hello. Anthony, isn't it?' she said with a shy smile, and my memory was jolted. Karen Bickford. Travelled on my school bus. Bus monitor, in fact. She was in her final year when I was a snotty Year Seven kid running amok. I remembered Karen because when I misbehaved on the bus, she made me sit on her lap as punishment, with her arms wrapped around my waist. You don't forget that in a hurry. In 1981 I spent most of my commuting time perched on her knee like a naughty ventriloquist's dummy.

Karen's story? Now twenty-five years old. Married at twenty-one. Divorced at twenty-four. No children – 'Thank God. Not with that bastard.' Had been out of town for a while but was now back working as a secretary in a local firm. Told me she couldn't believe how I'd grown. 'Well, I was only twelve when you last saw me,' I observed. She said she couldn't believe I was in a band. That she loved the music we were playing, that 'What's My Scene?' was her favourite song.

We drank, we chatted. I went back onstage, ignoring the looks and nudges from the other Spuds (Terry looked quite miffed, I was pleased to note), and watched Karen dance energetically during our final set. She kept shooting me glances and little smiles. Afterwards, we sat and talked some more (my voice was delightfully gravelly and hoarse in the wake of the gig), and Karen laughed when I reminded her of her not-so-cruel but definitely unusual bus-trip punishment.

Then she gave me a look. 'Well, actually, I hope you don't think I'm being too forward, but tonight, if you want, we can swap places,' she said. I drank up before she could change her mind.

Of course, I'll never know for sure how much of the Karen Bickford Incident was the direct result of my playing in a rock band. Or whether in fact it had any bearing at all. Even today, when I really should be getting on with my life, I sometimes find myself plagued by this question. Would she have approached me or shown such interest had I been in the crowd and not onstage? Had I been just another bleary drinker slouched against the bar? Might she not have spotted me lining up another beverage and thought to herself, Oh my God, there's that Anthony Griffis. Well, as I thought, he's amounted to nothing. Hope he doesn't recognise me. Who can say?

Other times it was easier to tell. When we embarked on short road trips up the coast, playing venues like Wauchope RSL and Laurieton Bowling Club (where the sign out the front proclaimed 'TONITE: LONE SPUDS', so that people weren't sure if we were a band or part of the buffet), we were treated like specimens from a far-flung corner of the galaxy. Groups of girls turned up to the gigs eager to see the 'new blood'. Remember when a new kid started at school? That's what it was like. We were curiosities, to be poked and prodded and examined. Because we had a glossy veneer of freshness, we were automatically deemed better looking and more intriguing than the local lads. Of course, we were demonstrably *not* better looking than a certain percentage of the local male population (except for bloody Terry, of course, who was better looking than everyone else, no matter where he was), but never underestimate that saying about familiarity breeding contempt.

On one such trip, Ian decided we needed to inject some life into our stage act and so purchased a collection of inflatable beach toys.

'And what do you expect me to do with those?' I asked.

'You know, play with them, whatever you want. They're props. Use your imagination.'

Dale walked past and shook his head. 'Out of buckets and spades, were they?'

Pink Floyd had a giant pig. Other notable stadium acts had enormous blow-up women towering over their stages, wobbling about on guy ropes like hot-air balloons struggling to rise. The Love Spuds had a preschooler's floatie ring with a grinning horse's head sprouting off it, and a multi-coloured beachball.

I was in a mood that night, feeling a little rambunctious. I bounced the beachball repeatedly off Terry's head as he sat glowering on his drum stool, mouthing, 'Fuck off!' at me. Then I threw it at Ian with probably more force than was strictly necessary, and he head-butted it, soccer-like, into the crowd, where he no doubt imagined it would be batted around in a display of cheery bonhomie. It was promptly deflated with the glowing tip of a cigarette. I was at a complete loss as to what to do with the floatie ring, so in the end I pounced on it during the lead break in 'Am I Ever Gonna See Your Face Again' and wrestled it ferociously, rolling back and forth across the floor like a man possessed. I delivered the last chorus lying on my back with my legs squeezed through the ring and the horsy head rearing up from my groin, a happy phallus. I then stood up and galloped in circles around Dale, yelling, 'Giddyup!' into the mic.

When it was all over, I stroked the horse's blue painted mane, made neighing sounds, and said something about not minding a little International Velvet meself, when the chance arose. The crowd in the Kempsey RSL auditorium were – well, I think perplexed is the most apt description. They must have thought they'd happened upon some avant garde theatre company going through its paces. I'm surprised we weren't tarred and feathered and run out of town on a rail.

'You're a fucking idiot,' Ian said afterwards, his face dark. 'Why'd you have to go on like a complete spazmo?'

I was livid. 'Says the bloke who bought me a floatie as a stage prop,' I snapped back. 'What was I gonna do? Tell you what, do us all a favour and steer clear of set dressing from now on. It's rock'n'roll, not fucking *Cats*.'

No career in rock music, however intermittent, ill-conceived or paltry, is complete without the obligatory outdoor festival appearance. Ever since the hazy days of the late '60s, musos the world over have yearned to take part in a recreation of Woodstock and the carnival atmosphere that accompanies all such events.

Over the years, bands have had the Isle of Wight, Glastonbury, Lollapalooza, the Monsters of Rock at Donnington Castle, and the Big Day Out. For the Love Spuds there was Wingham Brush, a two-day soirée on the banks of the Manning River, right next door to the last remaining patch of virgin rainforest on the New South Wales north coast.

The Wingham Brush Music Festival was the brainchild of community radio station 2BOB-FM. For a time, while we were still at school, Darren and I hosted a Saturday morning show on 2BOB. We used our two hours to indoctrinate the audience – all twelve of them – by playing favourite tracks from our own collections, and we interspersed those with sparkling repartee like 'What we got next, Dazza?' and 'Now we gotta bitta KISS comin' your way,' or 'Not that button, you idiot.' Incisive radio, you'd have to agree. No better or worse than most community radio, I suppose. At least we didn't pronounce INXS as INKS when back-announcing 'Original Sin', as I heard one young would-be jock do.

Of course, the festival was plugged endlessly in my Music Scene pages. Under the headline 'Top Bands For Brush Festival', I wrote: 'There will be a great lineup of the most popular bands on the mid-north coast. Check out these names: Boris and the Karloffs, Bliss Bombs, Freeway, Cheatin Hearts, the Love Spuds, the DTs, Anvil Chorus, Sound Company, Taylormade, Skumbagz, and Short Stories.' Check them out, indeed. Some of the lamest band names in history there. (Although I note with interest that the Skumbagz were still going strong. I *knew* painting your name on the bass drum ensured longevity.) As if sensing the slightly underwhelming nature of that rollcall, I went on, 'There will be other acts too, so it's guaranteed to be a great success. If you don't want to drive or can't drive, there will be buses to take you back to Taree.'

For forty-eight hours in November 1987 the normally peaceful park and barbecue area at Wingham Brush was awash with people who didn't. Dreadlocked folks eking out alternative lifestyles in tiny communities stumbled and tumbled down from 'the hills', as they say, keen to be a part of Wingham's Woodstock – two days of peace, love, drugs, and shitty covers bands all playing the same songs. Everywhere you looked, people were eating fire and juggling coloured balls. Not necessarily at the same time, mind. Others were so out of it they were juggling fire and eating the balls. I didn't spot anyone teetering about on stilts, but we'd just had a good spell of rain and the ground was soggy, so stilt-walking might have been tough going. The smell of hot dogs and frying onions mingled with the intense aroma of marijuana.

The stage was a semitrailer, and that fact alone excited me no end. I have always had a strange, inexplicable penchant for rock music being performed on vehicles. The Stones launched their

1975 North American tour by trundling around New York City on the back of a flatbed truck playing 'Brown Sugar'. And AC/DC did the same thing in the clip for 'Long Way To The Top', bringing traffic to a standstill as they rolled through Melbourne with Scottish pipers marching along behind. Our semi was stationary, but it gave me a little thrill nonetheless. What also excited us was the size of the PA and lighting rig. I'm talking about real lights here, clamped to scaffolding above our heads; lights that flashed in sync, bathing us in acid-green and red and blue. There was a mixing desk on a platform out the front of the stage, about ten metres away – an imposing chunk of faders and knobs manned by a lumbering bear of a man in a sleeveless shirt and cracked leather pants. As lead singer, I had not one but two foldback wedges at my feet, and when I uttered the requisite 'Tsyoo . . . check one, tsyoo,' my voice came back at me with a rounded clarity I had never experienced. I'll tell you one thing, we might have played better than we did that night, but we never *sounded* better. There is a distinction.

A high fence made of hessian cordoned off an area around the rear of the semi. This was the performers' private enclosure. Band members and invited guests only. How good was this? We even had little passes around our necks to identify us. I was beside myself. I must have walked in and out through the hessian flap two dozen times, just so people could see me walking in and out through the hessian flap. Inside, we drank the free beer on offer to the musos and watched other bands wander in, trailing girls and saying, ''S'awright, mate. She's with me,' to the questioning security guard. (A security guard!) What I liked best about this arrangement was that you weren't seen before you took the stage. You were away from the prying eyes of Joe Public – not that Joe Public's eyes were the least bit concerned – and it wasn't until the compere announced, 'Ladies and gentlemen, will you please welcome to the Wingham Brush Music Festival . . . the Love Spuds!' that you leapt up the few metal steps at the back of the semi and bounded onto the stage into the light. I was intoxicated. Of course, my level of expectation and excitement wasn't quite matched by that of the crowd, which either clapped politely or failed to respond at all. I suppose they could have cared less, but that would have taken effort, so they just left it at that.

The Spuds played at dusk on the first day, just as several thousand flying foxes took wing and streamed screeching from the rainforest canopy. We'd lobbied for this slot because we wanted the lights to take full effect. If you played in the afternoon – well, you were just a group of guys on the back of a truck. At twilight, with the lights flashing and hordes of leathery-winged mammalians slicing through the dim blue sky, you could almost imagine you were important, and that they were some giant, well-choreographed special effect.

We kicked off our 45-minute set – 'Good evening, Wingham Brush! You ready to rock?' – with 'April Sun In Cuba', and it had its usual effect on the few hundred people scattered on the grass. In the gathering gloom I could see shadowy bodies jumping about and men shifting their weight from foot to foot in the best tradition of hopeless bloke-dancing everywhere. I went through all the moves, ticking them off as I went – frontman by numbers. Foot propped on foldback wedge, *tick*; wrench mic stand across stage, *tick*; tango with it, *tick*; grab mic off stand, coil lead around fist, and stand with elbow cocked out like Bon Scott circa the clip for 'High Voltage', *tick*; run up and throw arm chummily around Dale's shoulders, *tick*; hoist Ian on shoulders while he peels off lead, *tick*; jump on drum-riser, grab spare stick and strike crash cymbal on Terry's signal, *tick*. With a pruned show like the festival, it was important to cram everything into our forty-five minutes. You didn't want to miss out.

Then Ian went and spoilt it by inviting a brass and woodwind section to join us onstage for 'Take A Long Line'. Suddenly the semitrailer was swarming with shambling hippies in their loose Eastern-print pants and bare feet, brandishing trumpets and trombones. Terry, Dale and I exchanged baffled looks. It turned out Ian had earlier started talking with a few guys who'd brought along their instruments on the off chance, and, you know, he thought it would be cool for them to join us for some rock/classical fusion, to really give our set an edge over the other acts. He'd just neglected to mention it to the rest of us, that's all.

Ian was always trying things. First it was the inflatable toys, then, only a week or so later, he hired a smoke machine, 'for that extra atmosphere'. Because I was unencumbered by an instrument, I was placed in charge of operating it. I overdid things a tad and ended up almost fumigating the entire Railway Bowling Club. And now this. 'Take A Long Line' lasted nearly twenty shambolic minutes and included, of all things, a flute solo, the flautist shouldering me out of the way so he could tootle breathily into my microphone like Ian Anderson from Jethro-bloody-Tull. Incongruous doesn't begin to describe it. Nor does the word 'peeved' begin to describe my state of mind.

In my humble, perhaps myopic opinion, there is something infinitely pretentious about rock bands using classical musicians or symphony orchestras. It's as if they're trying to say, 'Hey, our stuff is not really just boofheaded rock'n'roll, and the fact we've hired those cellists over there, who are dressed in black evening wear and actually reading from music sheets, proves it.' I remember, when the Eurythmics were still the

Tourists, Annie Lennox and co. appearing on some TV show in England. Midway through their New Wave number, out shuffles an ageing geezer with a herringbone coat, walrus whiskers, a French horn, and a bemused expression. He takes centre stage and starts bleating a tune that doesn't seem to bear much relation to the song, while Annie dances off to one side, tossing her head around and really getting into the whole groove. The poor man keeps glancing around, wondering if he should continue playing or stop and shuffle off again. But Annie urges him on because the whole pop/classical fusion vibe is just so amazing, you know?

And so our contribution to the Wingham Brush Music Festival ended with a honking of brass and some weedy, bespectacled stranger trilling on a recorder during 'Born To Be Wild'. Yes, a recorder. Like the ones you used to have to play at primary school. Thanking the stunned crowd – 'You've been great, Wingham. Enjoy the other bands. Seeya!' – we repaired to the hessian enclosure, where the festival's pervading atmosphere of peace and harmony was somewhat tarnished by two of the four Spuds staging an impromptu wrestling bout. We'd barely filed down the steps before Dale shouldered past me and leaped on Ian's back, knocking him to the ground. As we looked on in shock, he rained blows on Ian, who reacted instantly and squirmed around so he could return fire. From outside, this brouhaha must have looked cartoonish, the hessian walls bulging and billowing as my bandmates scuffled within, though it was difficult to see the funny side at the time. With the help of the security guard and several other astonished musos, we managed to separate them.

Dale was incensed. 'I've had a gutful of you running this show,' he spat through a bleeding lip as we hauled him off Ian.

'It's not your band. You fuckin' check with us before you get people up to play.' Shrugging us off, he rounded on the assorted hippie troubadours who only a minute or so before had been congratulating themselves on a good night's work.

'You lot, fuck off! Take your fucking recorders and flutes and any piccolos you might have hidden in your filthy fucking hippie rags and fuck right off, before I shove them up your fucking arses! Go on, mate, if you don't want that trumpet wrapped round your fucking neck. Piss *off*!'

Pacifists that they were, the hippies all left without so much as a word or a glance. As they parted the flap, I saw curious faces straining to see what the commotion was all about.

While I didn't condone Dale's actions, I was with him one hundred per cent when it came to the general thrust of his argument. It was bad enough having drunken patrons approach you in pubs every week asking if they could get up and sing a Chisel number, or having people swipe the set list from under your mic stand and pass it around for general consensus – 'Don't play that next one. It's shit. Play these two down here.' Now we were having our gigs hijacked by recorder-wielding ferals in pantaloons. It probably sounds petulant, but *we* did the hard work. *We* sweated away in rehearsals. It was *our* show. Dale was right, Ian was way out of line.

Naturally, I didn't have the gumption to voice this opinion, certainly not as vociferously as Dale had. Not when Ian was panting on his haunches, staring wildly at us. Terry shook his head in disgust. 'Fuck this,' he muttered. 'See you guys later. I'm out of here.' He vanished through the flap and into the crowd. Dale followed moments later, his jacket and shirt skew-whiff, Gail shooting murderous looks over her shoulder at Ian as they left. And I stood there listening to the muffled thump of the Bliss Bombs playing on the other side of the truck, wondering if my rock'n'roll career had suddenly and abruptly come to an end.

🎧

Not quite. The Love Spuds split soon after, Dale phoning to say he'd accepted a position as an apprentice jeweller in Sydney, but not before we played one last show at Jaxons. Relations were still frosty between the two guitarists, but with only one night to go they decided to put their differences aside and get through the gig without any altercations.

If this were a film, the club in this scene would be crammed with saddened fans wanting to see us off in style. There would be tears and there would be lovingly rolled joints thrown onto the stage, and the crowd would beg us not to disband. In the event, it was an unremarkable evening. A fair to middling crowd, for whom we were peripheral to the chief concerns of getting pissed and cracking on to members of the opposite sex. An unremarkable evening, that is, apart from the arrival of two members of the Angels – the bald guy and the drummer, from memory – who turned up midway through the show. We had supported them at the RSL earlier in the evening – a perfunctory thirty-minute set – then packed up, scooted to Jaxons, and set up again in time for our main event, the midnight kick-off. They caused quite a stir, taking their place at a table right in the middle of the room, and their gravitational pull sucked the crowd around them. Ian's last great flash of inspiration was to have us play an Angels' number in their honour.

'Here's one for our special guests here tonight,' he said into his microphone, and before any of us could argue he plunged straight into 'We Gotta Get Out Of This Place' (which, to be precise, isn't an Angels song at all, having been originally recorded by the Animals).

There was something so embarrassing, so annoyingly obsequious about playing this number in front of two completely impassive Angels that I cringed inwardly all the way through. I felt as though we were auditioning for them. When it was over, neither responded in any fashion. They just sat there, sipping beers, autographing drink coasters and basking in the adulation of their fawning subjects, who'd overcome their shyness and pulled up chairs. That was rubbing it in, and something clicked in my mind. Two bona fide rock stars were sitting there, right in front of me, no more than ten metres away, and yet there was a gulf between us. A yawning chasm that would never be bridged. For me, it was like looking at a distant star – the celestial variety, I mean – and knowing that the light from it has taken so long to reach Earth that the star itself might no longer even exist in the here and now. Their success radiated in a similar fashion. It had light years to travel. How many times, in how many towns, had these guys wandered into a local shitbox club after a gig and seen some pathetic group of no-hopers tooling away pointlessly? How many times, I wonder, did bands like us fall over themselves to play an Angels cover, hoping to elicit some kind of recognition, to be thrown some morsel of acknowledgement?

How did I feel when it was all over? Was I racked with grief that, as of tomorrow, I would no longer be playing in a band? Well, no, not really. It might sound strange, considering that I'd spent so much time and effort getting to this stage, so to speak, but what I really felt was an overwhelming surge of relief. I think it says something about my tenure as lead singer in the Love Spuds that I was still having to employ my imagination even though I was playing real gigs. Because, in the end, the reality of being in a rock band still bore no relation to my bedroom fantasies. This was a huge disappointment. I realised, even then, that playing covers could only invoke so much enthusiasm in the general public, and although we did the odd show that really cooked, gigs for which we were all on form and fired up, let's face it, how many times can you sing 'Like Wow-Wipeout' before you start to look as bored as your audience?

I didn't want to admit it, even to myself, but I was already, after less than twelve months, growing tired of waking up with my hair and clothes reeking of stale cigarette smoke and my throat sore from screaming. And I was tiring of RSL clubs and bowling clubs, tiring of their uniform dowdiness and the endless jangling and demented chirping of poker machines. Tiring of their greyness, their gaudy drabness, and the older drunk men who would berate us for wearing singlets while we lugged enormous speakers up the stairs, and who would go on endlessly about how they knew people who had fought and died so that we could have freedom. But not the freedom to wear singlets while lugging enormous speakers, apparently.

Even though fifteen years have passed since the demise of the Spuds, there are songs I still can't stand to hear on the radio. They are forever dulled, wrung dry, because I had to sing them dozens and dozens of times. I sang them until the words no longer held any meaning (not that most of them were exactly gravid with meaning in the first place). I would miss the money, sure, but that would be about it – in the short term, anyway.

Long after the crowd had gone and the two Angels had wandered off without even speaking to us, we sat amid the tangled leads and the partially disassembled drum kit and toasted ourselves. Caught up in the moment, Ian and Dale even hugged. Terry clapped me on the back and thanked me for taking care of his kit on all those occasions. 'Money well spent,' he laughed. And me? I smiled and drained my beer, and wondered if there was any sadder place than an empty club at four in the morning.

However . . . There's nothing quite like cavorting onstage with half a dozen near-naked women to rekindle your interest in the rock'n'roll lifestyle.

Let me put you in the picture. It's barely three months since the Love Spuds went their separate ways. Already I'm itching to sing again. (Maybe rock singing is like giving birth; you keep doing it because you forget the pain.) I'm fronting a new band at the Taree RSL. It's called Free Enterprise, which, after life in a group named after a vegetable with amorous intentions, seems just a tad unimaginative. In point of fact, I am only the part-time singer. The drummer Nev normally handles the vocals because the bulk of the band's appointments are weddings, birthdays and bush dances. They'll play everything from Steve Miller to 'Strip The Willow', depending on the crowd. They only call me in when they think they need a young buck out front to put on a bit of a show and drag down the average age.

This was just such an occasion. And as we crash into the first chorus of 'Honky Tonk Woman', my current girlfriend Belinda and five of her most nubile young friends appear from the wings clad in the briefest of raunchy underwear – teddies, stockings, suspenders, and high-heels. A parade of silk, satin and lace. As I watch them come out, I can hardly believe my eyes. They look incredible. As planned, they pout and slink and shake and strut and grind and tease and run their hands through their hair, in a performance which can only be described as inspired. (Well, it could be variously described, but inspired will do.) During the second verse, they each choose a band member to rub themselves against like affectionate felines, and the net result of so many barely concealed bums in such close proximity is one or two bum notes and bass stutters.

Belinda is giving me some extra-special attention. Her tongue is in my ear and I'm thrumming with lust. Bruce, our lead guitarist (and Nev's uncle), doesn't quite know what to make of it all. But then, Bruce is fifty-five. I'd warrant the only G-string he's ever seen is the one on his guitar. He's standing there in his sharply pressed fawn slacks and short-sleeved casual shirt, trying to concentrate and keep a straight face as a nineteen-year-old brunette rakes her fingers through what remains of his receding grey hair. I look at Chris (rhythm guitar, early thirties, married, two kids), who is in the process of having his shirt unbuttoned from behind by a girl who is grinding her pelvis into his backside. His grin is so wide, I fear his jaw might unhinge and the top of his head flip open.

The RSL audience has never seen anything quite like it. There is a crush of men at the front of the stage, a mosh pit in the days before mosh pits. They leap on each other, not so much jostling as wrestling for a better position, driven on by inguinal surges. They reach out, hoping a shapely, shiny, oiled leg might stray within reach. Some of the lads proffer five- and ten-dollar bills, in the hope our Honky Tonk Women might shed what little attire they possess. When the song finishes, the troupe wave and blow kisses to the drooling crowd and disappear.

The men bellow and roar like penned animals. They stamp their feet and yell for more. It is sheer bedlam. A shame our music has so little to do with it. But from that moment on, we have everyone's attention. There's a current passing through the auditorium. No-one dares leave lest they miss a return of the girls. But the girls will not be back; they have already changed and are exiting quietly through a side door, having agreed to meet me later so I can pay them a few token dollars for their efforts. Just before she leaves, Belinda catches my eye from the wings and blows me a kiss. She is now wearing jeans and a jumper which, for some hard-to-fathom reason, has been knitted in the design of a giant packet of cheese Twisties. One of her friends grabs her arm and she is gone.

There were those who claimed later that what they had witnessed was an outrageous, outdated, sexist, misogynistic display. A cheap, cynical, crass method of gaining people's attention while simultaneously pandering to the male ego. To those people I say an unqualified, 'Yep.' Although I prefer to view it as a savvy piece of marketing. I mean, we're talking about a band with arguably the most staid name in rock music history. You couldn't have done much worse had you actually called the group Billy Yawn and the Quite Boring Fellows. Or the Quick Nap. And poor old Bruce, as nice a man and as good a guitarist as he was, didn't exactly embody the quintessential rock'n'roll image. We needed something to pep things up. And the girls were it. The perfect tonic.

Convincing them to perform had been surprisingly easy. Very little persuasion had been required. I tentatively broached the subject with Belinda, flinching occasionally in case she slapped me mid-sentence. She munched on an apple, shrugged and said, 'Yeah, why not? Might be a laugh.' A few phone calls were all it took to assemble their ensembles. I'd suggested they wear swimwear or aerobic gear. It was Belinda who said, 'Let's go all out. Really turn the place on its head.'

It turned out to be a one-off performance. My Hugh Hefner-like vision of the girls becoming an integral part of the show, garnering publicity and whipping crowds into foaming frenzies all over the north coast, was not to be. There was a substantial backlash led, it will not surprise you to learn, by long-time RSL members who, apart from objecting to guys lugging gear in singlets, also appeared to have it in for girls parading around in their unmentionables. The bounds of good taste had been trampled. They were joined by a chorus of women who had been forced to watch that night as their boyfriends descended into savagery right there on the auditorium dancefloor. Whisky wasn't the only thing on the rocks that steamy Friday night.

Free Enterprise never again attained those dizzy, lace-frilled heights. Well, not with *moi* around, at any rate. More and more shows happened without me as the wedding and 21st-birthday bookings started to outstrip the pub and club gigs. Only occasionally would I be summoned, like the Caped Crusader, and off I'd roar to front a show at Wingham Ex-Services or some other beer den.

I don't mean to make it sound as if I were rescuing the band or anything like that. It's just that the calls usually came at the last minute, on the day of the gig sometimes, and I'd have to suddenly drop whatever else I was doing. The sporadic nature of these appearances didn't really faze me, though. I was grateful for the chance to perform, happy to just turn up and turn on. All care taken but no responsibility. And I enjoyed listening to Chris who, during the breaks, would regale us with sad and sorry tales of playing in bands in Sydney. The mere fact he'd played in the Big Smoke lent him an aura. He'd spent several years playing in a band with two of his brothers, doling out original compositions to half-empty houses. I can't remember the band's name, but one of their songs bore the unforgettable title 'Frank, I Can't Toss Salad', which fascinated me no end. That single song title made Sydney seem so sophisticated. In Taree, or any of the other regional centres dotted along the coast, you wouldn't get away with playing a song called 'Frank, I Can't Toss Salad'. Not unless the Choirboys had recorded it first. Only in the city could that happen, a place where people would happily shell out to see bands do stuff they'd never heard. It hadn't all been beer and skittles, though. Well, there'd actually been quite a lot of beer, gallons of it, in fact, but skittles were most definitely in short supply. Chris told horrifyingly funny stories of dismal failure and rejection. At one inner-city pub the manager paid them in full after just one number and asked them to pack up and leave because they were scaring away his pokie crowd. Another time they played to a room devoid of people other than their mixer, who promptly set the levels, made sure the boys were sounding good, and left as well.

'Ah, rock'n'roll,' Chris said, draining his beer as we laughed. 'Those were the days.'

After Free Enterprise, there was a variety of short-term, ill-fated 'projects'. Bands that could never quite get it together enough to play in public. In the late '80s I found myself trapped in a cycle of echoing bedlam in drafty hired halls; long nights locked away in rundown rehearsal rooms with slices of sound-sopping foam stapled to the walls, which vibrated with the dampened thump of other bands in neighbouring rooms.

For all the rehearsing, nothing much ever happened in the way of bookings. One band I was in, the Tennis Ladies, had a date at another outdoor festival but the lead guitarist made a mistake with the time. We arrived an hour and a half after we were supposed to go on, and the furious organisers refused to wedge open the program to make room for us. The lead guitarist, acutely aware that he was responsible for this fiasco, yelled at them for a while, then, amazingly, burst into tears. The Tennis Ladies never did play a fixture.

It was moments like that I appreciated what the Love Spuds and Free Enterprise had achieved. They might have recycled the same old songs ad nauseam, but at least they were organised enough to do it. I was beginning to realise that that in itself was a feat.

The Ripchords was the only other band able to muster the necessary savvy to put together a list of songs *and* organise a few paying gigs. The bass player, a guy called Robbo, even went as far as getting himself tattooed because he felt it would help with the image. A leering skull surrounded by hellfire was duly carved into the meat of his right shoulder. The tattoo bled and festered copiously for a few days. Blood trickled like demon tears from the empty eye sockets, and it made us retch to look at it. At its first outing, the skull was hidden beneath a white wad of cotton bandaging, somewhat spoiling the effect Robbo was striving for.

Robbo also invested in a radio-controlled bass. Suddenly he was no longer tethered to his amp by a lead, and Robbo roamed freely. Sometimes a little too freely, and too frequently. He was like an irrepressible pet, we just couldn't seem to keep him on the stage. He was always wandering off. You'd turn around and he'd be gone. Sometimes he'd stroll over to the bar and buy a drink – mid-song, mind – and stand there sculling and playing at the same time. Or he'd burst into the men's toilet, plucking away, and startle those lined up at the urinal, causing one or two mishaps and wayward aims. One night a busload of women on a hens' night descended on the pub, and when the bus pulled out again a couple of hours later, Robbo was on board, playing to a gaggle of giggling admirers.

The Ripchords was one of two bands hired to play at a party for a chapter of bikers. The stage – once again – was an open-sided semitrailer parked in the middle of a field. Beside it were parked row upon row of gleaming bikes. It was a bitterly cold Saturday night in August. Wraiths of fog swirled around our knees, and dew from the long grass soaked through our shoes and froze our toes. We were so cold we almost envied the pigs in the marquee, slowly rotating on their spits over glowing coals.

The bikers seemed unperturbed by the conditions, but then again they were encased in creaking leather, and their untamed facial hair kept the icy wind from their cheeks. The cold was such that my jaw seized up and I found it difficult to sing. I couldn't make my mouth work. Not that it mattered, because the band was so loud I don't think anyone could hear me anyway. The Ripchords wound the levels right up that night, figuring that the target audience wanted volume. A lumbering version of Led Zeppelin's 'Rock And Roll' drifted out across the field like a sudden storm, bringing the bikers reeling out of the marquee, spinning and jumping and stamping flat the grass in front of the stage.

We finished our set to tumultuous applause and made way for the lone stripper, a slender, silicon-chested blonde whose skin had turned blue and veiny from the cold. Braving the conditions, she held nothing back for her rapt audience. Towards the end of her act, she sprayed shaving foam all over her taut body and prised off her glittery G-string. It was apparent, from the ferociously manicured area beneath, that the foam wasn't purely a stage prop.

The second band was in trouble before they even started playing. As we lugged our gear off the stage, they heaved theirs on. Unfortunately their gear included a bank of keyboards. And their owner was wearing a blousy turquoise shirt. A ripple of consternation passed through the bikers. The band played one number, an original. The sound was big, clean and keyboard-driven, like REO Speedwagon, and they were promptly asked to leave. They promptly did so.

Having had our fill of roasted pig and bourbon, we went back on and played the rest of the night. We sounded like a factory production line. We gave them what they wanted and they simply loved us. We played 'Born To Be Wild' three times.

I have a recurring dream. I am up the front at a Rolling Stones concert and we are only moments away from showtime. The lights are down and I am assaulted by ear-piercing whistles. There's a crush of bodies; anticipation has taken on an almost physical presence, a glutinous substance oozing like perspiration from the pores of those around me. I am soaked in it myself, tingling with excitement.

Suddenly a cone of white light illuminates centre stage and the noise reaches new proportions. There's a figure standing in the spotlight, but it isn't one of the Stones. It's a man whose features I can never recall in my waking hours. The sound suddenly ebbs as confusion washes over the stadium. The man raises a microphone to his lips and his voice bellows from the huge black speakers.

'Er, sorry, ladies and gentlemen. I must apologise, but we seem to have a small problem. Unfortunately Mick Jagger has been taken ill and won't be able to perform this evening.'

There is stunned silence, then a cicada-buzz of worried murmuring. The man holds up a hand.

'It's all right, ladies and gentlemen, everything is gonna be all right. Mick's just got the flu. Nothing serious. And the Stones say the show must go on.'

Cheering and applause.

'They still wanna rock you, Sydney. Awwright?'

More cacophonous cheering.

'Now, then. Does anyone here know the words to all the Stones' songs?'

Stunned silence. Then simultaneously several thousand arms are thrown skyward, mine included. The man scans the crowd, eyes sweeping across the throng like searchlights until they come to rest, inevitably, on me.

'You there, sir. Are you sure you know all the Stones' lyrics?'

I nod until my head threatens to topple off my shoulders, my eyes bulging.

'Right then, up you get, my friend. If you could make your way to the stage, please.'

Amid riotous scenes, I am swept forward, hoisted high, passed over the crowd. People are slapping me on the back and cheering me and yelling at me to go for it. I feel numb with shock and excitement. The surreal scene continues, with the man shaking my hand and leading me backstage, my heart pounding, into a labyrinth of darkened tunnels where I'm to 'meet the boys'. I find myself surrounded by towers of steel scaffolding, the stage infrastructure. Roadies and technicians are bustling about, waving torches, the beams glinting off their laminated passes. They yell at each other in a variety of different tongues, all frantic purpose and last-minute desperation. The man is talking to me but I can't quite make out what he's saying.

I look away for a moment, and when I turn back I've lost him. He has simply disappeared, swallowed up in the crowd. In a panic I jostle my way through the backstage team, jumping up and down to see past shoulders, trying to spot the man who is leading me to the Stones' inner sanctum. He is nowhere to be seen. I turn down narrow passages, stumbling deeper and deeper through black-curtained alleyways. I can still hear the muffled roar of the 50 000-strong crowd, but now there is no-one around. I am alone, wandering around lost.

At this point I usually wake up. I've had this dream maybe a dozen times and I've never once made it onstage. Hell, I've never actually got around to even meeting the Stones. I get separated and lost every time.

This dream is, of course, a most basic adolescent fantasy. Unfortunately I am in my thirties. I'm not sure how Carl Jung or Sigmund Freud would interpret the fact that I never quite make it onto that chimerical stage. Something must be festering away beneath the surface, something interesting going on in my scarred psyche that prevents me from fulfilling my dreams, even in my dreams.

The reason I'm telling you all this is that sometimes, for the select few, this dream comes true. In fact, it is precisely how virtuoso guitarist Mick Taylor hooked up with blues legend John Mayall in 1965. Taylor was at a London gig, waiting to see his idol perform, when it was announced that Mayall's lead guitarist – some bloke called Eric Clapton, apparently – was a last-minute scratching. Believe it or not, John Mayall simply came on and asked if anyone in the audience could play guitar. (Can you imagine that happening today? Bono coming on and saying, 'Sorry, Edge is feeling a bit peeky. Anyone out there play any of our stuff?') Taylor was chosen from the drove and, thanks to his prowess, spent the next four years touring the world with Mayall's seminal band, the Bluesbreakers.

In 1969 Taylor left Mayall and joined the Stones, replacing a drug-hoovering, non-functioning Brian Jones. Taylor was just nineteen, a reed-thin, angelic-looking innocent with a baby face, a studious expression and a halo of golden hair. The six years he spent with the band are usually referred to as the Golden Years, the era in which the Stones recorded their best albums. He shocked everyone by resigning in 1974, leaving the fold to embark on a solo career which has, for the most part, bumped along the bottom.

On 11 August 1990 Mick Taylor came to Coffs Harbour, where I was then living. He was touring Australia on the back of a new live album, and, to my pant-peeing disbelief, the man John Mayall had literally plucked from obscurity, the man who, the year I was born, debuted with the Stones in front of more than half a million people in London's Hyde Park, was now poised to play the Coffs Harbour Hotel Motel, or the Hoey-Moey, as it was known, in those days a frayed beer barn with a rough reputation. After the initial excitement had worn off, I felt vaguely depressed on Mick's behalf. Imagine, one minute being at the pinnacle of rock superstardom, a demigod, and the next playing a pub in a New South Wales resort town.

By this time I'd left the newspaper and the Music Scene spread far behind. I was now a television journalist at a regional station, covering the requisite mix of local stories – the annual show, the courts, car accidents, the machinations of the local council, weekend football, various mutant fruit and vegetables, and, on this particular occasion, an ex-Rolling Stone hitting town.

At this point I was being gently, almost imperceptibly prodded towards maturity. I'd recently met a woman called Gabby and we'd started living together. Gabby was a few years older than me, a former trophy-brandishing bodybuilder. Her formidable muscles had thankfully subsided, becoming firm curves. She had travelled extensively, especially through Asia, and introduced me to tofu, tempeh and stir-fry. She too was passionate about music, but not the music I was passionate about. Her all-time favourite band was the Alan Parsons Project, an out-fit I considered unbelievably pompous and overblown, a relic from the truly dreadful progressive-rock movement of the '70s. Entire album sides given over to guitar solos and sweeping orchestral arrangements. Gabby loved the themed albums, *I, Robot* (based on the works of Isaac Asimov) and *Tales of Mystery and Imagination* (inspired by Edgar Allan Poe). It was during this time, I suppose, that I learned a little tolerance and acceptance. I loved the fact that Gabby was passionate about music. That was something I could understand. In the end it didn't really matter what music it was, just as long as she didn't play too much of it while I was around.

In return, Gabby tolerated my posters. I was at a difficult stage, in many ways still straddling that gulf between teenager and full-blown adult. My idea of knock-out interior design was a laminated poster of Keith Richards wearing a T-shirt with 'Who the fuck is Mick Jagger?' on it; one of Jagger himself clad in red- and white-striped doeskin tights; and an enormous, slightly torn poster advertising the Byron Bay Blues Festival, which I'd peeled from a hoarding after a late-night drinking session.

These I lovingly unrolled and stuck up on the walls of our rented house, where they floated incongruously next to Gabby's Nepalese Gurkha knife, Tibetan wall hangings, and rainforest photo series. Tricky times, indeed. We were experiencing a clash of cultures, of sorts. Gabby bore the visual pollution in teeth-grinding silence, and waited patiently for my tastes to develop beyond those of an acne-ridden adolescent.

I should also tell you that, musically speaking, there was precious little happening in my life at this time. Long gone were the days when playing in bands earned me more than my day job. Just about the only time I held a microphone now was when I conducted an interview for a news story. For a while I did what I mistook for a regular guest spot with a band that played at the pub where the TV crew congregated to become inebriated on Friday nights. The band, Hank and the Johnnies, covered the Stones' 'Miss You', and normally the lead guitarist – a camera operator at the station – would announce me. 'Right, where's Griffo, then?' he might say. Or, 'Oi! Get up here, Griffo. We're gonna do "Miss You".' Then one night I was drinking and talking to someone when I heard the opening bars. Oh well, no intro tonight, I thought. I excused myself and was confidently making my way towards the stage when the band's regular lead singer started singing, moaning about how he'd been waiting on a call from his lost lover and how a friend had phoned instead wanting to organise some Puerto Rican girls to come over and cheer him up.

I was on the dancefloor by this time and, burning with embarrassment, had to pretend I'd come up to dance. It was the only option. I had to make it look as if I'd never expected to sing, that I didn't, in any way, take their gracious permission for granted. I couldn't just turn around and walk back, that would look bad. And the toilets were at the opposite end of the bar, so I couldn't swerve away at the last minute, pretending I was making for the gents'. There being only five other people on the floor, I was unable to hide in the throng, so I put in a couple of achingly self-conscious minutes shuffling around by myself, giving the band little thumbs-up gestures, indicating my delight and approval of their rendition. Then I quietly slipped back to my table where my colleagues, who had seen through my pretence, greeted me with derisive laughter.

Recently, during the throes of moving house, I discovered

the dusty videotape on which had been recorded my interview with Mick Taylor. On the back is a sticker with the pencil inscription 'Mick Taylor interview. Hold for Griffo'. Not having watched the tape for some eleven years, it came as something of a shock when I did now. I must be honest and say I wish it had remained buried at the back of the cupboard. At the end of it I had a headache from having winced all the way through.

For a start, there's the shock of seeing my 1990 self. I'm wearing a black suit jacket over an open-necked white shirt. My mid-length hair, the perm long-since grown out, is immaculately coiffed, parted on one side and swept back at the rear into what look like folded wings. Thankfully I have my back to the camera for the most part. The few flashes of my face show fresh, boyish features as yet untarnished by time. God, but I look young. I do, however, recognise the look in my eyes. I am beyond nervous. This is brown-trousers time and no mistake.

Across from me Taylor sits sucking on a cigarette. Time *has* done some panel-beating work on him. I remember being taken aback when he walked in, schooner of Guinness in hand – the golden-haired, guitar-wielding Botticelli angel I'd seen in so many photos and videos now looking more like Worzel Gummidge. He's wearing a battered old pinstripe coat over a pale blue shirt, which in turn is only partially buttoned up over a white T-shirt. The curly blond halo of hair has been replaced by a nondescript reddish-brown do, longish at the back, flopping at the front. His fresh, cherubic features, reminiscent of James Spader, have been weathered and dragged down by time and gravity. A layer of fat has been fitted over his face like a latex mask. He arranges his thickened frame in the cheap vinyl armchair and blows blue smoke, which almost obliterates him in the shot.

'Oh. Sorry 'bout that.' Taylor waves the smoke away and we all laugh. My laugh is more of a bray, a little too long and loud. Taylor looks at the floor.

We've strategically placed a potted palm in the background, our idea of set dressing. A few fronds claw at the back of Mick's head. Other than that, the wall behind him is bare, glaring white under the camera lights.

The ensuing interview is singular proof that rock music fans should never, *never*, be allowed to interview the objects of their obsession. The only people who should be employed in the music press are those demonstrably uninterested in the topic. It might, in that way, be possible to avoid the kind of fawning, gibbering idiocy which came to pass on this occasion.

When the camera operator is finally ready and gives me the nod to start, I stun even myself with this gambit: 'Mick, looks like you haven't had much sleep, mate. Been a rough journey?'

I had no idea I was going to say that. If nothing else, it jolts Taylor out of his torpor. But then, being told you look like shit will have that effect. None of your 'So Mick, welcome to Australia. How's the tour going, mate?' stuff here. Even as the words issued like vomit from my mouth, I remember thinking, Why am I saying this?

Taylor struggles to regain his composure. In a distinctly defensive tone, he talks about how there was an extra show in Japan, a sellout, and how that made it tight getting to Australia in time for two shows in Brisbane and one on the Gold Coast, and that, basically, he's jetlagged and weary and tonight will be his fifth show in as many days, and what do you expect? His voice, although ravaged by fatigue and cigarettes, is warm and mellow, like good whisky. Mine, on the other hand, sounds high-pitched and slightly strangled. The lite beer of voices.

Nerves aside, after Taylor's English burr, my accent is pure nasal Strine. I'm speaking incredibly fast. The words trip and tumble over themselves in their haste to evacuate my mouth, which continues to declare itself a disaster area.

Question two is actually a statement: 'Pardon my ignorance, but it seems to have taken you a long time to get over the Stones and get your own career rolling.' That is my translation. What Mick actually hears is: 'Pardonmyignorance buiseemstohatakenyoualong,er,longtimeto,youknow,geoverthe Stonesangetyorowncareer,er,youknowrolling.'

Once he's deciphered what I've said, Mick's jowly face splits in a wry smile. 'That's not ignorant. That's quite perceptive, actually.' (I don't think he means that about me being perceptive. I think he's taking the piss.) 'It did take me a long time and there's a lot of reasons for that. One reason is that I'm quite lazy by nature, and for a long time I was content to just make occasional records with other people. Bob Dylan, you know, people like that. But I did start to get fed up with that about four years ago, and I really did have a strong desire to form my own band, which is something I've always wanted to do, but never actually done it. And since I have, things have been going very well.'

Taylor, understandably enough, is keen to talk about his current tour and album. I'm aware of this because his publicist told me. 'Don't pester him with questions about the Stones, yeah?' he said. 'He gets a little fed up with that. It's like ancient history, you know?'

So with great effort I ask a few perfunctory questions about the tour, but there are two factors at work. First and foremost, obviously, is my Stones passion. I have been granted a brief audience with someone who, in a past life, was actually in my all-time favourite band. No force known to man can prevent me from probing him about that period. The second factor at work is my newly acquired journalistic pragmatism. A story on Mick Taylor is only a story because he was once in the Stones. He might be a bloody good guitarist but it's the Stones connection that people are interested in. And so we wend our way towards the inevitable.

'Do you feel you live in the shadow of the Stones?' I ask after a while. 'That it doesn't matter what you do, people will always say, There's the bloke who left the Rolling Stones?'

Taylor shifts his weight and his answer sounds, to me, like a well-worn mantra. 'Well, I don't feel that I do. I'm not affected by the fact that I was once in the Rolling Stones, because it was such a long time ago. It seems like a different life. But other people tend to view me that way. When I first started doing this, I would say half of the audience came because I was an ex-Rolling Stone, and the other half came because I was a good guitar player. It's different these days. Most of the people who come to most of the shows come primarily because they want to see a good blues show, basically.'

Having said all that, he admits to pulling out a fair few Stones numbers during his shows, just to keep the crowd happy. Does he have any favourite tracks? I ask, and it is here that any professional demeanour I might have possessed slips and shatters at my feet.

'I do a version of "You Gotta Move",' Taylor says, 'which I think is from . . .' He looks at the ceiling, groping back over the years for the right album title. 'I *think* it's on *Exile on Main Street*.'

'*Sticky Fingers*, actually,' I say, not even a nanosecond later, pouncing on his mistake like an annoying A-grade school student with their arm permanently shot skyward. Once again the words have prised apart my lips and jumped out before I know what's happening. My tone is one of shocked amazement. *How the fuck could you forget that?*

An expression scuds across Taylor's face. It's brief, only a shadow, but I can read it. It's a look of glum realisation. He's not dealing with just another impassive journo sent to cover a story on him, but a full-blown, rabid Stones fan. Who else would spot a mistake like that?

'Is it? Oh. Right. Well, my memory's not that good,' he says with a resigned smile, eyes once more downcast.

As I watch the old tape, a line from *Macbeth* pops into my head and it seems to apply to the interview. Something to the effect that, having waded so far in this mess, turning back now would be as tedious as going on. Of course, Shakespeare put it a little more eloquently, but that's the general idea. With my cover now well and truly blown, I drop all pretence and launch myself into a full-scale frenzy of Stones-related questioning. The banality of the depths to which I sink is staggering.

'What is Keith Richards like?'

'He's a very difficult man to get to know, and I wasn't very close to him for a long time, but now I think he's the Stone I'm closest to.'

On I go, listing each Rolling Stone one by one, asking Mick for his take on his former bandmates. He appears to have surrendered by this time. Lighting another cigarette, he wilts into the creaking vinyl and rubs his forehead. He knows there is no escape from his past.

'There are seventeen-year-old guitarists going round,' I say, 'and music's a very hard business to break into –'

'It's even harder now,' Mick interjects.

'Exactly. And they would be saying, Why on earth would a guy get into the world's greatest rock band and quit?' I sound like a fussing mother scolding a child for spilling a drink.

Taylor sighs. 'Because things were different back then, people didn't think that way. I certainly didn't. I'd never been involved with the Rolling Stones from the beginning, anyway. And although I contributed a lot to making good and success-ful records during the six years I was with them, I didn't really feel fulfilled as a musician or as a creative artist, because it didn't allow me enough freedom to develop as an individual, you know? So, for me it wasn't really a hard decision to leave. Remember, before I was with the Stones I spent four years tour-ing the States and Europe with John Mayall's Bluesbreakers, so I've always viewed my career as being separate from any one group, however famous or successful it might be.'

As bad as it is, the interview seems even more woeful and cringeworthy in the light of information I've gleaned in the years since I met Mick Taylor. Information which, I have to say, sheds a somewhat unflattering light on life as a Rolling Stone. Taylor was regularly refused a writing credit on songs he'd helped craft, and so missed out on a larger royalty cut. Keith Richards was reportedly hostile towards his co-guitarist, con-stantly belittling and humiliating him in front of the other Stones. Taylor would often lay down tracks for a song, or record experimental parts, only to have Richards come in later and wipe the tapes. Lost and alienated in the Stones whirlpool, he took up heroin and slowly spiralled, until his wife begged him to get out while he was still alive. Years after leaving the band, Taylor was listening to a new Stones album and heard one of his own scorching solos, recorded half a decade previously, blis-tering the vinyl, uncredited and unpaid for. He had to sue to receive his royalties. To top things off, during one of his subsequent lean periods, Taylor decided to auction off the gold record he received for the Stones' *It's Only Rock'n'Roll*. It went for the grand total of seventy-five pounds.

And yet here was I, 'Gee whizz'-ing and 'Golly gosh'-ing my naïve way through our interview, chiding him for turning his back on the band. That he didn't clock me one and storm out is retrospectively impressive. Likewise his refusal to dump on his former colleagues. He doesn't have a bad word to say about them, not even when I ask the chestnut about whether they're getting a little too old to rock'n'roll.

'Back in the '60s, when all these bands were getting together and I was growing up and learning how to play guitar, we never thought it would be a lifelong thing,' Taylor says, lighting another cigarette. 'I mean, music should be a lifelong career and there's no reason why it shouldn't. But because we were young, I think we thought when our youth was over the music would be over too, and that no-one would be interested in it any more. But in fact it's turned out to be the opposite of that. If you make good music, then people are interested, no matter what age group it is. The only thing I can compare it to is people like Frank Sinatra, or B.B. King, or Sammy Davis Jnr. Anyone who's made a lifelong career in the entertainment business. Age has very little to do with it.'

After a plethora of other hard-hitting gems (Q: 'What was it like playing your first gig with the Stones?' A: 'Bloody nerve-racking.'), the interview ends as it began. Which is to say, on a fairly low point.

'Have there been times when you've looked back at your leaving the Stones, and thought, Bad move, Mick?'

Taylor smiles. It's a strange smile. Part rueful, part sarcastic.

His eyes twinkle, as if I'd just said something outrageously funny.

'Oh, a couple of times, yeah. Cuppla times.'

1990 was a good year for visiting blues maestros. Buddy Guy and Albert King also hit town. The latter was a very old man. A very old, very tall man. He flew into Coffs Harbour airport and had already wedged his enormous frame into the rear of a black limousine when I arrived, cameraman in tow. Breathlessly I raced across the carpark and more or less threw myself through his open window. I panted a request for an interview, and the big gnarled bluesman surveyed me impassively from behind black sunglasses. Then he growled tersely, 'S'pose so. Only wish you'd aksd me afore ah got mahself in this fuckin' car.' He unfolded his long, creaky limbs and climbed out again, a lengthy process accompanied by much puffing, grunting and cursing.

King was your classic crabby old man. That night, in front of a surprisingly packed house at the Sawtell RSL, he shambled onstage still dressed in the same clothes he'd been wearing at the airport, grumped his way through a couple of numbers, and then threw a spectacular tantrum. I was right up the front, of course, and noticed that he kept cupping his hand behind his ear, gesturing to his foldback speaker and pointing skyward, signalling that he couldn't hear himself and that his level needed to be turned up. He repeated the signal several times, and his gestures became more stabbing and violent on each occasion. I glanced back over my shoulder, peering through the crowd to where the besieged mixer twiddled knobs in vain, looking bemused. Eventually he shrugged his shoulders. He had no other tricks up his sleeve. Either he was going mad or Albert King was going deaf. It has to be said, the latter option was the more likely.

King's fuse burned low. Suddenly, in the middle of a song, he stopped singing and playing, waved impatiently at his backing band to stop, and yelled into the microphone, 'For the last fuckin' time, TURN THIS FUCKER UP!'

The crowd loved it. We'd never seen anything like it. King's petulance was rewarded with wild applause and cheering. After a minute or so, the towering bluesman resumed playing. Just a few bars later, before our disbelieving eyes, his guitar strap came loose and the instrument smashed onto the stage with a huge, deafening, discordant *KER-RUNG*. We cheered again. We hollered. This was the best show we'd ever seen. King muttered, 'Fuck this,' into the mic and stormed offstage, leaving his guitar face down on the boards and his band playing to a clamorous auditorium. Looking confused, they chugged through an extended, lyricless groove, while we chanted, 'Al*bert*!' and slow-clapped.

Rock audiences are a strange, masochistic breed. They are infinitely forgiving, and actually seem to enjoy being treated shoddily. It almost makes me wonder if these histrionics weren't part of the King repertoire, a tool for whipping crowds into a frenzy. Fifteen minutes or so later, when the anticipation had reached a delicious, unbearable level, King finally returned to the stage, acknowledged the rapturous hollering, and finished the gig. Afterwards, not one person claimed they felt ripped off. On the contrary, they were ecstatic. It's not every day you see a blues legend completely lose it. That alone was worth the price of admission. The fact he'd played one or two songs was a bonus. It's true, you know. I couldn't have been more thrilled if he'd beaten me with a large branch. And although I remember that gig as if it were yesterday, I cannot recall one single, solitary song. What a performer!

Buddy Guy's concert, at the same venue, was more conventional, though no less exciting. At times, Buddy's polka-dotted guitar seemed to have a life of its own. It chimed, it clucked, it wheedled, it teased, it berated. He squeezed excited squeals out of it. He made it growl. One minute he was wringing from it strings of cheeky, chuckling notes, the next he was sawing a splintered drumstick across the strings, making it scream like a punk violin. In the demeanour stakes, Buddy had Albert King beaten hands down. He grinned like an excited schoolboy all night, and Buddy Guy's grin is a sight to behold. The bottom half of his face was all teeth, a jaw full of large, white enamel tablets. Set into a front tooth was an enormous, glittering diamond, its facets twinkling under the hot white stagelights.

I'd interviewed Buddy earlier that day. He seemed perplexed by the fact that his hotel boasted a large windmill, of the Dutch variety, and kept asking me about it. Other than that it housed a restaurant, I could tell him little. He was charming and friendly. Mildly surprised, I think, that a local news crew from the Australian boondocks was interested in a blues guitarist from Chicago. I don't remember anything spectacular from our exchanges, but when we'd finished he asked if I planned to come to the show. I told him the tickets were already scorching the leather of my wallet.

'Come backstage after and say hi,' he said. 'I'll let 'em know you're coming.'

This was officially too much. Me? Backstage with Buddy? I couldn't believe it – Mr Guy and I kicking back after a red-hot show, sharing a few beers and talkin' the blues. Then I wondered,

Did he drink beer? Maybe not. What would be his poison? Whisky, most likely. Or bourbon. Yeah, they were more your classic blues beverages.

My imagination was gearing up again. Perhaps luckily, I didn't have much time to dwell on his surprise invitation. It was a frantic day. The Buddy Guy story was just one of several I had to complete for that night's bulletin. On top of everything, the weather girl was on holidays and I was filling in for her. But when, after the gig, I was finally ushered into his dressing room, Buddy Guy greeted me with that thousand-watt grin, shook my hand and said, 'Man, you is one versatile motherfucker. I watched your show tonight. Man, you do news, you do music, you do sport, you do the fuckin' weather. You do *everything*.'

Given that I'd just witnessed one of the greatest gigs I will ever see, I was taken aback. It never occurred to me that Buddy would bother watching the news, let alone be impressed by my humble news-gathering abilities. You always assume the stars you interview have something far better to do than actually look out for themselves on TV. There was something so disarming about the thought of him sitting down and watching not just his bit, but the rest of the local news as well that my vocabulary deserted me.

'Well, er, thanks,' I stuttered. 'Great show. Really fucking great. Thank you.'

'My pleasure. Pleased you enjoyed it.' Buddy beamed. He sat like a monarch in a comfortable chair, his hair clinging to his forehead in sweat-drenched ringlets, and a white towel draped around his neck. Perched on either armrest were two gorgeous black women, maybe a third Buddy's age, arranged in snake-hipped repose. No-one offered me a water, let alone a whisky or a bourbon. After a pause, I said I'd better be going.

'Thanks for coming by,' said Buddy Guy. 'And thanks for the story.'

'No problem.' That was it. I just didn't know what else to say.

Outside, Gabby and I met the bass player from Buddy's band, a weedy, bearded white guy who looked like he'd stepped straight out of a trailer park. He too had seen the story on the news. He thanked me, swigged his beer, turned to Gabby, whose curves were shown off to great effect by a sleek black catsuit, and said, without missing a beat, 'You really with him? Really? Watcha doin' with him?'

I couldn't believe my ears. An ugly, unknown, mangy dog of a bass player, who just happened to be on tour with the greatest bluesman alive, was coming onto my girlfriend, right in front of me. Acting as if I weren't even there. Bizarrely, pathetically, I felt proud. So, Buddy Guy's bass guitarist fancies *my* girlfriend, eh? Well, well, well.

'Yep. She really is, ' I chuckled. 'Can you believe it?'

He laughed too. Well, his mouth laughed. His eyes remained treacherous. 'No, no I can't,' he said.

I said right at the beginning that being a rock music tragic slowly eats away at your dignity. Mine was swallowed whole that night, and somewhere in my mind I thought I heard a satisfied belch as my obsession patted its well-rounded belly.

I did actually get to stand on the Rolling Stones' stage once. It wasn't a dream, either. There were no Rolling Stones on it at the time, unfortunately, just legions of roadies swarming all over the scaffolding, piecing together the giant jigsaw that was the set. But still, I was there, standing right on the spot where a gaffer-taped cross on the floor read 'Mick's mic stand' in black felt tip. I stood there gazing out across the green expanse of the Sydney Cricket Ground, savouring the moment, picturing a rippling tide of humanity stretched out before me. The stage seemed enormous, an impossibly daunting space.

Then, because I simply couldn't control the urge, I broke into 'Start Me Up', put my hands on my hips and did a little Jaggeresque mince across the front of the stage. Roadies stared, a few laughed. My little performance was recorded for posterity on video and made for hilarious viewing back in the *Beyond 2000* edit suite. Me, alone on the Voodoo Lounge set, strutting and posing.

This moment, in 1995, capped off an amazing few days for me. Finally, after all these years, they were here. The Stones were touring Australia for the first time since the early '70s, and they'd brought with them the biggest, most technologically sophisticated rock show in history. For weeks before their arrival, press releases yelled long lists of comical statistics and analogies. 'The Rolling Stones' stage and sound equipment fills twenty-four jumbo jets!' and 'The Voodoo Lounge show uses enough power during a single concert to run a small mid-western town for five years!' and 'The contents of Keith Richards' travelling bar would fill seven Olympic swimming pools!' and 'Mick Jagger's costumes are so loud, they can be seen from space!' That sort of thing. Jokes aside, it was an impressive technological feat. And that's why *Beyond 2000*, the science-and-technology television show I'd been working on for the past two years, leapt onto the media bandwagon.

The Stones' tour manager, a jovial rotund Cockney called Jake Berry, gave me and the camera crew a guided tour of the stage area while it was under construction on the hallowed turf of the SCG. He strode around at a furious pace, clutching a crackling two-way radio into which he barked a steady stream of instructions. Every so often he'd point to large chunks of moulded steel as they swung on cranes over our heads and say, 'See that? Fuckin' 'eavy, that.'

He took us everywhere. Up into a small tower that housed the mixing desk, which wasn't so much a desk as a banquet table, and the lighting area where the computerised light show was being programmed. I spotted a song list taped to a plexi-glass partition and almost erupted with excitement. There they were, all those songs that were ingrained in me, tattooed on my very being, listed one after the other. The lighting engineer explained that because the lighting was automatic there wasn't any room for mid-show spontaneity. 'No good Keith suddenly deciding to do "Satisfaction" if the lights are going for "Ruby Tuesday", is it?' he chuckled, and I chuckled right along with him. No siree, that would be no good at all.

Finally I could resist no longer and asked Jake if he'd mind if I actually got out *on* the stage. 'Be my guest, go right ahead,' he said affably. 'Jus' make sure they don't drop any of the speakers on you. Fuckin' 'eavy, they are.'

He led me to a little tunnel, a gap between black-curtained girders. 'That's the entrance.'

I gulped. 'You mean . . .'

'This is where the Stones will enter,' he said in hushed, reverent tones. 'Leads to the rear of the stage. Up you go, I'll let 'em know you're on your way.' Jake held the two-way to his cheek and warned someone called Johnno that I would be along shortly. ''E's one of the *Beyond Two Fahzand* crew. Yeah, that's right. TV show. 'E's got my okay. Jus' let him be, he's 'avin' a butcher's, awrigh'?'

Up I went, heart in my throat, wending my way between hulking black crates and heaving, sweating roadies. Suddenly the light hit me, the tunnel opened up, and there I was. The SCG, vast and empty, and Charlie's drum riser resting squat beside me. Cables and leads snaked like thick vines across the floor. Above me, suspended on either side of the stage, were two walls of speakers, dozens of empty black maws one on top of the other, waiting to expel gales of sound. Roadies were everywhere, shouting, joking, laughing, grunting, but I didn't really hear any of it. I was completely lost in my own reverie.

For some weeks we'd been trying to secure an interview with Mick Jagger, without much hope. That pessimism proved to be justified, and so the previous week I'd been dispatched to Melbourne, where the Stones were holding their one and only press conference. I would have to take my chances along with the rest of the media pack.

The conference was held at the Melbourne Cricket Ground, in a glassed-in VIP room overlooking the famous oval. At the far end the Voodoo Lounge stage brooded, glinting dully in the sunlight. The Stones' latest CD pumped from a small PA. The room was packed with reporters, photographers and TV cameras; the air hummed with nervous chat and expectation. You could sense the excitement, and again I felt that strange feeling of pride. I'd copped plenty of flak over the years for liking the Stones, but now look at everyone lining up for a piece of the action. Everywhere you went people were talking about the Stones. Even Triple J, which as a youth radio station prided itself on playing new music and ignoring dinosaurs from the past, gave over an entire evening to the Rolling Stones, talking about how amazingly important they were in shaping the course of rock music. Well, *derr*!

Once the Stones touched down in Australia, they were never out of the headlines. Photographers and television cameras staged late-night airport and hotel stakeouts, vigils that resulted only in blurry footage of what might or might not have been a Rolling Stone through a heavily tinted limousine window. There was a civic reception in Melbourne and preposterous front-page photos of Mick Jagger and Charlie Watts sipping wine with the Victorian Premier Jeff Kennett. Around this time I received daily phone calls and messages from people all over the country who were excited on my behalf. They knew how I must be feeling. For a whole fortnight I was swaddled in a strange, warm aura. I floated. It was almost as if the entire thing were being staged solely for my benefit.

Come the press conference, I was in a desperate state. A lather of excitement. I'd barely slept. I felt as if, somehow, my true loyalty must show through. That amid this jostling throng of bandwagon-jumpers and fly-by-night 'fans', I would stand out. That Keith might at some point lock eyes with me, raise a knobbly, skull-ringed finger and say, 'Hey, this cat down here's the real deal, man. He can stay. The rest of you, fuck off.' Their song catalogue was the soundtrack for my life. How could anyone else possibly feel this way, this deeply? (My God, reading that last paragraph back, I realise I've just set down the mental state of your average stalker.)

Only moments before the press conference was scheduled to start, a tall, broad-shouldered man approached me out of the crowd. He had curly, sandy-coloured hair and a booming radio voice.

'Well, bugger me. Anthony Griffis. G'day there. Brett McCormack. Remember? Taree High?'

I was thrown. The man pumped my hand as the gears crunched in my head. I remembered a Brett McCormack, all right, but the Brett McCormack in my head was a short, slight, freckle-faced shy youth whose voice, when he was compelled to use it, put one in mind of a fieldmouse with a sore throat. This stranger was reading my mind.

'Changed a bit since those days, I know,' he laughed, in a voice that sounded like it'd been piped directly from a pair of rockmelon-sized testicles strapped away beneath his black jeans. 'Late bloomer, I suppose. Hey, seen you a few times on *Beyond*. Good stuff, you come across well.'

'Thanks very much,' I said, somewhat preoccupied, stealing glances over one of Brett's meaty shoulders.

'Hey, weren't you nuts about the Stones back at school? Seem to remember you were their number one fan.'

'Yep, that's right. That was me. Still love 'em,' I said, forcing a matey chuckle. The Stones were about to make their entrance any second and I was hopping from one foot to another like an over-excited child. Now was most definitely not the time for playing catch-up with peripheral past acquaintances.

'Er, why are you here? What are you up to these days?' I asked, not in the least bit interested.

Brett pointed to the logo of a radio station on his black T-shirt. 'Became a jock.' His voice was warm honey. He refrained from cupping a hand over his ear as he said it, but otherwise he possessed the full radio announcer manner.

'Really? That's great,' I said. I followed that platitude with an appalling, unthinking, unintentional gaffe. 'I'm amazed. Wouldn't have expected it at all.'

Brett's smile froze. 'What, you think you're the only one allowed to go into the media?' he said darkly, shook his head, and strode off.

I kicked myself, but didn't have time to make amends. A man had suddenly taken to the podium. 'Okay, thanks very much, everyone,' he said. 'Well, the wait is over. It's time. Will you please welcome to Australia, for the first time in more than two decades, ladies and gentlemen, the Rolling Stones!'

A black curtain at the side of the room was swept aside and *they* filed in, to a standing ovation. Camera shutters chattered, flashbulbs flared. After fifteen years of rampant, single-minded dedication, here they were, only a few metres away from me. And my overwhelming impression? They were so *small*. They were short. They looked somehow *delicate*, almost frail. Their bodies were angular and wispy, their limbs scrawny, their faces an assorted scribble of plunging lines and creases. How did these creatures, now seemingly on the verge of extinction, ever manage to become the embodiment of so much sexual out-pouring, to spark so much mayhem and outrage around the world?

I couldn't quite take it all in. As the questions and answers passed, I stared at each Stone, studying the familiar countenances, not frozen in photos, but alive and moving, grinning and laughing in real time. I watched Ronnie Wood's extraordinarily jagged and pointy profile as he whispered something to Charlie Watts. Whatever he said made the dour drummer break into a laugh, his drawn face crinkling with mirth.

Of the questions I remember nothing, save for one journalist who used his alloted slot to say, 'Guys, on behalf of everyone here, I'd just like to say thanks for three decades of unparalleled rock'n'roll.'

Everyone backed this surprise toast with a round of applause, but it was slightly muted, as if they were thinking, You wanker. Even I, despite all my obsessions, almost gagged. The Stones themselves looked vaguely embarrassed. 'Well, er, thank you,' Mick said. 'Thank you very much.'

Then it was my turn. I felt like my vocal cords had become entangled in my throat. 'Er, guys, you've seen many changes in concert technology over the last thirty years. I'd just like to know, how have those changes affected the way you perform?' This question was dictated not by fandom, of course, but by professional requirement. Still, amid the plethora of questions on ticket-pricing, age, retirement and drugs, this one seemed to at least spark some interest among the Stones.

They looked at each other for a second, and Mick fielded the question. My vision blurred at the edges as the world suddenly shrank to a narrow tunnel, with me at one end and Mick at the other. I was being acknowledged. Mick Jagger was looking at me. Talking to *me*. I remember an extraordinary wrinkle, a deep faultline carving the left side of his face from tear duct to jawline.

'You have to perform differently,' he said in his distinctive drawl. 'You have to make bigger gestures, and also your choice of numbers is slightly limited, insofar as you really want to play more of the well-known numbers than you would if you were playing a smaller venue. That's because you've got to outperform the gizmos, so to speak. And not let them overwhelm you. So it's a very fine line, which you've always got to worry about.'

When he'd finished, I said thanks and took my seat. The questions rolled on and I sat there feeling as though I'd emerged from a drugged sleep.

I saw the Stones three times on that tour. Once in Melbourne and twice at home in Sydney. The first time, the night after the press conference, it was almost too much to take in. My eyes were everywhere, scooping up details like a greedy child at a lolly counter. There was so much sensory data, I couldn't process it all. Afterwards I wandered, almost staggered, from the MCG, completely shellshocked, feeling exhausted and mildly depressed in a strange way I couldn't quite put my finger on. So it goes, I suppose, when dreams are finally realised.

In Sydney, two nights later, my brother came with me. We showed the usher our tickets and followed him as he strode off down the centre aisle. Thousands of people milled around, teenagers probably wanting to see what all the fuss was about, legions of greying baby-boomers, and some even older. One woman, whom I would have placed well into her seventies, incongruously wore blue-rinsed hair that had been set for the occasion and a voluminous black Rolling Stones T-shirt, which hung off her scrawny shoulders. The usher kept walking until the stage seemed to loom over us, until I thought I was going to wind up *on* the stage again. When he finally stopped walking, we were only eight rows back. 'Can you believe this?' Darren kept saying. 'Can you fuckin' *believe* this?'

From the first chiming chord, everyone was on their feet,

dancing, clapping, fists pumping the air. I didn't throw myself around too much because I was worried I might miss something if I started tossing my head. I wasn't there to dance, I was there to see the band. I stared, fixated, at the spot where I had stood, a spot now occupied by Jumping Jack Flash himself. Keith, bare-chested, with strange metallic clips like mousetraps dangling from his rat's-nest hair, strode the stage like a grizzled pirate on the deck of his clipper. He came and stood, legs splayed, right in front of us. At which point Darren let out a howl. '*KEEEEEEEEF!*' Everyone was roaring for the haggard Human Riff. Joints rained down all around him. He laughed, looking genuinely touched, scooped one up, and stuck it behind his ear.

Midway through 'Brown Sugar' I suddenly, and quite unexpectedly, found myself in a headlock, my mouth covered by one of Darren's brawny, freckled forearms. My brother's sweat-sheened face was shoved up against the side of my head and he was yelling the words right into my ear canal. Then, just as suddenly, he released his grip, pushed me away, and laughed a huge, excited laugh, slapping me on the back of the head. I laughed too, wiping his perspiration from my lips. A tender moment between brothers.

That night the Stones pulled out a searing version of 'Midnight Rambler'. In the middle of the song Jagger produced a blues harp and the band embarked on an extraordinary jam. They closed ranks, coming together centre stage, playing, it seemed, as much for each other as for us. Jagger's lips and tongue scoured the harp while Keith chopped and wrenched at his pale guitar. It was pure, hardcore blues, tight and stripped down. For a brief time you could forget about the bells and whistles, the enormous stage and lights, the inflatable figures.

They were irrelevant. So too Keith's legendary drug usage and Mick's endless sexual dalliances. We were seeing the real Stones, skinny old white English guys possessed by music, cranking it out with awesome venom. It seemed as though thirty years were channelled into that mid-song jam. This was my moment of singularity, my Lourdes. It was akin to having a religious vision and I was utterly transported. There were tears on my cheeks.

As the concert ended and fireworks thundered in the night sky, casting a smoky pall across the ground, the woman next to me said, 'Oh my God, I'm bloody exhausted. That was so power-ful. Like watching *The Piano* and *Schindler's List* back to back.'

I just looked at her. Lady, I thought, you've got no idea. That doesn't even *begin* to describe it.

At the next night's show Gabby asked me to marry her. The Stones were smack bang in the middle of 'Beast Of Burden' when she swung herself in front of me, held my shoulders, looked long and hard at me, and proposed. I was jolted. I knew right away this wasn't a joke. She meant it. Well, of course she meant it. Why else would she say it if she didn't mean it? I had to get my head together, and fast. Treat the situation with the gravity it deserved.

And so I laughed. 'What?'

Gabby said, 'I'm serious, Anthony.'

'Don't be silly.' My mouth was working way too quickly. My brain couldn't keep up.

'I'm not being silly,' she said, still gripping my shoulders. 'I'm asking you to *marry* me.'

'Well . . . What, you want an answer *now*? Can't we wait and talk about this after the concert? Tomorrow morning?'

'You have to think about it? You've had four years to think about it. You should have some idea by now.'

Feeling flustered and trapped, my anger flared. 'Well, no then. I'm sorry, Gab, but the answer's no.'

She said nothing. Just looked at me, eyes brimming with tears. Then she resumed her seat and started to cry. She was the only person sitting down in the entire stadium. I couldn't decide whether I felt angry, depressed or regretful. Or all three. She'd planned this. She'd thought it through, decided that a Stones concert was the special moment, the moment that would hold the most meaning for me. One part of me thought it was brave and sweet. Another, cynical and angry part of me viewed it not as a thoughtful gesture, but a tactical ploy. A trap. Get me when I'm at my weakest, when I'm so lost in the music that I'll be swept up and carried away. Say yes to anything. Now she'd gone and spoiled the whole night. There was a sour taste in my mouth. My heart was leaden. I'd handled things very, very badly.

Gabby abruptly grabbed her bag and the eighty-dollar T-shirt she'd bought when we'd arrived and left, shouldering her way through the sweaty forest of heaving bodies, fiercely wiping her eyes as she went. I stood for a moment longer, immobile, a waxwork. Everything had taken on an unreal quality. Adolescent fantasy and adult reality had suddenly met head on, like matter and antimatter colliding, and the result was a tangled wreckage. Up on that stage, which glowed like a spaceship, the symbols of my dreamy youth were careering through yet another anthem. Now it almost seemed as if they were mocking me. In light of what had just happened, the fact I was even here, for the third time, somehow made me feel immature and ridiculous. There was another world out there. An adult world where people my age, people like Gabby, got on with adult life and did adult things. Like getting married, buying houses, taking out home and contents insurance. Learning the art of Thai cooking. They didn't spend hundreds of dollars on tickets to see the same rock band three times. That was profligate and childish.

And so I walked out on the Rolling Stones. I followed Gabby, picking my way through the rows, squeezing past happily oblivious concert-goers. As I went by each person, I heard them yelling the lyrics along with Mick, so that every line was delivered by a different voice, male and female, a chorus escorting me to the exit.

Gabby was already getting into a taxi when I caught up with her. For a short while we sat in gravid silence.

'Not much good, eh?' said the driver.

'What?' I asked.

'The Rolling Stones. Not much good?'

I sighed inwardly. How was I going to explain why we'd left early? Then I spotted the path of least resistance and wandered off down it. I heard myself utter words I never thought would pass my lips regarding the Stones. 'Nah. Not really much chop.'

'Bloody overrated, I reckon,' he went on, pleased to have had his suspicions confirmed. 'And that Jagger's a bloody pansy. Sick of hearing 'bout 'em.' He went on, delivering a familiar litany about inflated ticket prices and ageing rock stars who should be in retirement homes.

'Anyway, they're nothin' next to the Beatles,' he concluded, typically. 'Now, *there* was a band.'

'Let me out here, please,' Gabby suddenly said. Her eyes were red.

'Where are you going?' I asked as the taxi speared into the kerb near Oxford Street. Gabby didn't reply. She jumped out, slammed the door, and vanished into the crowd of Sunday night pedestrians.

'Bloody hell. She really didn't like them, did she?' said the driver. 'She's pissed at you for even taking her along.'

Something inside ruptured. 'Mate, just can it,' I snapped.

We crawled through the streets. On the radio, people were phoning in to say how amazing the concert had been. The driver growled something and jabbed the button to change stations. Beside me in the dark I discovered the T-shirt Gabby had left behind in her overwhelming urge to escape. I still have it, somewhere. It's never been worn.

17 September 2000
Four months after Bait's Goulburn gig

It happens like this: Darren, who lives in central western New South Wales, learns that a CD showcasing the area's musicians is being produced. The New South Wales Ministry for the Arts has apparently thrown some cash at the project, under its Rock Music Initiatives program. Anyway, Darren phones the brains behind the scheme, discovers that the selection process is not yet finalised, dashes off a solo composition in just under ten minutes, records it badly on his ageing tape deck, sends the cassette away, and a week or so later receives a call saying they love it, he's in, and he's been booked into a studio to record the song properly. He calls me.

'Get up here, mate. We gotta song to record. We're gonna be on a CD,' he says in a state of breathless excitement.

And so I find myself in the car, pre-dawn on the day after the Sydney Olympics opening ceremony, driving to Orange with the radio on to keep me awake, wondering at the type of person who phones a station at 5:30 in the morning to complain about an Aboriginal woman lighting the Olympic cauldron. I change stations, music fills the car, and once again those pubescent feelings, dormant for so long, are stirring.

Bait's gigs have been few and far between. We've played only once since Pat's surprise fortieth bash at Goulburn, and that was at a disastrous football-club fundraiser, during which the club secretary drew his own raffle ticket from the tupperware bowl three times and claimed prizes on each occasion. Later, when Bait took the stage, the room immediately emptied, people stampeding to the poker machines in the next room.

Not that we didn't have plans aplenty. We attempted to get ourselves booked at a few pubs around my area. A friend who writes musical scores for TV recorded a demo for us and we hawked it around the traps, to no avail. Some places wouldn't even listen to it. Others had stopped having bands because there was more money in lining the walls with poker machines. One publican who turned us down claimed our stuff was too modern for his clientele. Hello? The Blues? Too modern? Maybe I'd wandered through a mysterious time portal and stumbled into 1963. When I caught sight of some of his punters, I was certain of it. We thought we'd struck gold when the manager at one pub said he liked the cut of our jib. He told us we'd come along just at the right time because he was looking to book some new acts, and he mentioned something about a regular gig, once a fortnight. When I went in to see him again to nail down the deal, he'd been sacked.

'Sorry,' said his replacement, a pouty young babe with platinum-blonde pigtails, a midriff top and an eyebrow-piercing. 'We're going for a new direction. I'll be booking DJs, you know, dance music. None of that old stuff.'

Then, to top it all off, my TV-music-penning friend phoned me. 'Hey, I need a bit of bluesy harmonica for the new Foxtel stuff I'm doing.'

I felt a little warm glow seep through me like honey. 'Well, mate, I'm flatt–'

He cut me off. 'Don't take this the wrong way, but do you know anyone who plays really good harmonica?' Emphasis on the 'really good' part.

But this is different, I think to myself as I near Orange. This is the real deal. *Finally*. The culmination of all those years of lugging and sweating and screaming. At last there will be a pay-off. We're going into a *studio*, to *record*, to be on a *CD*. The producer is some guy called Rocky Rochelli, a name that even has the right rock'n'roll ring to it. The only hitch is that I haven't actually heard Darren's song yet. All I know is that it's called 'If You Don't Want My Love', but Darren assures me it won't take long to get my head around the lyrics.

'There's a bit in the middle where you can blow some harp as well,' he says.

Years ago, when my bedroom fantasies were in full bloom, my image of a recording studio was lifted from television and photographs. There would be one room with an enormous mixing desk. On the desk are dozens of coloured knobs and buttons. This is where the producer sits, nodding along to the beat and nudging faders, a soggy spliff jutting from the corner of his mouth. In front of the mixing desk is a panel of glass, a window into the studio where the band is playing. This room is soundproofed and everyone wears headphones. There are partitions and little booths where the vocals are laid down and overdubs recorded. The microphones all have little screens in front of them to protect them from flying spittle and popping 'p's.

For all that commonsense tells me not to expect a set-up like this in Orange, I can't get the image out of my head. It is ingrained in my brain. Darren will play in one part of this vast studio and I will be in the booth with the cans on. When I sing, only my voice will be heard, because the music track is being piped directly into my headphones. And when we've done a take, Rocky Rochelli will lean forward, flip a toggle, and say, 'Nice one, you've got the job,' or some such witticism. And my voice will come back, filling the control room, 'Ah, maybe just one more, Rocky. There's a little something I'd like to try in that second verse.'

The studio isn't like that at all, of course. It is in fact a garage in the backyard of Rocky Rochelli's Tuscan villa-style home on the main drag heading into Orange. Rocky Rochelli doesn't look very rock'n'roll at all. He's a tall, thin man in his early forties with short, wavy black hair, glasses, and a pleasant, open face. There is no control room. In place of the mixing desk and NASA-esque array of buttons, there's a computer keyboard and mouse. There are no partitions, no window, no headphones, no soundproof booths. Two microphones rest on stands in the middle of the room. They are without shields. I'll have to watch my 'p's, if not my 'q's. If Rocky wants to speak to us, he doesn't have to flip a toggle, he just has to talk, and we'll hear him loud and clear because we're standing right behind him.

Darren fishes the scribbled lyrics from a bulky old briefcase. He was right, they shouldn't take long to learn. Here, reprinted with kind permission, are the words to 'If You Don't Want My Love':

I just wanna love you
More than I can say
I just wanna love you
More than I can say

But if you don't want my love
I'll be on my way

I just wanna kiss you
More and more each day
I just wanna kiss you
All hours of the day

But if you don't want my love *(repeat x 2)*
I'll be on my way

I will do anything
Anything you say
I will do anything
Any little thing you say
But if you don't want my love
If you don't want my love
If you don't want my love
Said if you don't want my love
I'll be on my way
Bye bye

Pretty simple, eh? My brother mightn't trouble Bob Dylan in the lyricist stakes, but he certainly makes up for it in the music department. For 'If You Don't Want My Love' he has crafted a chunky, catchy, blues-based tune overlaid with just a hint of menace.

I sing what I think is a warm-up vocal, a soundcheck. Rocky records it and says he doesn't want to do it again. That one is perfect. I feel a little let down. After three hours in the car, that's it? I want to do more. I want to draw the whole thing out. But Rocky says it fits with the rawness of the track.

'I like it like that,' he says. 'Let's not try to do too much to it, or fiddle with it. I reckon it'll work better if you keep it raw.'

'Raw' seems to be Rocky's favourite word. Uttered from

someone else's mouth, it could be construed as disparaging. Not when Rocky utters it. He seems genuinely enthusiastic about the song, and we are grateful for that. Darren overdubs a lead guitar part, trying to suppress a grin the whole time. Then Rocky, unable to contain himself, shows us a whole range of effects he could place on the track with just a mouseclick, if he wasn't so adamant about keeping it raw. One I love makes my voice sound like a crackly old 45, all thin and static-laden, like Al Jolson, and I insist that Rocky use it on the third and final verse. Darren isn't sure. Rocky isn't sure. But I insist. I love it. There is absolutely no reason for it whatsoever, there is no call for it, but what the hell, I'll probably never again see the inside of a recording studio, even one like this, so I want to have some fun.

'When will the CD be out?' I ask when we've finished.

'No idea,' Rocky replies. 'Soon, I hope.'

More than twelve months later, *The Sound of Colour* is released. (So named because most of the musos hail from Orange.) To our surprise and delight, 'If You Don't Want My Love' is track one. We try to mask the delight part because we know it's just a collection of local yokels. Parish pump music, really. But hey, number one is number one is number one. In a music career peppered with so many failures and letdowns, this minor feat takes on Everest-conquering proportions. And somewhere inside, hope is springing eternal and I'm dreaming of a time, way off in the future, when Bait devotees all over the planet are bombarding second-hand shops and scouring the Internet for a copy of that rarest of rarities, *The Sound of Colour*.

The CD is launched at a glittering function at the Orange Ex-Services Club. All the artists on the CD have been invited to perform, but only four have turned up: Bait; a girl whose contribution is a double-bass-slapping jazz number; a young

Aboriginal balladeer with a truly beautiful, soaring voice; and a laconic country-and-western singer whose song deals with the hardships of life on the land and contains the phrase 'she's bloody dry' over and over.

I should really do something about my imagination. Once again, it's been wandering off of its own accord, priming me for disappointment. Here was I thinking that the launch would be held in the club's auditorium, when in fact it is being held in the smaller of two conference rooms, which can only be reached by negotiating a labyrinth of corridors, traipsing through an undercover carpark, and then taking an asthmatic elevator to level two. When we eventually arrive, we see that at one end of the room there is a small PA. Next to it is a lectern, and a screen with an enlarged version of the CD cover projected onto it. At the other end of the room is a table stacked with white cups and saucers, a silver urn, and plates of biscuits.

'Very rock'n'roll,' Darren sighs.

On another table are copies of the CD, on sale for fifteen dollars a pop, and laminated nametags which we are instructed to pin to our shirts. I count a total of twenty-five people – mothers, fathers, proud grandparents, friends – chatting on chairs around the edges of the room and treating the space in the middle as if it might be littered with trapdoors. Through a window I can see the neat, impossibly green square of a bowling green.

There are speeches and thankyous. Food is brought out. Platters of spring rolls and dim sims and curry puffs and meatballs appear from a kitchen one elevator, a carpark and a warren of corridors away. Rocky Rochelli is invited to the lectern and talks about the CD, about his thoughts and impressions of each act. When he talks about us, that word 'raw' is uttered again. And when he says it, a few people laugh, reading it as code for 'pretty bloody awful, really'. He says some nice things about why he thought Bait should kick off the CD. There has apparently been some consternation regarding the order of appearance. One or two fellow *artistes* are allegedly miffed at our number one ranking. Mindful of this, we decline the offer of playing first, leaving that honour to the country-and-western singer. With his wife and two young girls watching raptly, he strums his acoustic guitar and delivers his lament in a voice as dry as the parched earth about which he sings.

The jazz singer is up next. There is no double bass, so Rocky accompanies her on snare drum and brushes. Her voice is rich and powerful, obviously trained. In the middle of the song, against the rasp and slap of wire fronds on hide, she embarks on some extraordinary, improvised vocal callisthenics. Boop-boop-be-doops and high-pitched, back-of-the-throat ululations that sound a little like a squealing saxophone. At which point the younger of the country singer's two children claps her hands melodramatically over her ears, shakes her blonde pigtails, cries out, 'I can't stand any more!' and launches herself onto her mother's lap in tears. As the red-faced woman bundles her distressed daughter from the room, the singer, consummate professional that she is, ignores the interruption and powers on to the end, scatting and trilling with unabated ferocity.

Quite a few people have already departed by the time we storm through 'If You Don't Want My Love'. While Darren tunes up, I suddenly feel compelled to offer a pre-song ramble.

'People have said this song is too simple, that it's very basic, lyrically-speaking. Well, to them I would point out that "She loves you, yeah, yeah, yeah" ain't cutting a lot of lyrical mustard either.' There is a titter. I realise I've succeeded only in illuminating our song's weakness. Now they will be listening intently to the words, so that they can laugh at us. We churn out a solid rendition, I think, marred only slightly by me holding the harmonica upside down during the solo and, as a result, hooting a completely different set of notes to the one on the album version.

And that, ladies and gentlemen, is it. The launch started at 7pm. By nine, Darren and I have somehow found our way back to the main bar and are drinking ouzo while absently funnelling spare change into a poker machine. The machine accepts our offerings with bleeping, burbling gratitude, and gives us nothing in return.

The following night, in something of a bolt from the blue, we're booked to play in a local pub. Four hours. That's not a long time when you're drinking and enjoying yourself, but it can seem like an eternity if it's only 10pm and you're running out of songs.

Figuring that we'll need somewhere in the vicinity of sixty songs, and worried that we don't have enough material to get us through, Darren takes the day off work and we rehearse in his garage. For hours. There's the standard batch of songs that we know we know – thirty in all. According to Darren's calculations, all we need to do is conquer another thirty numbers and the gig will be sweet.

As the afternoon wears on, Darren becomes panicky, his cigarette breaks more frequent. I'm feeling weary, having already plodded through half a night's worth of material. My throat is sore and it dawns on me that I'll be struggling to do some of the songs a second time. This is a grim realisation, one I elect not to mention to Darren as he stands at the back door absently tapping ash into a pot plant.

'We don't have enough. It's never gonna be enough,' he mutters over and over, running his fingers through his hair.

'Well, you booked us,' I croak. 'And it's a bit fucking late to be worrying about it now, isn't it? We either ring 'em up and cancel, or we just make shit up as we go along.'

'Can't cancel. Too late for that.'

'Well, then, there you go. Why did you say yes anyway, if you thought we didn't have enough songs?'

'A gig's a gig. And I could use three hundred bucks about now.'

I shake my head. As usual, the lure of playing, of being paid to play, overrides commonsense. I can't say anything else. I'd have said yes, too.

We drive to the gig with all the cheery expectation of men being led to the gallows. There is an air of impending doom in the car, though that might just be the chicken curry we had earlier. You know the saying 'wrong side of the tracks'? This pub is precisely that. On the wrong side of the tracks. By about five metres, in fact. The railway line runs right past its door. Darren tells me the pub used to have a reputation as a bit of a rough hangout, but that it has had a recent makeover. He's right. The walls are heritage-green and the timber tables and chairs are dark and rich. Tastefully framed prints adorn the walls, works depicting pioneering days – timbercutters sawing logs, bullock drivers, and bearded men standing outside slab huts with curling wisps of blue smoke rising from their chimneys.

There are quite a few people about, and – oh, happy day – they are mostly female. This is mildly surprising. Large groups of young women, dressed to the nines, cluster around haphazardly joined tables, laughing and smoking and sucking gin and tonic through straws. Every so often, they screech laughter. Maybe we haven't wandered onto the wrong side of the tracks after all, I think, although they do look slightly misplaced. As if they somehow don't belong in this neck of the woods. Not so long ago, this watering hole would have had spit and sawdust on the floor. Was a lick of paint really all it took to draw in the crowds?

Surprise number two. The pub is equipped with a good-sized stage, another recent addition. As we set up, Darren and I are exchanging glances that say, 'Well, this is looking up. Mightn't be so bad after all.' Then, ten minutes before we start playing, the women leave. Every. Single. One. They rise and disappear into the night, leaving as an audience three young lads who are already well on their way to full-scale inebriation, three of my brother's workmates, and a small group of older men at the back bar who are trying to watch the trots on the telly. When Darren comes back clutching beers, he explains the exodus.

'There's a male revue on at the pub down the road. The Chippendales or something. Wouldn't you fuckin' know it?'

I have a peculiar feeling of resignation. Almost detachment. What did I expect? Did I really think that word of our gig had spread around town? Did I really think, even for a second, that they were there to see us? There is something strangely fitting about them all filing out before we've even started. An annoyingly optimistic person might say it's better than them leaving *after* we'd started. At least this way we know it has nothing to do with our music. There's a sagging somewhere in my head as my motivation finally gives out and deflates like a balloon with a slow leak.

We start with a standard blues. I blow some harp. Darren plays some nice fills and licks. We finish. Apart from a smattering of applause from Darren's workmates, we are ignored. Utterly ignored. All I can hear is chatter. Up the back, one of the older guys wanders over to the television and turns up the volume, because race six from Harold Park is about to get under way. He wanders back to his stool and drains his schooner.

Two songs into our four-hour gig I arrive at a deeply sad-dening realisation: for the first time in my life I don't want to do it. I really don't want to be here. I'm actually bored. While I'm singing, I watch the drinkers talking and idly wonder if we can call it quits if they all go home. Time crawls. After about forty minutes, we take a break, the announcement of which draws a sarcastic clap from the punter up the back.

'Now I might be able to hear the fuckin' races,' he says loudly to the lanky young bartender, who laughs as if to say, Yeah mate, I'm with you.

Darren's mates come out with the requisite words of support and encouragement, although it's obvious they feel embarrassed, and they stay no longer than politeness dictates.

'Loved that harp-playing, mate,' one of them says to me as they shrug on their coats. 'When Darren told me you played harp, I thought he meant one you play between your knees, one with strings, you know?'

We all laugh. 'Yeah, mate, electric harp,' I say. 'I can see it now. During a solo you could play it with your teeth and have fireworks shooting out the top of it. It'd be great.'

With their departure we're down to nine people. Darren and I drag ourselves back onstage and I don't even bother with ban-ter. Between each song I just let the sound of the trots fill the pub while I guzzle beer and chat with Darren. Soon we're playing only for each other, trying out new songs, dredging up long-forgotten numbers and dusting them off. It doesn't matter if we stumble, or if we bail out of a number halfway through, because nobody's listening. At least we don't have to worry about not having enough material. If worse comes to worse, we'll just repeat songs. No-one will realise.

I look at my brother and feel a pang of regret. He's better than this. He's always been better than this. The decade following the breakup of the Ripchords he spent on his own solo tour of sorts, travelling between jobs and cities, too preoccupied with day-to-day survival to worry much about music. Then, in 1997, came the one brief, soaring peak on his fame'n'fortune flatline, when he was invited to try out as the new drummer in one of his favourite bands, The Mark of Cain. I was living in Ireland at the time, and suddenly received a spate of excited, echoing phone calls. It finally seemed as though one of the Griffis boys was on the cusp of rock reality. I badgered him with questions, drinking every little detail. He had apparently been into a studio, a real studio, and laid down an audition piece. It was like the old days in his bedroom – he wore headphones and played along to a few Mark of Cain songs. Then the original drumming track was lifted off and replaced by Darren's. He even met the band, chatting with them in a hotel room for over an hour.

Inevitably, I suppose, the call came through: he hadn't got the gig, although he was in the last three. I think I was more shattered than Darren. To him, it was an adventure, and in however small a way, his talent had been acknowledged.

If I'm to be honest, I have to say I've probably always known, deep down, that Darren is the real thing and I'm a counterfeit. An imposter. A mimic. I've never really found my own voice, just aped other people's styles. Maybe that's an inevitable outcome of spending so much of your formative years in your bedroom pretending to be someone else. It's certainly a by-product of playing covers for years. After all, if you never write your own songs, how can you expect to forge your own voice?

During the third interminable set, four drunk, middle-aged women wander in, grinning and flushed in the wake of the buff'n'buns show on the other side of the tracks. We're in the middle of 'Brown Eyed Girl' and they immediately rush to the dancefloor.

'Sorry, ladies, our clothes are staying on,' I say.

'Thank Christ for that,' one of them cries out, and they're all cackles and squeals. The four twist and wobble and shake, screaming out the 'Sha-la-la-la' chorus. This perks us up a little, but it doesn't last. When we embark on our 'Gloria'/'Jailbreak' medley, it doesn't have quite the same effect it had in Goulburn, and I can see their interest waning. One of them asks if we know 'Moondance'. I do, but Darren isn't sure of the chords, so she shrugs and the four retreat to the other end of the bar, where they order drinks and fend off the drunk old men.

We take our last break just after midnight. Ordering another beer, I say to the lanky young bartender, 'Whaddya reckon, mate? There's only four people here and they don't give a shit. How about we call it a night, yeah?'

He plonks the drink down in front of me and shakes his head. 'No way. We're paying you for four hours. You can bloody well play till one.' Then he adds, 'Maybe there'd be more people if youse were playing the sort of stuff we normally have on in here.'

I bristle. I'm not going to stand here and take shit from this pimple-pocked cowpoke. 'We're playing exactly the sort of stuff Darren told your boss we'd be playing when he booked us,' I say. 'He told you we don't play Conway-fucking-Twitty. He told you we played blues and rock. Anyway, everyone had gone before we started, so don't blame us for the poor turnout. Blame the fucking strippers down the road.'

I seem to have finally elicited some interest from the few patrons left. Bleary faces are turned in my direction. Darren comes over and escorts me from the bar. 'Come on, mate. Don't worry about it. Fuck 'em. Let's just get it over with and get outta here.'

We go back on and do an angry, truncated set, pulling out the hardest songs we know. In a last-ditch belligerent gesture, Darren turns the volume right up and I scream myself hoarse, giving it my vein-bulging all. We round off the night with an AC/DC medley, incorporating 'Hell's Bells', 'You Shook Me All Night Long', 'It's A Long Way To The Top', 'Whole Lotta Rosie', and 'High Voltage'. In a ridiculously exaggerated ending, Darren rakes the plectrum back and forth across the strings, faster and faster, until each strike is indistinguishable. I give a one-finger salute to the bar but no-one sees me do it because no-one is looking at us.

Afterwards, we're coiling leads when one of the three young lads who have been ensconced all evening and who are still drinking solidly shambles over to us. He looks to be in his early twenties, certainly no older. His black hair hangs in a shapeless bowl cut, and a wispy moustache is struggling to conceal his upper lip. His large, dumpy frame is barely contained by a blue tracksuit, and his eyes are slits. We brace ourselves for trouble.

'Hey, good one, fellas,' he slurs. 'That was some good shit.'

'Er, well, thanks,' Darren says.

'Not really my type of music, ay, but I can appreciate what you was doin'. Real clever, ay, the way you guys manipulated them songs. Reckon they sounded like the originals, 'cept for the fact you were just playin' 'em on acoustic guitar. 'Part from that, they were spot on.'

'Thanks. Pleased you enjoyed it.'

'Nah, did but. Really fuckin' good, ay.'

It's becoming increasingly clear that we're not going to shake our tracksuited admirer quickly. Typical. The guy ignores us all night, now he feels like a chat.

'You guys known each other long? You'd have to, yeah, to be able to play stuff like that? Been friends a while?'

'Brothers, actually. So yeah, I suppose you could say we go back a ways.'

'Brothers, ay? Fuck, that's excellent. Nah, really excellent, man. It's great you blokes get on well enough to play together like that. Good ta see. My brother stabbed me. Nah, fair dinkum, he did. That's why I'm on compo now, can't work. Yeah, stabbed me six times. Slashed me 'cross the guts [gestures], slashed me down the inside of me thigh [gestures]. Yeah, reckon it's great you guys get on well like youse do, man. 'S'way it should be, you know?'

We don't quite know how to respond to this. As it turns out, we're not expected to.

'I'd love to get up there and sing them songs and stuff, like youse do, ay. I was gonna ask you earlier if you knew any Green Day, y'know, any shit like that, that I could get up and sing. But mate, youse were too good and I knew that if I did get up, I'd only forget the words and fuck it all up, an' I didn't wanna do that to ya, y'know? Make a fuckin' idiot of meself, ay?'

Just then our newfound fan notices that one of his friends, a thin guy with close-cropped blond hair, is looking a little the worse for wear. He's gradually sliding lower in his seat, and his face has a greenish tinge.

'Oh shit, there he goes,' Tracksuit says, with a weary resignation that suggests this is not a new phenomenon. ''Scuse me, fellas,' he says and shambles off to attend to his mate. Curiously, he doesn't try to move him, or actually take him home. Instead the bartender brings out a white plastic bucket, which they wedge under the young man's chin so that the bucket rests on his chest, his face framed in the opening. He looks like a horse with a nosebag strapped on.

'You right, mate?' Tracksuit keeps asking. 'You gonna be right?'

The reply is a muffled moan, which Tracksuit interprets to mean, 'Yes, fine thanks. You go on back and talk to the band some more.' He pats his bucket-bound mate almost tenderly on the shoulder. 'You just rest there, man. Won't be long and we'll get you home.' He grabs his half-empty beer, then turns his attention once again to us.

'Sorry 'bout that, fellas. What was I sayin'? Oh yeah, I reckon you guys could be big but, ay? Nah, really. I reckon you could.' He pauses, giving this matter weighty consideration, then a chubby finger raises itself off his glass and wavers in our direction. The finger is accompanied by a note of caution. 'Now, I'm not sayin' you're gonna be world-famous or nuthin', 'cos maybe you won't, know worra mean?' He's carrying on like a talent scout from EMI. 'But, seriously, I'd reckon there'd be a few people round Orange who'd know your names right off the bat, yeah?'

'One or two, yeah,' Darren says, trying not to laugh.

He nods craftily, pleased to have his theory proved correct. 'Fuckin' right. Doesn't surprise me in the least, ay.'

There are sounds coming from the bucket. It appears Tracksuit's friend is depositing into it several of the dozen or more beers he has consumed over the course of the evening, along with a goodly proportion of mulched potato chips.

'Oh shit. Sorry, fellas. Better take him home, ay?'

As Tracksuit helps his friend, Darren nudges me. 'Give him a CD.'

Good idea. I grab one of the two dozen *Sound of Colour* CDs we have in our possession and present it to Tracksuit, who's struggling to help Bucket Boy out of his chair.

'There you go, mate. A little present. We're on this CD. Track one.'

Tracksuit looks down at the CD, as if I've just deposited gold bullion in his palm. 'You're fuckin' *jo*kin'. You're on here?'

I turn it over and point. 'There it is. Track one, Bait, "If You Don't Want My Love".'

'Bullshit, man. There you go, I told you youse were good. An' here youse are on a fuckin' real CD. Unbe-fuckin'-lievable.'

'Well, she's all yours. Enjoy.'

'No way, man. No fuckin' way. Thanks very much. Fuckin' excellent. *Excellent.*'

Bucket Boy is retching again, so they manhandle him outside, still clutching the receptacle to his face. Before the door swings shut, Tracksuit turns back.

'This is just about the nicest fuckin' thing anyone's ever done for me. Cheers, fellas. See youse.'

Considering that Tracksuit's own brother allegedly tried to fillet him, I fear he might not be exaggerating. What he will think when he regains consciousness later in the day and plays the CD is anyone's guess.

Darren's wringing our money out of the begrudging barman, and when he comes back, his fist full of fifties, I announce my retirement. 'That'll do me, I reckon. No more of this crap. No more shitty gigs.'

He laughs. 'Yeah, right. Sure. Till the next time there's a chance to grab a mic and sing a Stones song, that is.'

He's probably right. Fact is, I know it will never take much to prise me from a crowd onto a stage. I'll protest, of course, but not too much. Partly because if I stall for too long I might miss my opportunity, and partly because I don't think I can protest convincingly. Anyone who knows me knows I will be wanting desperately to get up there. It will always be an itch never quite scratched. I'll have to be content with brief appearances, guesting with other bands, being that drunk wanker who asks if he can come up and sing something, except I'll be able to say, 'It's all right mate, used to play in bands myself. I won't fuck it up, promise.'

I suppose I'll keep on sporadically having that dream where I'm at a Stones concert and Mick takes ill, although I think I should stop telling people about that. They're starting to laugh at me, at the sheer, unreconstructed adolescence of it all. Maybe my subconscious is still only fourteen. Then again, maybe the key to not dreaming it any more is to finish it. Maybe one day, in the dream, I won't get lost. I'll actually make it all the way into the bowels of the stadium. There I'll shake hands with Keith ('Wotcha, mate.'), Ronnie (''Ow ya goin'?') and Charlie ('Evenin'.'), and they'll hand me a song list.

'You right with these?' Keith will rasp, and I'll nod.

'Yeah, no worries, mate. I won't fuck it up, promise.'

And while I'm limbering up, I'll spy Mick sitting in a corner, behind a rack of outrageous stageclothes, with a fluffy robe on and a clump of white tissues held to his red-raw nostrils, and he'll give me the thumbs-up sign. 'Break a leg, mate,' he'll croak. 'Thanks for covering for me.'

'Pleasure,' I'll say. 'Don't you worry about a thing. Just take it easy. See you later.'

And the next thing I know I'll be running up a tunnel, just

behind Ron and in front of Charlie, and the crowd, which back-stage sounded like pounding surf, will erupt as we unleash a perfect version of 'Start Me Up'. And about two hours later, as fireworks explode in the night sky above the stage and the Stones thunder through the climax of 'Jumping Jack Flash', I will stand panting with my torso bare and sweat-slicked, raise my arms in a rock'n'roll salute, and let the crowd's euphoria wash over me like a cleansing tide.

Thank yoouuu . . . and goodnight!